Interpretations of Fascism

Renzo De Felice

Translated by
Brenda Huff Everett

Harvard University Press
Cambridge, Massachusetts
and London, England
1977

Originally published by Gius. Laterza y Figli,
Rome, Italy, as *Le interpretazioni del fascismo*

Library of Congress Cataloging in Publication Data
Felice, Renzo de.
  Interpretations of fascism.
  Includes bibliographical references and index.
  1. Fascism.- 2. Fascism—Italy. I. Title.
JC481.F3613   320.5'33   76-30590
ISBN 0-674-45962-8

Introduction

by Charles F. Delzell

For some time after the Liberation of Italy from Fascism in 1945 a considerable proportion of that country's historians and social scientists seemed to be in no hurry to turn their professional attention to the study and writing of the history of Mussolini's Blackshirt dictatorship. No doubt political expediency, as well as the very real difficulties of gathering source materials and thereafter gaining access to them in the archives, contributed to this situation. When scholars did bring themselves to study and write about that era, they confined their attention almost exclusively to Italian Fascism rather than try to tackle the broader, more elusive problem of whether there was such a thing as "generic" European fascism (with a small "f"). It was not until the late 1960s that an Italian historian shifted the focus of his attention to the possibility of such a generic movement and began a systematic survey and analysis of the international literature on fascism. This was Renzo De Felice, a prolific young scholar at the University of Rome whose paperback book, *Le interpretazioni del fascismo*, first published in 1969 and later republished several times with additions, is now presented in English translation.

To be fair to Italian scholars, one should quickly note that the study of "generic" fascism (apart from what was written in the interwar period) is largely a product of the 1960s and 1970s. It was especially stimulated by Ernst Nolte's difficult but important book,

Three Faces of Fascism: Action Française, Italian Fascism, National Socialism, and by Eugen Weber's *Varieties of Fascism: Doctrines of Revolution in the 20th Century*. Most of the research has been undertaken by North American, British, and Western European scholars, though writers in Eastern Europe have also made contributions. To judge from the multiplicity of interpretations thus far proposed, it is unlikely that a consensus about fascism will emerge soon among scholars who come from a variety of intellectual disciplines and ideological persuasions. Indeed, the diversity of informed opinion regarding the reasons for fascism's appearance, the nature of its appeal, and the direction of its thrust continue to be little short of amazing, as the reader of Professor De Felice's useful book will see.

Born in Rieti in 1929, Renzo De Felice pursued his university studies under the guidance of the late Federico Chabod and Delio Cantimori and now holds the chair in the history of political parties at the University of Rome. He is also the editor of the review *Storia contemporanea*. In the late 1950s De Felice turned his research to the Fascist era. Fortunately, he was able to gain access to many of the important documents that were slowly being systematized in the Archivio Centrale dello Stato in Rome. He has shown remarkable zeal in studying these materials and has also been instrumental in publishing many of them. Moreover, he has been very helpful in bringing about a more liberalized policy of scholarly access to archival holdings on the Fascist era.

Apart from the present book, De Felice has achieved recognition for a number of important works that can be grouped into several categories. (See the Selective Bibliography of Works by Renzo De Felice at the end of this book.) First, there were his studies of the late eighteenth century and of the Italian Jacobins. Of note, too, were his studies of Gabriele D'Annunzio's occupation of Fiume and his editing of correspondence and other writings of that condottiere. De Felice found time to compile a collection of documents pertaining to Italian Fascism and some of the other parties in 1921-1923, and his lengthy study of Italian Jews under Fascism is particularly significant. He has also investigated various aspects of Italo-German relations during the Fascist era.

But, most important of all, is De Felice's massive, multivolume, archivally researched biography of Mussolini, of which four thick tomes have thus far been published. This major work is in many respects a "life and times" of Mussolini and is characterized more by a preponderance of documents than by interpretation or narration. It is not surprising, therefore, that the appearance of each installment of this biography has stirred interest and controversy, a number of critics charging that the author, who declares that he is strictly objective and nonpartisan, has really been too indulgent in handling his subject. The appellation, "Mussolini the revolutionary," which was employed in the title of the first volume, was questioned by Leftist critics, particularly with respect to Mussolini's role in the years after his expulsion from the editorship of the Socialist party newspaper *Avanti!* in 1914. Others expressed doubts about the validity of De Felice's sharp distinctions between Italian Fascism as a "movement" (which he has characterized as "positive" and "vital") and Fascism as a "regime" (which he concedes was both "oppressive" and "repressive").

When the fourth volume, subtitled "The Years of Consensus, 1929-1936," was published in 1974, a veritable storm of dissent erupted in Italy. Many critics, including articulate veterans of the anti-Fascist struggle, contended that the author had pictured greater mass support for the Duce in those years than was really the case. Some also questioned the generally favorable marks he gave to Mussolini in his handling of the Ethiopian War. It has also been noted that the author paints a Duce whose earlier ideological debts to Georges Sorel and Vilfredo Pareto have been replaced by the influence of Oswald Spengler. Thus, the German's suggestion that caesarism would provide the sole chance of renewal from a stifling plutocracy is said to have undergirded Mussolini's imperialism of the 1930s. The criticisms and replies have not been confined just to the book-review pages of the Italian press and professional journals; they have also been aired on Italian television and have appeared in the "Letters to the Editor" section of the London *Times Literary Supplement* in the wake of a biting review by Denis Mack Smith of Oxford that appeared in the October 31, 1975, issue of the *TLS* under the heading, "A monument for the Duce."

Some critics have declared that De Felice tends to let himself be taken in at times by propaganda in the Fascist documents and that he fails to make equal use of evidence set forth by anti-Fascists. Although most of the critics have set forth their views in a professionally responsible manner, a few have gone perhaps too far in suggesting that the author is "philo-Fascist." To some of these charges De Felice has responded with vigor in an interview he gave to Michael A. Ledeen, an American historian who resides in Rome. This was first published in Italy in 1975 as a paperback: *Intervista sul fascismo*, ed. Michael A. Ledeen; a year later it appeared as *Fascism: An Informal Introduction to Its Theory and Practice*. More recently, the exchanges between Mack Smith and Ledeen in the *TLS* of January 9 and 16, 1976, as well as a letter from Ledeen that did not appear there, have been published in Italy: Denis Mack Smith and Michael A. Ledeen, *Un monumento al duce? Contributo al dibattito sul fascismo*.

Some of the statements in the Ledeen—De Felice interview have opened the way for new questions to be put to the Italian scholar, particularly with respect to his suggestion that "Fascism was therefore the attempt of the petite bourgeoisie in its ascendancy —not in crisis—to assert itself as a new class, a new force" seeking political participation and power. "These elements asserted themselves as a class seeking to gain power and to assert its own function, its own culture, and its own political power against both the bourgeoisie and the proletariat. To put the matter briefly: They wanted a revolution" (*Fascism: An Informal Introduction to Its Theory and Practice*). In the earlier volumes of the biography, De Felice had contended, like most other historians, that Mussolini's success in seizing power owed much to the support of a lower middle class that feared displacement and proletarianization in a time of crisis. De Felice now declares that he has precise documentation to prove his new contention. But until this is made available, it would seem, as Mack Smith has observed, that scholars are left with only a hypothesis. There seems to be a real possibility that Italian historians may be embarking on as wordy a debate over an "emergent" middle class as specialists in English history engaged in a few years ago over the question of the rise of the gentry.

De Felice's *Le interpretazioni del fascismo* unquestionably deserves to be made more accessible to an international audience, as the Harvard University Press has perceived. The English translation by Brenda Huff Everett, which I have had an opportunity to check, is of the fourth edition of 1972. (Since then a fifth and a sixth edition have also appeared but with almost no changes.) The translator has made a commendable effort to clarify some of De Felice's text by breaking up a number of long sentences and paragraphs and recasting the author's sometimes convoluted Latinate syntax into the English active voice.

Every author of an interpretive study of this kind is free to select the writers he wishes to discuss. De Felice's coverage of writers who have sought to interpret the various fascistic movements is quite extensive; yet there are some omissions that are a bit surprising. Thus, among the specialists who have written on Italian Fascism, one fails to find mention of Gaudens Megaro, Roberto Vivarelli, Aldo Garosci, F. William Deakin, Christopher Seton-Watson, and Ivone Kirkpatrick, for example. Many readers will find it odd that there is no sustained discussion of Nazism. Doubtless this deliberate omission stems from De Felice's denial of a common identity between Fascism and Nazism. He contends that the differences between the two ideologies are more numerous and significant than the similarities—a highly dubious proposition, in the judgment of the present writer, and in the face of what Mussolini himself affirmed in his September 28, 1937, speech in Berlin on the Axis: "Although the course of the two [Fascist and Nazi] revolutions may have been somewhat different, the goal they have sought and reached is the same: the unity and greatness of the people. Fascism and Nazism are two manifestations of that parallelism of historic positions that links the life of our nations." The rest of the Duce's speech on that occasion pointed out specific elements held in common in their *Weltanschauung*. (Quoted in Charles F. Delzell, ed., *Mediterranean Fascism, 1919-1945*.)

According to De Felice, Fascism was born "on the Left" and stands in the political and cultural tradition of the Enlightenment and the French Revolution, with their ideas of progress and faith in the "new man." Nazism, on the other hand, he insists, was from the beginning a movement of restoration, of Right-wing radicalism; it harked back to the old, unchanged Aryan German. For this reason, too, he argues that Italian neo-Fascism has little to do with classical Fascism, and that Mussolini is no longer their model; rather it is a movement of Right-wing radicals or neo-Nazis. In spite of his exclusion of Nazism from his category of generic fascism, De Felice does make a number of references to Hitler's Germany in *Le interpretazioni del fascismo*.

The author divides this book into two major sections. In Part One, he surveys fascism as a generic European phenomenon and discusses much of the literature on the subject, while in Part Two he turns to Italian Fascism, concentrating here on the writings of Italian scholars. As the Table of Contents provides only a listing of the categories of scholarship to be discussed, rather than specific authors, it may be helpful here to identify some of the latter and place them in De Felice's frames of reference.

In his initial chapter, he offers a typology of the forms of power that generic fascism assumed. He proceeds in the next chapter to divide the various interpretations of fascism into three broad categories: "classic," "minor," and "social science." The classic ones are further broken down into three groups: writers who have perceived fascism to be a sudden "moral sickness" of Europe (Benedetto Croce, Friedrich Meinecke, Gerhard Ritter, and Golo Mann, for example); those who have looked upon it as the logical and even inevitable product of the historic development of certain countries like Italy and Germany—fascism being a kind of "revelation" of these countries' ingrained historical propensities (Denis Mack Smith in the case of Italy, and Edmond Vermeil, William M. McGovern, Peter Viereck, and others in the case of Germany); and those Marxists who have regarded fascism as an anti-proletarian reaction that is the more or less inevitable product of capitalistic society (for example, Maurice H. Dobb, Paul A. Baran, Paul M. Sweezy, August Thalheimer, Otto Bauer, Boris R. Lopukhov, Georgy Dimitrov, and Richard Löwenthal).

In a shorter chapter devoted to some of the "minor" interpretations proposed between the 1930s and 1960s, De Felice examines first the views of two Catholic philosophers, Jacques Maritain and Augusto Del Noce. Another minor category is the school that has sought to interpret fascism as a manifestation of a wider phenomenon, Totalitarianism, a tendency that became conspicuous in the West during the early phases of the Cold War and especially among some of the social scientists (such as Carl J. Friedrich and Zbigniew K. Brzezinski, Hannah Arendt, and to some degree the historian Wolfgang Sauer). Finally, De Felice's minor interpretations include the category represented by Ernst Nolte, the German philosopher-historian who has tried to describe fascism as a "metapolitical phenomenon." Although De Felice believes that, strictly speaking, Nolte has no clear-cut disciple, he suggests that the works of René Rémond and George L. Mosse, as well as those of Del Noce, bear some affinity to Nolte's interest in the intellectual and cultural history of Right-wing movements, and he comments at some length on the rather abstruse thought of the last-named Italian Catholic philosopher.

In Chapter 4, De Felice endeavors to provide a notion of the scope and importance of some of the social science interpretations of fascism. With regard to the psychosocial group of writings, he comments on Wilhelm Reich's sexual-economic theories, on the findings of Theodor W. Adorno and others with respect to the characteristics of the "authoritarian personality," and on Erich Fromm's theory set forth in *Escape from Freedom*. He also has some comments on the studies of Talcott Parsons and Harold W. Lasswell. The section on sociological interpretations of fascism includes certain works of Karl Mannheim, David J. Saposs, Svend Ranulf, Nathaniel Stone Preston, Seymour Martin Lipset, Gino Germani, and Jules Monnerot. Under the rubric "socioeconomic interpretations," De Felice considers the studies of A. F. K. Organski, Barrington Moore, Jr., and Ludovico Garruccio that have sought to correlate fascism with a specific stage in economic and political growth and modernization.

Part Two, which deals with Italian Fascism as interpreted by Italians, may well be the most interesting to those readers who have not been able to consult the relevant literature in Italian. In Chapter 5, entitled "Stages in the History of Fascism and the Problem of Its Origins," De Felice observes how Angelo Tasca, Federico Chabod, Pietro Nenni, and Gaetano Salvemini have dealt with these problems and then offers his own views. In the ensuing chapter, which covers interpretations of Fascism prior to the crisis brought on by the Blackshirts' assassination in June 1924 of Giacomo Matteotti, leader of the revisionist Unitary Socialist party, De Felice takes up a number of writers. The best known and probably the most important figure was the liberal democrat Luigi Salvatorelli, whose book *Nazionalfascismo* was a pioneering and very perspicacious effort to analyze the nature of the new movement not only in terms of its attraction to the lower middle class but its continuity with the prewar Nationalist party. Most of these early writers (such as the socialist Giovanni Zibordi, the communist Antonio Gramsci, and the former socialist Ivanoe Bonomi) perceived the importance of the shift from the original Milan-based Fascism to the reactionary "agrarian Fascism" of 1920-21 that developed in the lower Po Valley. There was similar general agreement that Fascism was the product of bourgeois reaction to the "Red biennium" of Italian Marxism, but there was lack of censensus as to whom this reaction was directed against, as De Felice goes on to clarify.

Chapter 7 deals with interpretations of the years of the "regime," 1925-1943. Here the author finds three subgroups worthy of attention: studies published (or at least initially written) in Italy during 1925-26 before the last vestiges of freedom of the press came to a halt; studies published by Italian anti-Fascist émigrés; and studies published by the Fascists themselves. In the first category the most significant books, he thinks, were those by Guido Dorso, Francesco S. Nitti, and Luigi Sturzo. The second category of émigré writers he breaks down into four groups: those who were active in the predominantly socialist Anti-Fascist Concentration organized in Paris between 1927 and 1934 (such as Filippo Turati, Claudio Treves, and Nenni); various politically heterodox but anti-Fascist writers like Giuseppe Donati, Mario Bergamo, Francesco L. Ferrari, Camillo Berneri, Giuseppe A. Borgese, Silvio Trentin, and—most important—those identified with the new liberal-socialist movement, Giustizia e Libertà (Justice and Liberty), founded in Paris in 1929 by Carlo Rosselli and dominated by him until his assassination by Fascist agents in June 1937; the Communist émigrés (especially Palmiro Togliatti); and, lastly, those émigrés who sought to write works of a professional historical nature (notably the ex-communist Tasca and, to a lesser degree, the radical Salvemini and the socialist Nenni). As for the studies published by Fascists, De Felice recalls Giorgio A. Chiurco, Roberto Farinacci (whose book was really written mostly by Giorgio Masi), Luigi Villari, Gioacchino Volpe, Giulio Colamarino, and Giovanni Gentile.

Chapter 8, which considers the historiographical debate that began after the Liberation, starts out with a discussion of Croce's controversial assertion that Fascism was a disjointed "parenthesis" in Italy's history. During the 1940s and 1950s, according to De Felice, most historical scholarship (for example, Giacomo Perticone, Nino Valeri, Emilio R. Papa, Antonio Graziadei, Lelio Basso, Armando Saitta, Paolo Alatri, Chabod, Salvatorelli, Giovanni

Mira, and Gabriele De Rosa) pursued the courses set forth in the three classic traditions described in Chapter 2. Among the post-World War II apologists for the regime De Felice notes Attilio Tamaro, Edoardo and Duilio Susmel, and Giorgio Pini.

In Chapter 9 the author comments briefly on the recent Italian treatment of Fascism—the writings of the 1960s. He feels that the contributions of the social sciences and of sociology in particular have been meager; on the other hand, he observes that at least two philosophers, Del Noce and R. Mazzetti, have offered some useful discussion of the relation of Fascism to intellectual life. It is the historians, however, who have done the most to clarify the nature of Fascism, he contends, and these have included outspoken Marxists like Enzo Santarelli and scholars who have tended to take a more eclectic approach (Alberto Aquarone, Simona Colarizi, Ferdinando Cordova, Francesco Gaeta, F. Margiotta Broglio, Piero Melograni, Giuseppe Rossini, Salvatore Sechi, Paolo Ungari, and, of course, De Felice himself).

In his interesting conclusion, De Felice identifies those elements of generic fascism that must be stressed in order to attain historical understanding. He also offers his views on fascism's relation to capitalism and to class struggle. Lastly, he discusses the allegedly "totalitarian" and "revolutionary" aspects of fascism.

It is to be hoped that this English translation of the observations of an outstanding and controversial Italian scholar on the historiography of fascism will contribute to a keener understanding of the subject and help to encourage other scholars to broaden and deepen the coverage and analysis of the burgeoning literature on this complex phenomenon.

Contents

Part One

Interpretations of the Fascist Phenomenon

1

Fascism as a Problem of Interpretation

The earliest attempts to interpret the Fascist phenomenon were more or less contemporary with the emergence of Fascism and paralleled its development. Although these interpretations originated in Italy, the dialogue soon extended to other countries, and Italian Fascism became the subject of journalistic and political reportage, as well as of an occasional memoir. Aside from its cumulative value, this early literature on Italian Fascism was generally superficial, so much so that books by Pelham H. Box and Herbert W. Schneider and some studies of corporative structure are distinguished as isolated attempts to plumb the deeper meaning of events.[1] Few saw in Fascism a potential threat to Europe as a whole; it was not until the early 1930s that it was viewed as a phenomenon whose implications extended beyond the boundaries of Italy. At best, an occasional author conceded that Italian Fascism might exert a limited influence in Eastern European countries lacking sound liberal traditions, efficient and stable parliamentary systems, and advanced economic or social development.

With the exception of the Marxists, most observers viewed Fascism only in relation to Italy and with reference to the special characteristics inherent in that country's postwar development, the weakness of its liberal-democratic tradition, and the deficiencies of its political and bureaucratic classes. (Only Giolitti was exempted from this charge.) References were made to the Italian "tempera-

3

ment" and to "saints and sinners" endowed with strong but evanescent passions, whose limited political and social conscience encouraged a type of strong government inconceivable in England, the United States, and France, but which could be useful in the Italian situation. The firm hold this interpretation of Fascism had on front-ranking intellectuals who were well acquainted with the history and culture of Italy is shown in works by G. M. Trevelyan and, especially, Paul Hazard.[2] Examples proliferated during the years following the Matteotti assassination. Nor can we escape the fact that, in Anglo-Saxon countries particularly, some individuals viewed Italian Fascism benevolently and wished a somewhat similar system for their own land.[3]

In the early thirties the successes and ultimate victory of National Socialism in Germany provided Fascism with content and significance it had previously lacked. In Europe and America many ceased to consider it an insignificant, peculiarly Italian phenomenon. As Cole wrote:

> Fascism, to be sure, had conquered Italy well before that, and Fascist tendencies had emerged in a number of other countries—for example, in Hungary and in the Balkans—not to mention China. It became, however, a world danger only with the rise of Hitler; for only in his hands did it become a third force challenging on a world scale both Socialism and Communism on the one hand and capitalist parliamentarism on the other, and thus raised the issue whether it was properly regarded as a new, and perhaps final, form of imperialist capitalism or as an altogether different creed and way of life.[4]

With this new international aspect Fascism lost much of the favor it had enjoyed in some circles.[5] It could no longer be viewed as an exclusively Italian phenomenon; it came to be seen as a social and political manifestation of actual or potential concern to all countries heretofore guided by liberal-democratic governments, or, as the Communists maintained, countries with a capitalist economy. Despite its limited scope, the emergence of a Fascist movement in England had wide repercussions. After the publication in 1933 of John Strachey's notable book, warnings and alarms multiplied.[6] All countries now participated in prolific and lively debate about the nature and historical import of Fascism, its programs, and its implications for Europe and the world.[7]

The predominantly practical objectives of the anti-Fascist struggle, its passions, interests, and needs, gave this debate an increasingly political turn in the late 1930s and culminated with the outbreak of World War II. Generalizations abounded; the least significant and most pathological aspects common to various forms of Fascism were emphasized, while the differences were underestimated; importance was ascribed to certain aspects and denied to others. Excessive stress was placed on the use of nationalistic, coercive, and terroristic elements to achieve consensus, a pitfall that even the German and Italian varieties of Fascism had avoided. The result was a tendency to view demonologically a phenomenon that indisputably had aberrant aspects, but that nevertheless had its own rationale and could be explained historically.

Despite these limitations, there was no dearth of serious studies of lasting importance.[8] Indeed, the vast literature on Nazism-Fascism between 1933 and 1945 provides valid antecedents for recent interpretations of the Fascist phenomenon. But its real value lay elsewhere. Because such literature was conceived of as a function of the anti-Fascist struggle, its immediate impact was political, or ethical-political. Through a vast series of channels and by means of infinite illustrations and schematic outlines, it contributed substantially to the development of propaganda and the anti-Fascist struggle both in the democratic and in the Communist camps. It gave rise to ideas and political and moral values that made it possible for World War II to assume a decidedly ideological character and for the foes of the Tripartite Alliance to survive and win that war as a veritable crusade for freedom and civilization.

Nor was the cultural significance of this literature limited to isolated interpretative outlines and sketches. Here also it engendered the major interpretations of Fascism that dominated and, to a degree, continue to dominate our politics and thought: Fascism as the product of a moral crisis in European society during the first half of the twentieth century; Fascism as the result of retarded and atypical economic development and national unification in European countries such as Italy and Germany; and the Marxist notion that Fascism was the senescent or dying stage of capitalism, or, at the very least, the final product of class struggle.

European thought paused a long time over these three interpretations. For fifteen years they remained virtually uncontested. It
cannot be said, however, that they were accepted unquestioningly.
On the contrary, their respective advocates often confronted each
other in lively debate, in the course of which each tried, and often
succeeded, in demonstrating his adversaries' weakness. Nor were
attempts lacking to reconcile the interpretations and to reduce all
three to a common denominator, that is, a moral disease.[9] It is,
however, a fact that during these years—despite these discussions,
which were especially lively in Italy and in Germany—the debate in
Europe on Fascism continued to revolve substantially around these
three interpretations; other voices were virtually silent. Even the
Fascist survivors have been unable to confront these interpretations
with one of their own.[10]

An inquest into the causes of this situation would entail a
lengthy study of European thought after World War II. Briefly, although different circumstances obtained, some points were held in
common. Extremes of ideological and political thought at the time
caused the three interpretations to be categorized as sharply defined
political and cultural concepts: Liberal (moral disease), Radical,
and Communist. On the other hand, the Fascist problem was not so
urgent as other problems that arose or reemerged at the end of
World War II. Also, at that time European thought suffered psychological effects that caused it to be exhausted, nauseated, and
reticent before a situation that it had quite often been incapable of
understanding in the past. Some people tended to consider that the
matter was definitely concluded and could be explained conceptu-
ally on the basis of the arguments they had employed when they
participated in the political and military struggle against the Fascist
powers.

For many years, however, the situation has been changing.
Everywhere there is renewed interest in the problem of Fascism, its
characteristics, social significance, causes, and historical interpretation. Especially among the younger generation, a growing number
of historians has been joined in pursuit of the question by sociologists, social psychologists, political scientists, economists, and even
philosophers. Because it is not possible here to undertake a detailed
examination of the reasons for this changed attitude, we shall con-
fine ourselves to certain very general and clear observations.

For the first impetus to change we must observe the effects produced by the debate that took place years ago among the advocates of the three classic interpretations of Fascism. This debate attempted to reduce Fascism to a mere manifestation of class struggle at home and imperialism abroad. But, at the same time, Fascism was viewed as an outgrowth of nationalism. Finally, there was a categorical refusal to consider an explanation that took into account both of these alternatives, or any others. Thus, the debate proved the inadequacy of all three interpretations when viewed individually and the futility of attempting a reconciliation among them. It was necessary to consider other alternatives, to renew the systematic study of the problem, and to investigate approaches that had been barely considered or even totally neglected by European thought.

The historical interpretation was foremost among these new approaches. It came to the fore at a particularly favorable time—when the major ideologies that had governed the first half of the century and had given rise to the three classic interpretations were undergoing a crisis. These ideologies, although not in eclipse, as some thought, were becoming less monolithic and politically less exclusive; they were themselves transformed as they came into contact with new facts. Debate about Fascism became less closely bound to positions and passions that had marked the years in which the phenomenon occurred, and the problem became more complex than merely understanding or justifying it.[11]

A second, more specific but no less important, reason for change is the effect on cultural and philosophical thought of the reverberations and dissemination during the 1950s and 1960s of sociological, sociopsychological, and socioeconomic research into the nature of mass society, collective behavior, and economic development. (In the United States sociology and psychology were applied to the study of Fascism as early as the late 1930s.) More than one student of Fascism looked to these new studies as a means of avoiding the pitfalls posed by the three classic interpretations. There is no doubt that the social sciences threw new light on a series of important problems concerning the nature and character of the Fascist phenomenon that heretofore had been underestimated or ignored. However, this new form of inquiry soon developed an excessive and irritating tendency toward rigid interpretation that was just as one-sided and schematic as that of its predecessors. Fascism was to be understood by means of models—psychological, sociological, socioeconomic, and so on. And these models, by attempting to encompass all forms of Fascism, soon obliterated a realistic view of the problem.

Besides these two, strictly scientific mandates, there was a third, more practical, reason for change. In a certain sense it might be labeled political, and it had significant influence on the new interest in the problem and nature of Fascism. At the end of World War II, with the elimination of the German and Italian Fascist regimes, movements, and parties, as well as those that had emerged during the war in all parts of Europe occupied by Axis forces, the term "Fascist" came to be employed in an increasingly indiscriminate and generic manner. It was used to characterize the Franco regime in Spain, the only Fascist government to emerge from the war unscathed; it was used to indicate the neo-Fascist movements in Germany and Italy that harked back to the historical experience and ideals of Fascism and National Socialism. But the term was also used to characterize the Salazar regime in Portugal and the Peronista government in Argentina; and it was applied to certain regimes in postcolonial Africa and Asia. After 1958, and De Gaulle's accession to power in France, it became fashionable to refer to a Fascist revival there. Finally, and on an even more general level, the extreme Left and certain radical groups have used the adjective in an increasingly broad, indiscriminate, and distorting sense.

A few examples prove this point. During the Cold War, and recently as well, more than one aspect of the policies of the United States and of certain governments allied to it have been labeled Fascist by the Soviet and Chinese Communist movements. Similarly, many governments in Latin America and elsewhere have been labeled Fascist, although strictly speaking they were no more than manifestations of traditional conservative tendencies ascribable to a particular historical experience.[12] The same has been true of the regime of the Colonels in Greece. And, more recently, the Chinese have referred to the Soviet Union as a "social-Fascist" state. The extreme left wing of the Berlin student movement has been accused by the philosopher Jürgen Habermas (identified with the Frankfurt Left) of running the risk of slipping into a kind of "Fascism of the

Left." The need to put an end to this indiscriminate and distorted use of the adjective "Fascist" has become so practically and scientifically imperative that it has been proposed that its use be banned, at least temporarily, from our vocabulary. It is necessary to establish once and for all what is meant by Fascism.[13] We must develop a model to which we may refer with reasonable certainty; and we must decide whether it is to be considered an individual phenomenon dictated by a specific historical moment in determined countries and brought about by contingent, nonrecurring circumstances, or whether it should be viewed as but one of the possible forms of political and social organization that mass societies encounter at a given stage in development.

It is hard to predict what influence these three mandates for change will have on future studies of Fascism, just as it is too early to forecast how they will affect the history of Fascism. Renewed interest on the part of European and American historians has led to two types of investigation. Attempts have been made to fill in the blanks about Fascism in the 1930s and 1940s by studying individual national manifestations of it and by trying to draw analogies and pinpoint differences among its various forms. This will result in more precise control over the various interpretations of Fascism, whether they be classic or more recent. Moreover, all the interpretations have been reexamined with a view to inserting them into the framework of current thought.[14] Important contributions of this sort have been made by the University of Reading's Seminar on Fascism, in April 1967, and the International Symposium, held in August 1969 in Prague under the auspices of the Czechoslovak Academy of Sciences.[15]

It is to be expected that Italy and Germany should be the countries most interested in a systematic study of Fascism. However, studies elsewhere also have shown a tendency on the part of historians to remain open to the greatest possible variety of suggestions and a reluctance to discard a priori any hypothesis.[16] Scholars are taking advantage of every opportunity afforded by the social sciences; yet at the same time they are trying to return studies on Fascism to an exclusively historical dimension, avoiding generalization and systematizing. This seems to imply that Fascism will no longer be viewed as a phenomenon characteristic of an epoch, as

Nolte has contended.[17] In Europe, at least, the various interpretations are taking on precise national and historical dimensions related to the specific economic, social, cultural, and political events
that characterized so-called Fascist regimes or movements in individual countries between the wars.[18] Although it is becoming increasingly obvious that the various manifestations of Fascism had
much in common, that they felt the need to support each other, and
that they suffered similar demises, this does not alter the fact that
their origins were largely dissimilar and that each retained peculiarities that make it difficult to speak of them as a truly single phenomenon.

If we accept this premise, the real problem lies in defining to
what extent Fascism can be considered a phenomenon of suprana-
tional dimensions. In my judgment, this tendency should not be
carried to an extreme. Rejection of the postulate of a single Fascism,
although with minor national variations, does not imply the denial
of a minimum common denominator among the various manifestations of Fascism that arose between the wars.[19] Rather, the problem
lies in neither restricting nor diffusing that common denominator
too much. If we restrict it too much, it is impossible to understand
why Fascism occurred, albeit with distinctive features, in various
countries at approximately the same time, and why it has virtually
never recurred. If we diffuse the common denominator too far, we
will underestimate the significance of specific historical circumstances in the various countries where Fascism emerged. This road
leads once again to generalizations. Geographical areas and historical circumstances intrinsic to Fascism are ignored; but it is arbitrary
to speak of Fascism in the historical context without them.[20]

If we are to consider Fascism one of the major historical
events of our time, use of the word cannot be extended to countries
outside Europe, nor to any period other than that between the
wars. Its roots are typically European; they are inalienably linked
to the changes in European society brought about by World War I
and to the moral and material crisis occasioned by conversion to a
mass society with new political and social institutions.[21] These circumstances prevailed throughout the Continent, but especially in
those countries that confronted change in conditions of backwardness, weakness, and economic and political abnormality. If we take

this transformation as a starting point, bearing in mind the social and economic development and the historical characteristics of the countries involved, we can deduce from the individual manifestations of Fascism a general notion of the phenomenon. We can distinguish within it elements that are old, conservative, and inherited from the past, as well as factors that are new, transforming, and typical of modern mass societies with Fascist regimes. And we can seek to scale the respective incidence of the phenomenon in its complexity.[22] A more extensive, rigid study tracing other aspects of Fascism, or even other characteristics sometimes labeled as Fascist, to a single common denominator would be as difficult as it would be distorting. Suffice it to recall, for example, that although racism and anti-Semitism were essential to National Socialism, they were not a part of Spanish Falangism and the Franco regime. Nor were they an integral part of Italian Fascism, which adopted them late and largely for reasons of political convenience and to avoid being at odds with other Axis powers. In Italy they were not elements of the prevalent ideology and political life.[23]

As a preliminary working hypothesis, I propose this twofold typology:

Typology of countries. Fascism established itself wherever:

social mobility, particularly of a vertical nature, was the most rapid and intense;

a predominantly agrarian and latifundium-type economy existed, or massive residues of this sort of economy were not substantially integrated into the national economic complex;

there was an economic crisis (inflation, unemployment, high cost of living, and so on), or such a crisis had not been completely surmounted;

there was a confused process of crisis and alteration of traditional moral values;

there was a crisis of either growth or senility within the parliamentary system that caused either the Socialists and Communists or certain sectors of the bourgeoisie to question the very legitimacy of the system and occasioned the feeling that there was no valid alternative government;

war had aggravated or left unresolved certain national and colonial problems such as Irredentism and the presence of powerful alien minorities, thereby encouraging nationalistic tensions and the rise of revisionist tendencies with regard to the configuration of Europe as determined by the treaties of Versailles, Trianon, Saint-Germain, and others.

Typology of forms of power. Fascism established itself through:

mystical concepts of life and politics based on the primacy of irrational activism and faith in direct and revolutionary action; denigration of the ordinary individual and exaltation of the national collectivity and extraordinary personalities (elites and supermen), thus providing the basis for the myth (so essential in Fascism) of the 'leader';[24]

a political regime of the masses (in the sense of a continual mobilization of the masses and a direct relation between the leader and the masses), based on a single-party system and a party militia and enforced by a police regime and control of all information and propaganda media;

verbal revolutionarism, coupled with substantial conservatism[25] and alleviated by social concessions of a welfare nature;

an attempt to create a new managerial class, existing as the expression of the party and, indirectly, of the petty and middle bourgeoisie;

the creation and improvement of a strong military apparatus; an economic system based on private enterprise but characterized by expansion of the public sector, by transfer of economic leadership from the capitalists and entrepreneurs to high state officials, and by state control of the major aspects of economic policy including mediation in labor controversies (corporativism) and promotion of autarky.

Each part of this typology is meaningful only to the extent that it achieves historical verification and fits the specific national manifestations of Fascism. It appears impossible to proceed toward a definition of the Fascist phenomenon except through such a broad typology—whose value is negative, in that it prevents an almost unlimited expansion of the Fascist model to include historic reality, which has nothing in common with it. Within this framework we must proceed with caution to avoid two ever-present dangers. The first is that of categorically attributing to Fascism, as inherent in its very nature, economic and social choices and changes that it

brought about but which were largely dictated by objective needs
for social development and by the dialectic of the state and community. Instead we must determine the roles played by the needs of
the totalitarian states, by Fascist ideology, by the interests of the
parties involved, and by objective needs for change—all of which
were quite often brought about—as was typically the case in Italy
—by *commis d'Etat* to which the Fascist label can be applied only
secondarily. Secondly, we cannot forget that beneath the authoritarianism and anti-Bolshevism of the better part of its class distinctions, Fascism basically reflected, though in confused and contradictory fashion, the need to rebuild human integrity that had
suffered at the hands of social and economic change brought about
by the war.[26]

If we accept this line of study and evaluation of the phenomenon, it becomes obvious that the individual interpretations offered
heretofore are insufficient, partial, or too exclusive for the compil-
ing of a single interpretation reflecting Fascism's various manifestations. But it is also obvious that each of them contains a part of the
truth and can contribute to a better understanding of the Fascist
phenomenon in its broad framework. They cannot be rejected a
priori, and the book of H. Stuart Hughes, *Contemporary Europe:
A History*, provides new evidence of the results that can be attained
from such a combination of methodologies and interpretations.[27]
Hughes's passages devoted to the "nature of the Fascist system" are
the most balanced and convincing that I have read in an overall interpretation.

The present volume, which has been conceived in these
terms, aims to provide an overview of the principal Italian and
foreign interpretations of the Fascist phenomenon, as well as an
outline of the debate that arose among the advocates of these interpretations.[28] It is my conviction that the historical discussion of
Fascism can no longer be terminated at the interpretative level, but
must try to reconstruct the history of each example of Fascism. The
various interpretations provide working hypotheses for and a conceptual stimulus to the search for the historical significance of a series of movements and regimes that, along with the democratic and
the Communist ones, played so great a part in the moral, social,
and political life of Europe during the first half of this century.

2

The Classic Interpretations

Fascism as Europe's moral disease

This is probably the interpretation that gained most favor among continental European intellectuals. Most of its advocates have been Italians and Germans. There also have been significant and authoritative reverberations on the other side of the Atlantic, especially among scholars with European backgrounds.

The interpretation was propounded by the Italian Benedetto Croce in a November 1943 *New York Times* article, in a speech on January 28, 1944, at the first congress in Bari of the Committees of Liberation, and in an interview in March 1947.[1] On these occasions Croce expounded on the interpretation's two fundamental premises. First, that Fascism "was not conceived nor desired by any one social class, nor supported by any single class"; it was "a bewilderment, a civic depression, and a state of inebriation caused by the war." Second, this bewilderment and inebriation were not exclusively Italian, but affected almost all the nations that had participated in World War I. In Italy they had gained the upper hand, "thanks to illusions, tricks, and threats"; but this was not true in Italy alone, because, "as a tendency, effort, aspiration, and expectation," Fascism was world-wide, just as "the whole contemporary world celebrated the person of the Superman and the Leader." As such, Fascism was a "parenthesis" corresponding to "a lowering of the consciousness of freedom."

In Germany the most authoritative advocate of this interpretation was Friedrich Meinecke, who in 1946 made it the subject of *Die Deutsche Katastrophe*. He was followed by numerous other authors, though for reasons of space we shall study only Gerhard Ritter and Golo Mann. Just as Croce had concentrated on Italian Fascism, Meinecke was interested in explaining German National Socialism. His analysis has a general interpretative value, however, because he asserts that National Socialism was not a phenomenon deriving only from German evolutionary forces; however horribly unique an example of German degeneration Nazism seems, it had certain analogies and precedents in the authoritarian systems of neighboring countries.

According to Meinecke, National Socialism and Fascism represented an "astonishing deviation" from the evolutionary line along which, until then, Europe had developed. To explain this deviation he refers to Jakob Burckhardt, who detected "the germ of the great disease" in "the optimistic illusions of the Age of Enlightenment and the French Revolution," as well as in "the mistaken striving after the unattainable happiness of the masses of mankind, which then shifted into a desire for profits, power, and a general striving for living well." Along this deviant road lay a gradual dissolution of traditional social ties and the creation "of new but very powerful ties." The principles and individuals that came to the fore forced the masses "into discipline and obedience" and persuaded them to renounce freedom in the name of happiness.[2] This moral crisis was the consequence of the "mobilization of the masses," brought about by the French Revolution, and of the Industrial Revolution.[3] Meinecke is explicit:

> Technology's expansion into all walks of practical life has in general called into existence a great number of new crafts and careers. It thereby finally created a new social class whose psychological structure is markedly different from that of previous social classes, both those of the old agrarian state and those of the new bourgeoisie which has blossomed out of the agrarian state. An intellect sharply concentrated upon whatever was utilitarian and immediately serviceable took possession of mental life. Through it great things could be achieved, resulting in an astonishing progress in civiliza-

tion. Man's other spiritual forces, so far as they were not
suppressed, avenged themselves either by those wild reac-
tions . . . or fell into a general decay and debility.[4]

World War I worsened the crisis, especially in Germany.
Most of the moral values that had guided Western civilization were
sacrificed on the altar of victory and of power gained at any price,
and both old and new negative forces were exalted. This crisis was
exacerbated in Germany by the "depressing influence" of defeat
and the Versailles Treaty, and then by the great economic crisis.
The balance between rational and irrational impulse was irremedi-
ably altered between these parameters, especially insofar as youth
were concerned:

> An intoxication seized upon German youth at this time,
> both upon those who had borne arms in the World War and
> upon those who had grown up under the debilitating effects
> of the Versailles peace. On the material side they craved em-
> ployment, an income, and opportunities for advancement.
> In the field of ideas they craved something which gave play
> to feelings and phantasy—to ideals which were worth living
> for. The Weimar Republic, to be sure, was founded on a
> great ideal, for which a whole politically ripe nation ought
> to have lived and fought—the ideal of an established na-
> tional community uniting both working class and bour-
> geoisie, the ideal that all groups formerly avowedly hostile
> to the state should be permeated by a sound national feeling,
> not exaggerated but embracing all human values. Combined
> with this ideal in the Weimar Republic was the firm determi-
> nation to throw off, or at least to loosen, one by one the
> fetters of the Versailles Treaty. . . .
> Such a program, however, involved much too much rea-
> sonableness and resignation on the part of the craving youth
> of 1930. "You have offered us no ideals," they cried out
> against the Weimar supporters; "you cannot fully satisfy us"
> —and they meant it . . . in both the material and the ideolog-
> ical sense. There is a natural impulse in all youth to form
> associations which stimulate impulses for speedy action
> wherever possible. So in the early thirties many young peo-
> ple, worthy but wholly unripe politically, began to organize

themselves as the Storm Troops [SA, *Sturmabteilungen*] of the Hitler movement. Hitler, one may say, came to power through a typical but dazzled and blinded youth movement.[5]

These are the main lines of Meinecke's analysis, from which he derives his interpretation of National Socialism and, by extension, of Fascism. The great German historian stressed, however, that there were significant differences among the various forms of Fascism:

> the character of the German people of Hitler's day resulted from a continuous shifting since Goethe's time of psychological forces—a disturbing of the psychological equilibrium between the rational and the irrational. The calculating intellect was excessively exaggerated on the one hand, and the emotional desire for power, wealth, security, and so forth on the other hand. As a result the acting will power was driven onto dangerous ground. Whatever could be calculated and achieved technically, if it brought wealth and power, seemed justified—in fact, even morally justified, if it served the welfare of one's own country. The new ethics of national egoism, the doctrine of *sacro egoismo*, had to be added to give this shifting of the psychological forces the proper blessing.[6]

With regard to this last point, Meinecke refers to a "Machiavellian" rebirth and a transformation of Machiavellianism from an aristocratic phenomenon, to a middle-class occurrence, and finally to an event that had much in common with the masses. Ritter develops this concept in *Die Dämonie der Macht*. For him, too, Fascism was the fruit of a dramatic moral crisis which was translated into a frantic search for material well-being and also into a need for "a surrogate religion." Through it the masses, especially the lower middle class ("that typical mass humanity of modern times") found a means of escaping from the straitjacket of class struggle and of finding a solution to the social problems of the age of capitalism. All of this occurred, in Germany especially, in the wider context of a break in the ethical framework that hitherto had dominated relations between morals and power. Moreover, there was a distorted rebirth of the old Machiavellian ideals that had never really disappeared in Europe.

> The "Totalitarian" state that thus emerged can be viewed as the culmination of a historical process that began with the Christian Middle Ages, with its bipolarity extending throughout the life of Western man, right up to modern paganism. There is no longer any place outside the community of the state where man can face his God on his own cognizance; nor is there an apolitical community of participants in a common conviction or religious faith . . . In the political sphere there are no longer any ethics of love, only the morals of a struggle that no longer allows for respect . . . Moral conscience and political conscience are irretrievably commingled. That terrible confusion of ideas is born whereby success in power politics of external affairs is confused with moral right, blind fanaticism for power is confused with "reason of state" and creative energy, and for which all moral judgment over political action is lost . . . In this way the demon of power, instead of disappearing, rises to the condition of full-blown Satanism.[7]

The debate initiated by Meinecke, Ritter, and their followers is couched in more precise terms by Golo Mann. The schematic general interpretation of the phenomenon becomes a vehicle for a comprehensive review of historical events in Germany from the French Revolution to the present. The general interpretative thesis is articulated, honed, and applied to previously neglected aspects of the problem by means of a parallel discussion of events and of their background. Mann contradicts those who refuse to consider Fascism, and National Socialism in particular, as an unpremeditated outburst of irrational and demonic forces brought into play by precise causes and occasioned by the profound crisis provoked by World War I ("a singular event in history, bound to the individual and the moment, an event that can never be exactly reproduced"). He also refutes those authors who consider Fascism a logical outpouring of a series of ideas, emotions, and forces that had been incubating for decades, and which progressively came to represent the historical antecedents of Fascism. As Croce's had been,[8] Mann's reply is extremely firm:

> The failure of the Republic [of Weimar] proves nothing about the historical validity of what came after it and much too much honour is done Hitler by historians who want us to believe that all that Germany did for hundreds of years was to prepare itself for the inevitable end, for National Socialism. Particular ideas and sentiments which Hitler used, pan-German nationalism, imperialism, desire to have a strong man, and anti-semitism had of course long been there in the German soul yet such ideas alone did not constitute an historically effective force. Although we think that we can hear Hitler's voice in slogans of the pan-Germans, the late Bismarckians, the supporters of Ludendorff, the *Vaterlandspartei* and the *Freikorps* together do not add up to National Socialism. It is not identified by these elements. Other things were needed for its rise: The economic crisis and this unique individual. The economic crisis helped the breakthrough of the individual; in 1933 it therefore helped feelings to emerge which originated from the year 1919 and which basically were already out of date in 1933. Such perverse happenings are possible in history. What had in fact started with Bismarck and what the First World War brought to fruition was the interregnum: the inability of the nation to settle its internal conflicts according to the rules and to give its state a satisfying meaning. The rest was not predetermined. If the one man had not existed, anything might have happened, but not National Socialism as we knew it. *He happened to exist.* In an interregnum the strongest takes over and it was Hitler who happened to be the strongest.[9]

It is just as false to view Fascism merely as the product of specific interests that use it knowingly to conquer power. In this respect, too, Mann is explicit. It has been stated repeatedly that the army and the industrialists nurtured National Socialism and brought it to power in Germany.[10] Neither hypothesis is true:

> If many young officers swore by Hitler, their views were not shared by their superiors; the Army was part of the peo-

ple and could not be isolated from what was happening
among the people. The generals were deeply mistrustful of
this mob raiser and did not want to see him in control, much
less in unrestricted control. Yet they were opposed to the Republic and themselves incapable of replacing the Republic
by anything else. The same is true of industry, particularly
of the heavy industry of the Rhineland. It did not "make"
Hitler, as historians of the Marxist school have wanted to
persuade us; the German steel magnates were not that imag-
inative. Only a few outsiders among them provided the Nazi
Party with money during the period of struggle.

The real reasons for the success of National Socialism must
be found elsewhere. A large number of Germans did not want Hitler, "and even most of those who voted for him freely did not want
what he finally brought." If Hitler succeeded, it was because these
same Germans, including the military and the industrialists, "did
not want the Weimar Republic." Above all—and this is the true crisis, the moral crisis—they did not want it, but they did not know
what they wanted instead, "or if they knew they lacked the courage
to act." Unable to offer a constructive political alternative, in the
long run they had "reluctantly accepted the strongest anti-republican offer."

They were all in the same position, the opinionated pro-
fessors, the old bureaucrats, the young romantics, the war
veterans' associations, the *Herren* clubs, all those who refused real support to the Weimar democracy and who
wanted something else without themselves knowing what, a
return to what had been before or a step forward, a strong
system, a strong lead, something national, something splen-
did.

This occurred in a country where the masses were particularly concerned with their immediate well-being. They had no rally-
ing points, and after the "great economic crisis" their only concern
was to extricate themselves. In sum:

there was much scepticism in Germany, much cynicism and
rootlessness. Most people did not believe what their rulers
said but when asked officially whether they supported "their

government's policy" they voted yes. Life was hard, how hard had recently been demonstrated by the years of economic crisis. Now that there was work again and opportunity of promotion and reasonable security, people's attitude was that it would be foolish to risk everything for the sake of mere political differences. Success justified those at the top.[11]

In a country where National Socialism provided the Germans "a home, a spiritual shelter," it succeeded in providing them with the experience of a popular "community," which the Weimar democracy had not, and it allowed them to "participate," or to believe they were participating in this community.

Essentially these are the characteristics of the European, especially the liberal Italian and German, interpretation of Fascism as a product of contemporary moral crisis. Scholars in other countries —José Ortega y Gasset, for example—followed almost the same reasoning. Hans Kohn, a Czech-born American, in *The Twentieth Century* treats the problem of Fascism and its interpretation. His work repeats and vigorously develops the thesis of Fascism as a moral disease. But it adds an element present in other authors, but which Kohn alone has made an integral component of the interpretation: the concept of Totalitarianism. Kohn emphasizes that the full historical significance of Fascism can be grasped only if it is linked, in the long run, to the glorification of life and power and the disdain of reason advocated by a long line of modern philosophers. And, in the short run, it must be linked to the crisis produced by World War I. This crisis unthroned individual reason. (In a felicitous metaphor, Kohn asserts that although Descartes' *cogito ergo sum* summed up the contemporary moral posture of our civilization, henceforth it would be contained in a new formula: *agitamus ergo sumus*.) It also caused the disintegration of traditional moral values and, at times, of the rule of law. It provoked a series of economic transformations that "destroyed the strength, and in some cases the existence, of that middle class which had been the backbone of nineteenth century civilization." And it fostered the "massification" of European society:

> Glorification of life and distrust of reason led to a new *Verzauberung* of the world, its derationalization, the reap-

pearance and recrudescence of leaders and slogans, a new
triumph of magicians and witch doctors, equipped this time
with all the newest devices of technique and mass hypnosis.
What had been an esoteric teaching among the intelligentsia
before World War I became after the war a fundamental issue with the younger generation. In the growing complexity
of the world, after the unprecedented catastrophe of the
World War, the bewilderment of the masses led them to a
growing impatience with, and distrust of, reasonableness,
compromise, and slow progress. This happened just at the
time when it would have been most important to mobilize
all rational forces and all patient efforts, all critical faculties
and all tolerant fairness, for ordering the postwar world so
as to avoid even graver catastrophes.[12]

Now Kohn introduces the concept of Totalitarianism. The
cleavages that divided mankind became "unbridgeable abysses
across which there seems no longer an understanding possible," so
that contrasts themselves become conflicts that can only be resolved
by force and the destruction of the adversary. From this crisis of
reason were born other beliefs, one more exclusive than the next,
but all expressions of a single crisis. It was the birth of Totalitarianism, and Fascism was one—though not the only one—of its primary
and most important manifestations. It was a manifestation that basically was not dissimilar to Soviet Communism. In this respect
Kohn writes:

> While Descartes stressed the legitimacy of doubt and the
> right of the thinking individual, modern totalitarianism has
> reasserted the same claim to absoluteness as medieval faith.
> The outlook on life of those who have adopted fascism or
> communism has nothing in common with the Western tradi-
> tion of reason. Its liberalism was prepared to admit that
> alongside one's own path to truth there may be others. This
> attitude permitted liberty of thought and tolerance and
> formed the basis for the growth of individualism. What the
> West had won thus in breadth and freedom, it lost in cer-
> tainty. The fanaticism of the totalitarians springs from the
> absoluteness of their faith. The consciousness of the saving
> truth gives them their assurance: the opponent is always

wrong; there can therefore be no compromise. In this secularized orthodoxy, the hardness that shrinks from nothing is a true service to the attainment of the goal. The totalitarian certainty of victory is based on an eschatological confidence free from all moral contexts. The dethronement of reason and the rise of the new totalitarian myth threaten the growth of a unified world and all the progress which the nineteenth century had achieved.[13]

Thus, Kohn completes the definition and interpretation of Fascism formulated by a Croce or a Meinecke. Moreover, he illuminates the new features of Fascism and Totalitarianism not found in traditional conservative and absolutist regimes. Traditional regimes result from the authoritarian imposition of a relatively small group of leaders whose aim is to maintain or restore a determined political and social framework. Rather than activate the masses, the leaders rely on their passiveness. Fascist and Totalitarian regimes, on the other hand, look to a new political and social order, and, at least on certain levels and at determined moments, activate the masses, taking advantage of their immaturity, their moral and material crisis, and their sense of disillusionment and cynicism brought about by the crisis.

Totalitarian dictatorships are phenomena peculiar to the twentieth century through their "democratic" character; they are mass movements. Though they started as seizure of power by minorities, and in the case of Russia by a small minority, they succeeded because they gave form to the shapeless dreams of the national masses and voiced with almost frightening daring and oversimplification their confused and hardly conscious wishes. The mass following of men like Stalin and Hitler cannot be explained by terror alone. A bond of fundamental affinity unites the leaders with their peoples, not any outstanding attractiveness in the leader himself . . . Hitler did not conquer the German masses, he represented them . . . "This was his true strength." Hitler's success was based on the fact that he "democratized" or vulgarized for the masses some of the great intellectual and political traditions of Germany.[14]

Fascism as a result of the historical development of certain countries

Of the three classic interpretations, this one has had the best reception in political and lay circles, either on its own or in conjunction with the Marxist interpretation. Its most fervent advocates in all countries have come from certain sectors of radical thought. Even the highest intellectual circles have been influenced by it, especially during the years immediately prior to and following World War II.

According to this interpretation, Fascism is the logical and inevitable consequence of a set of obstacles characteristic of the historical development of certain countries, particularly Italy and Germany. For most countries these obstacles are fairly recent and the result of the delay, fragility, and exasperation with which the countries achieved economic development, unification, and national independence. The middle class in these countries was able to develop only along pathological lines; it was under constant pressure, therefore, to fall back on conservative alliances and essentially illiberal and antidemocratic forms of power to assert its own predominance. As a result, the moral and material participation of the masses in the country's government and national unification was virtually excluded, and Fascism was the logical and necessary result of this reactionary, antipopulist policy. Thus, it is asserted, there is a valid connection between Fascism and the traditional authoritarian and imperialistic traditions in these countries.

In other countries the obstacles dated back to a remoter past and were also of a psychological and moral nature. Some questioned whether Italian Fascism might not be "the final explosion of a disease rooted in the Italians and corresponding to habits of insubordination, lack of civic pride, a delight in swindling whatever government might be in power, absenteeism, corruption, and vices bred by centuries of despotic government and transformed by the D'Annunzian rhetoric of millions of unemployed adventurers, and by the exasperation provoked by the currents of fury and despair that exploded in Italy at the end of the war."[15] This interpretation, however, was most often applied to Germany. The authoritarian, militaristic, imperialistic, pan-Germanic, and anti-Semitic German intellectual and political tradition and the elements of continuity *apodictically)*

between it and National Socialism were the keystones of this interpretation. They provided material for a series of specialized studies and research whose conclusions had and continue to have wide dissemination among laymen and in the mass media. Chronologically, the most important of these studies are: *Doctrinaires de la Révolution allemande, 1919-1938,* by Edmond Vermeil, 1939; *From Luther to Hitler: The History of Fascist-Nazi Political Philosophy,* by William Montgomery McGovern, 1941; and *Metapolitics: From the Romantics to Hitler,* by Peter Viereck, 1941.[16]

These studies are stimulating because they highlight the fundamental historical differences among the various Fascist movements and regimes. Advocates of this interpretation, however, too often limited its formulation to mechanical and peripheral contrasts and similarities. Moreover, they apodictically juxtaposed it to the other interpretations, particularly the moral-disease theory, without testing it in broader research. They stressed only those aspects of reality of immediate concern, without examining the full historical complexity of the problem. The few attempts to correct the situation are unconvincing, weak, and fail to explain a number of crucial problems. One such problem is how Germany and Italy, despite so many obstacles, were able to conceive and consolidate the unified State, create a national market, and dictate effective economic, social, civic, and political development. Above all, these studies have not confronted the fundamental problem of the transformations in European society brought about or hastened by World War I which led to the new social and political conditions, nor have they investigated the effectiveness of these transformations in bringing about decisive new social and political conditions in the realm of the traditional. Typical of this approach to Fascism are the accusations directed against Gerhard Ritter and, in particular, against his monumental work on German militarism.[17] He is accused of not detecting "in Prussian and German history from Frederick the Great to Adolf Hitler a single and substantially continuous chain of examples of 'military reason of State,' in which there might exist difference of degree but not of principle."[18] *Italy: A Modern History* and other writings on Italian Fascism by Denis Mack Smith are dominated, as Walter Maturi has pointed out, by an obsession to prove that "everything in Italian history from 1861

on leads to Fascism."[19] This English historian carries his charges to
the point where, to cite a single example, Cavour's *connubio* (union
of parties) was but one moment of an imagined pattern of "Italian
parliamentary dictatorship, and it differed only in degree whether
under Cavour, Depretis, Crispi, or Giolitti, or even under Mussolini during the first years of power."

Having made this general statement, I must point out that in
Italian thought this interpretation developed with certain characteristics of its own that have earned it the label "revelation." More
important, it has acquired significance that is partially different
from what it had in other countries. In Italian thought the revelation thesis, after its embryonic enunciations (that had more political than historiographical value), developed to the extent that it
conflicted with the position of Benedetto Croce, particularly with
two of his assertions, one of which was that Fascism was an "acci-
dent," a "parenthesis" in Italian history. (Actually, Ivanoe Bonomi,
on the last page of his *Dal Socialismo al Fascismo* [1924], was the
first to speak of Fascism as a parenthesis.) The second instance
where the revelation theory crossed swords with Croce, though of
a methodological, or even philosophical, nature, was intimately
related to the first. According to this assertion, "historical causal-
ity" should be rejected so as to avoid falling back into a new sort of
"skepticism or historical Pyrrhonism." The parenthesis thesis—so
radical and, in actual fact, so largely dictated by political rather
than historical considerations—has aroused criticism and rebuttals
that are just as radical. Such was the case not only among Croce's
opponents but also among certain scholars who adopted the moral-
disease position—Chabod, for example. But because of the political
undertones of the question, these criticisms and rebuttals eventually took on features leading to a great misunderstanding among
many Italians. Many scholars thought that discarding the indefen-
sible parenthesis thesis was tantamount to denying the moral-disease interpretation. For them the parenthesis became the salient
characteristic of the moral-disease interpretation (often even referred to simply as the parenthetical interpretation). However,
Croce's discussion of the Fascist parenthesis is not found in Meinecke, Ritter, or other advocates of the moral-disease theory; on the
contrary, they explain the disease by referring explicitly to a series

of transformations dating back to the French Revolution. It is clear that it is in no way a necessary corollary and that its omission does not make it vulnerable in its own right.[20]

The interpretation of Fascism as the logical and inevitable product of the historical development of certain countries has been steadily losing ground among historians. There are at least three reasons for the decline. One is dissatisfaction with the paucity, inconsistency, and even sectarianism of the interpretation's contribution to the wider debate on Fascism and reconstruction of recent historical events in countries where Fascism occurred, such as Germany and Italy. Another reason, related to the first, is that many advocates have nullified the contribution of this historical interpretation by allying it too closely with the Marxist interpretation. The third reason can be found in the massive and irrefutable criticism levied against this interpretation by supporters of the moral-disease interpretation and even by some Marxists, not to mention the criticism launched by advocates of more recent interpretations.[21] There is no reason to linger here over the criticism of the advocates of moral disease because I have already addressed the subject in discussing Mann's position and also because I shall refer to it in Chapter 8, when we observe how first Croce and then Chabod refuted the "revelation" interpretation.

For the purposes of our discussion it will suffice to review the essential aspects of this criticism. First, no one can seriously maintain that Fascism is not subject to historical explanation or that it should be considered an irrational occurrence. There is no doubt that in the nineteenth-century history of countries such as Italy and Germany one can isolate "certain themes that later expand under Fascism and see in them the seeds that later bore fruit" (Chabod). Second, this does not mean, however, that Fascism was inevitable and the logical historical result of prior events in those countries. On the contrary, it was avoidable to the very end. If Fascism triumphed, it was not so much because of the preexistence of these "motifs" and "seeds"—which in the nineteenth century had neither a decisive nor a primary role—as it was because of the change brought about by World War I and the "massification" of society. Only in this new situation, and because of the faults and errors of the existing ruling class, did these "motifs" and "seeds" that had been secondary become primary. Other quite new and decisive factors were added to them; and from their sum Fascism ensued.

Gerhard Ritter summarized this twofold criticism better than anyone else when, in his book on Carl Goerdeler and the anti-Nazi opposition, he stated:

> It is not irrelevant to that rise [Hitler's] that political self-consciousness awoke later in Germany than in Western Europe, and from its first appearance in the wars of independence from 1813 to 1815 had a pronouncedly military character which was intensified by the experiences of 1864-71 and even by those of the First World War. The catastrophe of 1918 interrupted that rapid political and economic progress begun under Bismarck, but it could not destroy the enormous vitality of the German people, their economic power and their political self-confidence . . .
>
> None the less, it is fundamentally untrue . . . to say that National Socialism was the result of earlier German history, the last consequence, the fulfilment of German tradition . . . National Socialism is at bottom not an original German phenomenon, but only the German form of a European one —the phenomenon of the one-party state—and that is to be explained not as arising from an old tradition, but as arising from a specific contemporary crisis, the crisis of the liberal society . . .
>
> A decisive factor is that modern industrial society and the uniformity of the masses characteristic of it, do not favor the liberal ideal of free and autonomous personalities that are spiritually and economically independent; it is, however, all the more favorable to the democratic ideas of popular equality and sovereignty. Modern technology offers the means to mobilize people, or rather the newly sovereign masses in a completely different way from the past. Mass demonstrations, so-called "direct action" was always able to replace serious parliamentary discussion. Masses seek efficient action, not discussion; they obey their own sentiments, not rational considerations; they heed the impassioned appeal of the demagogue, not the advice of wise experts; they want a guide, not the pondered consideration of problems and alternatives; nor do they want the freedom to choose for themselves. In such a society the opportunities available to a

demagogue are enormous if he knows how to present himself as the representative and the exponent of the popular will: especially when a parliamentary government doesn't rest on secure internal foundations and parties but is always concerned with its popularity and unable to meet difficult obligations . . . The greatest weakness of our time is revealed in the paucity of its faith, the uncertainty of its convictions, the relativity of its moral values, in the scepticism in the face of everything that presents itself to men as absolute necessity. It is found in the nihilistic decline of sincere ideals to simple ideologies, in the not taking seriously of ethical-spiritual decisions as such, and of mere gossip in the place of a clear awareness of personal responsibility. The fact of possessing a fanatical faith in himself, in his mission and in the Nationalist Socialist religion gave Hitler the utmost superiority over many intelligent but sceptical and irresolute politicians of the Weimar Republic; because the masses have a need to believe in a man and a cause. The same fanaticism that raised him up, pushed him to self-divination and the insane adventures that came to an end with his fall.[22]

Although the interpretation of Fascism as the logical and inevitable product of the historical development of certain countries was decried, we cannot discard it as worthless. In Italy it has certainly contributed to discrediting the notion that Fascism was a parenthesis in our history; and it has clarified the significance of the historiographical debate on moral disease. History itself has been enriched, for this interpretation has attracted the attention of scholars to a series of problems, movements, and ideas (the "motifs" and "seeds" recently mentioned) whose presence had often been underestimated. Indeed, its major contribution, however indirect, has been to focus the attention of scholars on Fascism's real or presumed "motifs" and "seeds." This research and the discussion it engendered have increased our awareness of certain antecedents of Fascism, so that the debate has developed along new lines. Studies now focus on the influence of these precedents on Fascism, or on its individual manifestations, and on their gradations and place within the various phases of Fascism. Even though the problem is still under discussion, a tendency has emerged from these studies (let us recall Ritter and Talmon, to mention only the best known names) to list among Fascism's ideological components not only traditional elements, of a conservative and authoritarian kind, but others that previously had not even been considered or had been discarded as foreign to Fascism because of their radical-democratic, populist, and even revolutionary nature.

Fascism as a product of capitalist society and as an antiproletarian reaction

Chronologically, this was the first interpretation studied. Because of it, during the 1920s Fascism was considered a phenomenon that not only was present in Italy but also was evident or potentially could arise in other countries. Its central thesis is extremely precise: along with the basic premise that Fascism must be viewed and explained within the social and political framework of contemporary capitalist society and its contradictions, it asserts that Fascism was the embodiment—or at least one of the political, social, and ideological embodiments—of capitalism's struggle against the workers' revolutionary movement. The Communists were the chief advocates of this thesis, but it was also defended under various guises by several authors with Marxist backgrounds who had no connections with the international Communist movement. Arturo Labriola, for example, was among the first to adopt the thesis in 1924 in *La dittatura della borghesia e la decadenza della società capitalistica* (The dictatorship of the bourgeoisie and the decadence of capitalist society).

Today the main thrust of this interpretation can be deduced from the writings of Maurice H. Dobb, Paul A. Baran, and Paul M. Sweezy. In a book published in 1937, Dobb considered the connection between certain recent political movements such as Fascism and "the disintegration in the position of wide sections of the so-called 'middle class' " and the economic crisis and the postwar dysfunction of capitalism as "particularly intimate"—even though, he admits, the facts have not been sufficiently evaluated and the "generalization rests on particular interpretations of political happenings." For him there is a similar connection "between Fascism as an ideology of political and economic nationalism and Imperialism as a system characteristic of an epoch."

The events of the past few years afford abundant evidence to support the view that the historical rôle of Fascism is a double one. First, that of breaking and disbanding the independent organizations of the working class, and doing so not in the interest of the "middle class" or the "small man" but ultimately in the interest of Big Business. Secondly, that of organizing the nation both spiritually by intensive propaganda and practically by military preparations and authoritarian centralization for an ambitious campaign of territorial expansion. True, it employs for these purposes—particularly for the former—a unique demagogy of "radicalism," yoked to a highly modernized propaganda-machine, and seeks to build a social basis for itself in mass organizations created around these demagogic demands. This, indeed, constitutes a distinctive characteristic of it as an historical movement. But the "revolution" when it comes is at most a "palace revolution," and once the Fascist State is in being it is the masses, not Capital, which are regimented, and the radical programme, not surplus-value, that is jettisoned. If the Corporate State has economic significance, other than as a means of controlling labour-disputes, it would seem to be as machinery of giving State sanction and support to a more complete and rigid monopolistic organization of industry. . . . Fascism has been called a child of crisis. In a sense it is; but the aphorism is too simple. It is a child of a special sort of crisis, and a complex product of special features of that crisis: namely, a crisis of monopoly capitalism which derives its special gravity from the fact that the system finds the road blocked for it both to an extensive and a more intensive development of the field of exploitation. To break through these limits, novel and exceptional measures—measures of political dictatorship—become the inevitable orders of the day. If one is to summarize shortly the historical pre-conditions of Fascism, one can speak, I think, of three factors as pre-eminent: a despair on the part of Capital of finding a normal solution for the impasse created by the limitation of the investment-field; considerable and depressed "middle class" or déclassé elements, ripe, in the absence of an alternative rallying-point, to be recruited to the Fascist creed; and a working class, privi-

leged enough and strong enough to be resistant to normal
pressure on its standard of life, but sufficiently disunited or
non-class-conscious (at least in its political leadership) to be
politically weak in asserting its power or in resisting attack.
The first of these conditions is most likely to be characteristic of an imperialist country which is thwarted of the fruits
of colonialism on which it previously relied. With regard to
the second and third conditions: it will clearly be those middle strata, previously nourished directly or indirectly on the
imperial connection, which will most acutely feel the pinch
of such a situation; and it will be a nation whose economy
has previously rested on colonialism which is most likely to
have produced an "aristocracy of labour," with an ideology
and a political movement corresponding thereto. It is clearly
more than mere coincidence that the classic homes of Fascism should be in two countries which were so evidently
thwarted of their colonial ambitions by the outcome of the
Great War; as it may well be also that similar tendencies
should first strike their roots in Britain, the original cradle
both of parliamentary democracy and of trade unionism,
simultaneously with the first serious appearance of "middle
class unemployment" and of portentous signs of a decline of
Britain's position as a financial and exporting centre.[23]

In spite of its obvious weaknesses, Dobb's argument is very
clear: Fascism and Nationalism are too closely related to Italian and
German colonial matters. But it fails to take up one of the questions
that has long been central to the Marxist interpretation: whether or
not capitalism at a certain stage of its development inevitably leads
to Fascism. As we shall see, for many Marxists the answer was
affirmative. Prevalent opinion today, however, rules against a
thesis of inevitability. A typical position is that of Baran and
Sweezy, who in *Monopoly Capital* treat the problem:

> The history of recent decades is particularly rich in
> examples of the substitution of authoritarian for democratic
> government in capitalist countries: Italy in the early 1920's,
> Germany in 1933, Spain in the late 1930's, France in 1958,
> and many more.
>
> In general, however, moneyed oligarchies prefer demo-

cratic to authoritarian government. The stability of the system is enhanced by periodic popular ratifications of oligarchic rule—that is what parliamentary and presidential elections normally amount to—and certain very real dangers to the oligarchy itself of personal or military dictatorship are avoided. Hence in developed capitalist countries, especially those with a long history of democratic government, oligarchies are reluctant to resort to authoritarian methods of dealing with opposition movements or solving difficult problems, and instead devise more indirect and subtle means for accomplishing their ends . . . By these methods . . . democracy is made to serve the interest of the oligarchy far more effectively and durably than authoritarian rule. The possibility of authoritarian rule is never renounced—indeed, most democratic constitutions make specific provision for it in times of emergency—but it is decidedly not the preferred form of government for normally functioning capitalist societies.[24]

This denial of the inevitability of Fascist evolution from capitalism is of decisive importance to our discussion.[25] It raises anew the problem of Fascism's historical significance.

During the twenties and thirties the rigid and mechanical interpretation of the relation between capitalism and Fascism proposed by the Communist International had come under fire from critics even within the Marxist camp. Arthur Rosenberg maintained that Fascism should be viewed essentially as a phenomenon of underdeveloped capitalism seeking modernization. For example, in Italy—a country that was still semi-feudal—even though Fascism, prior to the economic crisis of 1929, had not resolved the agrarian problem, it had effectively developed the means of production: "the State Capitalism with which the corporative system had endowed Italy ensured that the country would be ruled by efficient capitalist groups."[26]

August Thalheimer, a founder of the German Communist Party, from which he was expelled in 1929, investigated two serious problems in *Über den Faschismus* (1930). First he questioned why Fascism, if it was the "open dictatorship of Capital," as the Communist International asserted, had taken root in Italy, Poland, Bul-

garia, and Spain but not in the more developed capitalist countries
such as the United States, England, Germany, and France. He asserted that if "the Fascist form of State had taken root specifically in
those countries that are far from the top of the list in terms of capitalist development," this did not mean that Fascism rigidly corresponded to a specific stage of economic development; nor was the
possibility to be excluded that it might take root in countries where
capitalism was more advanced. On the contrary, in certain advanced capitalist countries the middle class displayed a strong tendency "to destroy or limit the parliamentary system" and "to create
stronger political guarantees" to insure its own rule. In "critical situations" such a tendency could "lead to open forms of dictatorship
of Capital that, however, do not have to be identical to Fascism."
Indeed, for Thalheimer, this was but one of the particular manifestations of the open dictatorship of Capital. "The middle class resorts to the dictatorship of Capital as soon as its society is threatened by the strongest assault of the proletarian revolution: when
the bourgeoisie has exhausted its defenses, when all classes have
been laid low and the middle class looks for the safest way to establish its social dominion."[27]

At this point Thalheimer undertook his second theme. He
probably reached it as a result of his observation that, although
Fascism was "the open dictatorship of Capital," power was in the
hands of an elite that was not the expression of Capital nor of the
true bourgeoisie. His solution was slightly mechanical, but, given
the premises, it was effective and, in the final analysis, right on tar-
get. Referring back to what Marx and Engels had written about
Bonapartism, Thalheimer defined Fascism as a political and social
system similar to Bonapartism.[28] As had been the case under Napoleon III, the bourgeoisie was reduced to extremes and found that in
order to salvage its own social existence it had to sacrifice its own
political power and subject itself "to the strength of the newly independent executive power." This executive power, however, was
not the expression of a specific social base. Rather, it was an amalgam of rootless economic and social elements that were unable to
act as a class but were at the same time "the flesh and bones of private property and of bourgeois society and therefore able, despite
their annihilated political power, to defend and protect their social

power against those other classes that advocated revolutionary abolition of individual bourgeois property, and to defend themselves against the proletariat and the proletarianized sectors of the peasant class." Thus, according to Thalheimer, if Fascism-Bonapartism was characterized by independence of the executive branch, by annihilation of the political rule of the bourgeoisie, and by subjugation of all other social classes to the executive, its substance, its social and class content, "was still the domination of the bourgeoisie and holders of private property in general over the working class and over all the other social strata exploited by Capitalism." For that reason Fascism could be defined as a manifestation of the open dictatorship of Capital.

Others more realistically maintained that Fascism was a form of political power that placed itself above both the capitalist bourgeoisie and the proletariat, and that it carried out a "capitalistic-militaristic" dictatorship in favor of well-defined and limited conservative interests. This point of view should be studied in conjunction with the noteworthy essay "Der Faschismus," written in 1936 by Otto Bauer, one of the most important leaders of Austrian Social Democracy. To illustrate the various phases of relations between Italian and German Fascism and their respective middle classes, Bauer went to considerable pains to select the most exclusively political means by which Fascism had seized the reins of power. For him it was impossible to speak of Fascism in countries such as Poland, Hungary, Yugoslavia, and Bulgaria. He contended that counterrevolutionary governments in these countries merely imitated Fascism occasionally. For Bauer the roots of Fascism were to be found in the Great War and in the postwar economic crises. In the first place, the Great War had destroyed civilian life and stripped it of class labels. It had made it impossible for vast masses of soldiers to reinsert themselves into civilian life, and had thus caused them to assume a militaristic, antidemocratic, and nationalistic orientation. In the second place, postwar economic crises had impoverished, disillusioned, and exasperated a vast portion of the lower middle class and peasantry. It had also decreased the profits of the capitalists, making them eager to recoup their losses at the expense of the working class. Thus, on the one hand, we see the upsurge of Fascism with a typically lower-middle-class nationalist ideology, "oriented simultaneously against great Capital and the proletariat." On the other hand, we see Fascism receiving progressively greater support from the bourgeoisie—this support was crucial to its success, Bauer maintains. "The Fascist movement, from the beginning a mass movement of the lower middle class and of the peasants, achieved power only when the capitalist class decided to make use of it in order to crush the working class."[29] This is not to say that the bourgeoisie had become Fascist or contemplated turning power over to the Fascists. "The capitalist class made use of this rebellious and plebeian movement; but initially it never considered turning over the reins of power" to the Fascists and in the main had outright contempt for the Fascist leaders. Once Fascism had been mobilized, however, the bourgeoisie became its prisoner, because to deny Fascism would mean exposing themselves to proletarian reprisal. Thus, Fascists were granted positions in the government, and the bourgeoisie in turn became subject to its pressure—to the point of being expelled from the government and seeing their parties disbanded. The new elite that rose to power did not come directly from the ranks of the bourgeoisie. In Bauer's opinion, this did not mean that the capitalists had lost power as a class; on the contrary, power had increased for some:

> Under Fascist dictatorship, Capitalists and the larger landholders—by virtue of their power over the economy, over the course of business and public credit—can exert an influence on the dictators that is no less direct than the influence it exerts over bourgeois democracies. On the other hand, the bourgeois and peasant masses—restricted by their organizations, the suppression of freedom of the press, and electoral competition—are reduced to silence and are no longer able to defend their interests. Whereas in a bourgeois democracy the bourgeoisie dominates even though it may be under the tutelage of large Capital, under Fascist dictatorship only large Capital and large landholders dominate, and the masses of the bourgeoisie and the peasants are deprived of all power.[30]

Bauer astutely noted that, despite this preeminence of large Capital and large landholdings, tensions and conflicts were constantly arising in Fascist regimes between the ruling class and the

Fascist elite in government. These were caused either by "the 'guided economy' that had resulted from the economic crisis and was subsequently developed by Fascism, or by Fascist economic decisions that offended first one and then another group among the ruling Capitalist class and so placed the Fascist ruling caste at odds with these Capitalist groups." Moreover, Fascism's steady shift toward a war economy further weakened certain sectors of the capitalist class (such as finished-products industries, and trade) to the advantage of others (the armaments industry and the landed aristocracy).

More recently, G. D. H. Cole has denied that Fascism should be considered "the final throw of capitalism in decline, though Fascism of course received large help from capitalists in its rise to power, and in its measures for accomplishing the destruction of the working-class movement." It was, we read in his monumental history of Socialist thought,

> the ally of capitalism in this struggle; but it was not the mere lackey of capitalist interests. Its growth was greatly influenced by the economic conditions of the time, and by the moods of frustration which economic adversity stirred up in the minds of the young; but it was, all the same, not fundamentally an economic movement, but rather the manifestation of aggressive nationalism appealing to the violent passions of the underman. To attempt to characterise it in purely economic terms is to miss the essential key to its driving force and to leave out of sight its most dangerous quality —its irrepressible drive towards war. Hitler would most likely never have come to power in Germany had there been no great depression to throw millions of Germans out of work and to impose very bad working conditions on those who were able to keep their jobs. But this does not mean that Hitler, or the movement he inspired, was exclusively, or even mainly, a product of economic conditions, even if these were the main cause of his rise to power. The Nazi movement was in its essence political rather than economic: it arose out of the thwarted feelings of a defeated Germany intent on national self-assertion and revenge. It used the German capitalists, rather than was used by them; and the Germany which it created was far less capitalistic than mili-

taristic and driven on by a fanatical belief in the superiority of Germans to the rest of the human race.[31]

True Fascism—the Italian and German varieties especially, not those forms for which it was a convenient label justified on the basis of a few common elements—was not a new form of imperialistic capitalism. On the contrary, it was "a doctrine and a way of life that were totally different," a third force opposed both to "parliamentary capitalism" and to Socialism and Communism. This third force drew its strongest support from elements in the lower middle classes "that bitterly resented the equalitarian ambitions of the working classes, and found themselves adversely affected by economic depression and shortage of superior jobs carrying social prestige."[32] This lower-middle-class element, Cole wrote,

> was of great importance in both Germany and Italy; and its influence differed greatly from that of the conservative elements that rallied to Fascism; for it was concerned, not with the retention of an existing social order, but with the setting up of a new order that would present to it the opportunities for power and advancement which the existing order denied.[33]

Actually, in both Italy and Germany, when it came to power Fascism suppressed its more radical and subversive elements in order to ally itself with feudal and capitalist forces. This did not mean that Fascism became feudal or capitalistic; it retained its distinctive real and potential political and social characteristics.

In criticizing this interpretation of Fascism as a product of capitalist society and an antiproletarian reaction, the position of scholars such as Dobb, Baran, and Sweezy must be viewed in conjunction with another work, by Sweezy and Leo Huberman. I shall not argue with this extremely appropriate and important contribution, although it seems to add substantially more grist to Cole's mill than to the rigid interpretation of the relation between capitalism and Fascism. It explains why Baran and Sweezy insist that capitalist oligarchies are reluctant to make use of Fascism and prefer democratic governments. According to Huberman and Sweezy, Fascism has five principal characteristics. Four of these fit clearly into the classic Marxist scheme: an ideology of the extreme Right; a milieu of democratic and bourgeois origin; an expedient mixture of elections and of illegal violence; and a determination to destroy every Leftist threat to social order. What conflicts somewhat with the classic Marxist scheme is the fifth characteristic, relating to the forces that in large measure support Fascism—the "elements that consider themselves unjustly excluded from the existing economic and political establishment." Thus, "in generalizing on the Italian and German experience, it can be said that Fascism is the specific form that counterrevolution assumes in a democratic-bourgeois context. It opens the way to wealth and power to elements foreign to the establishment, while at the same time guaranteeing the status quo against those who seek a radical revolution."[34] Though quite correct, this analysis places the middle class at the center of Fascism and, therefore, confirms Cole's thesis of Fascism as a third force.

The foregoing are the essential characteristics of the interpretation of Fascism that has dominated, or been inspired by, Marxist thought. Although it has been the object of countless essays and papers of a general ideological and political nature, no comprehensive scientific study of the Fascist phenomenon has been made from this perspective to date. The only attempt of this sort remains *Fascisme et grand capital*, written in 1936 by the French Trotskyite Daniel Guérin. With a perspective limited to the Italian and German situation, the book reflects the time and circumstances in which it was written.[35]

During the 1960s Marxist thought concerned itself increasingly with ever more systematic study of the individual manifestations of Fascism.[36] The results have often been both informative and historiographically important. These studies show an occasionally significant effort to rise above (though always within the framework of Marxist methodology) some of the more typical schematizations of the past. They confirm the impression that for more than one Marxist historian the Marxist interpretation is becoming too narrow, and that there is a trend toward a broader, more specifically historical vision concerned with individual manifestations of Fascism rather than the overall phenomenon.

During the 1920s and 1930s the Marxist definition of Fascism focused on two aspects: the relation between Fascism and capitalism, and the social forces that contributed to the emergence of Fascism. The same problems are at the heart of the debate today. In the twenties and thirties, however, they were almost exclusively the province of the Communist Third International. This fact explains the schematic value of some of the assertions, their vacillations and instrumentalism, and especially the political and unscientific nature of the interpretation of Fascism during that period. These drawbacks became increasingly pronounced as the Communist International became less autonomous and reflected ever more the government policies of the USSR. This weakening of the Third International was accompanied by the reduced possibility for concrete, unprejudiced debate on Fascism within official Communist circles and finally led to its cessation. The detrimental effects were felt everywhere: in the Communist movement's anti-Fascist struggle; in the political definition of Fascism (recall how the Social-Fascism theory and the Fascist label were applied to domestic opponents of Stalinism, especially the Trotskyites); and in the historical studies of Fascism with which we are concerned.[37]

In the Soviet Union during the 1920s these studies were numerous and full of suggestions and noteworthy contributions. At the beginning of the 1930s, however, the cloak of total political conformity fell over them. Typical in this regard is what Boris R. Lopukhov, whose work gives a useful impression of Soviet writing during this period, said in 1965 about studies of Italian Fascism.

> Soviet studies made an important contribution to the research of the general problem of international Fascism. At the end of the twenties and the beginning of the thirties this problem was the center of attention by the Communist International. However, even in the early thirties the negative influences of the cult of personality were already being felt in Soviet historical literature . . . The influence of the new climate was felt in the attempts to represent and schematize reality and in the tendency to substitute the concrete study of reality with the repetition of various general resolutions of the Communist International pertaining to Fascism.[38]

Insofar as the relation between capitalism and Fascism is concerned, the position of the Communist International (after several early, short-lived waverings) was that Fascism was a phenomenon characteristic of the historical period through which capitalism was passing. It was the final stage of development of the capitalist regime within various countries, just as imperialism was the expression of the struggle for world markets among various capitalist states. As early as its Third Congress, in the summer of 1921, the Communist International asserted that capitalism had accomplished its mission: the promotion of the development of production.[39] It had reached a stage of irreconcilable conflict not only with the needs of historical development but also with the most elementary conditions of human existence. In the judgment of the Third International, capitalism was already in decline. The war and the cyclical economic crises had resulted in an increasingly revolutionary situation, even though capitalism attempted an economic and political counteroffensive. Capitalism was trading on the dissatisfaction and the crisis of the middle class and seeking to use it as a "white guard."

This diagnosis was substantially confirmed at the end of 1922 with the convening of the Fourth Congress, which coincided with Fascism's coming to power in Italy. It was repeated during successive years in a series of position papers revolving around four concepts: (1) the breakdown of capitalist society; (2) the inadequacy of the state's legal instrumentalities, which caused capitalism to have recourse to extralegal means of struggle and especially to Fascism (while middle-class parties and Social Democracy, in particular, assumed Fascist characteristics to a greater or lesser degree); (3) the internal contradictions within bourgeois society, which were supposed to lead to the defeat of Fascism and to the victory of the revolutionary proletarian movement; and (4) the contention that, in view of these circumstances, the struggle against Fascism meant also a struggle against capitalism.[40]

In September 1928 the Communist International published the following formula; it was to remain its position for the next few years:

> In the imperialist epoch the intensification of the class struggle, the expansion of the elements of class war—particularly after the imperialist world war—led to the bankruptcy of parliamentarism. Hence the "new" methods and forms of governing (e.g., the system of "inner Cabinets," the opera-

tions of oligarchic groups behind the scenes, the deterioration of "representative assemblies" and distortion of their
function, the restriction and elimination of "democratic free-
doms," etc.). In certain historical conditions this process in
which bourgeois-imperialist reaction conducts its offensive
assumes the form of fascism. The relevant conditions are:
instability of capitalist relationships; the presence in large
numbers of socially declassed elements; the impoverishment
of broad strata of the urban petty bourgeoisie and the intelligentsia; discontent among the rural petty bourgeoisie;
finally the constant threat of proletarian mass action. To
secure greater durability, solidity, and stability for their
power, the bourgeoisie are to an increasing degree com-
pelled to abandon the parliamentary system in favour of
fascist methods of rule, which are independent of party relationships and combinations. Fascism is a method of directly
exercising the bourgeois dictatorship, ideologically disguised
under ideas of "the national community" and representation
according to occupation (i.e. in fact representation of the
various groups of the ruling classes). It is a method which
uses its own peculiar brand of social demagogy (anti-semitism, occasional attacks on usury-capital, impatience with
the parliamentary "talking-shop") to exploit the discontent
of the petty-bourgeois masses, the intellectuals, etc.; and
which corrupts by creating a compact and paid hierarchy of
fascist fighting squads, a fascist party machine, and a fascist
bureaucracy. Fascism also seeks to penetrate the ranks of
the working class by winning over its most backward strata
by exploiting their discontent, the passivity of social-democracy, etc. Fascism's chief function is to annihilate the revolutionary vanguard of the working class, i.e. the communist
strata of the proletariat and their leading cadres. The combination of social demagogy, corruption, and active white
terror, and the most extreme imperialist aggressiveness in
foreign policy are characteristic features of fascism. When
the position is particularly critical for the bourgeoisie fascism resorts to anti-capitalist phraseology, but once it is certain of its power it is revealed more and more openly as the
terroristic dictatorship of large capital, and discards its anti-
capitalist lumber.

According to changing political circumstances, the bourgeoisie resort either to fascist methods or to coalitions with

social-democracy, while social-democracy itself, particularly at critical moments for capitalism, not infrequently plays a fascist part. In its development social-democracy displays fascist tendencies, which does not, however, prevent it, when the political situation changes, from coming out against the bourgeois government as an opposition party. For normal capitalism both fascism and coalition with social-democracy are extraordinary methods. They indicate the existence of a general capitalist crisis and are used by the bourgeoisie to halt the advance of the revolution.[41]

The final important pronouncement of the Third International with respect to Fascism came in the summer of 1935 at the time of the Seventh Congress. It was elaborated by one of the Comintern's foremost leaders, the Bulgarian Georgi Dimitrov, who spoke on "the Fascist offensive and the duty of the Communist International in the struggle for unity of the working class against Fascism." Having set aside the theory of Social-Fascism, the official Communist movement was about to launch its Popular Front policy. This change had no repercussions whatsoever on the problem which concerns us. The evaluation of Fascism was not modified; if anything, it became further entrenched. Indeed, according to Dimitrov's speech, not only countries where Fascism was in power were Fascist, but Fascism could also exist in countries where it did not have a large base and where the middle class was still plagued by internal conflict. "Fascism does not immediately decide to liquidate the parliament, and it allows a certain degree of legality to the other bourgeois parties and even to the Social Democrats."[42]

On this same occasion, the Communist International, through Dimitrov, pronounced its final word as to which social forces had contributed most to the expression of Fascism. Thus we arrive at the second problem at the heart of the debate in the twenties and thirties. For several years Marxist opinion had been far from unanimous on this matter. Most Soviet scholars had maintained that Fascism was the expression of the struggle in which capitalism and the upper middle class were united against the proletariat. Others had referred to Fascism as the struggle of rural areas against the city; still others had stressed the lower-middle-class elements. The same differences of opinion prevailed on the political level. This passage from the manifesto to the Italian workers, approved November 5, 1922, by the Fourth Congress of the Communist International, is indicative of the situation:

> You must remember that, while the revolutionary forces in Italy are not as weak as the panic-mongers say, the fascist forces are much weaker than their friends and admirers maintain. Not only will a substantial part of the radically-minded democracy turn away from them; in the camp of your direct class enemies itself there is no unity.
>
> The fascists are, primarily, a weapon in the hands of the large landowners. The industrial and commercial bourgeoisie are following with anxiety the experiment of ferocious reaction, which they regard as black bolshevism.[43]

This implicit definition of Fascism shows a different and more nuanced opinion than that professed by the majority of the Italian Communists under their formula of "capitalist reaction." It was a judgment closer to Lenin's when he compared Fascism to the Russian Black Hundreds and emphasized its agrarian aspects; it was also reminiscent of the judgment formulated by Antonio Gramsci.

At the same Fourth Congress Karl Radek's examination of Italian Fascism differed substantially from that made by Bordiga. The Italian conceded that the lower middle classes had incubated and fed Fascism, but he considered the latter, nevertheless, "a large unified movement of the ruling class" able to dominate all private interests. The Pole maintained, on the other hand, that the most important matrix of Fascism was provided by the lower middle class and the intellectuals, with their disquiet and illusion that Fascism could constitute an effective intermediary between capital and labor.[44] It is very significant that in June 1923 the Communist International approved a resolution on Fascism that constituted a remarkable attempt to understand and plumb the depths of the phenomenon.[45] According to that resolution,

> Fascism is a characteristic phenomenon of decay, a reflection of the progressive dissolution of Capitalist economy and of the disintegration of the bourgeois State.

Its strongest root is the fact that the imperialist war and the disruption of the capitalist economy which the war intensified and accelerated mean, for broad strata of the petty and middle bourgeoisie, small peasants, and the "intelligentsia," in contrast to the hopes they cherished, the destruction of their former condition of life and especially their former security. The vague expectations which many in these social strata had of a radical social improvement, to be brought about by reformist socialism, have also been disappointed. The betrayal of the revolution by the reformist party and trade union leaders, their capitulation to capitalism, their coalition with the bourgeoisie to re-establish the formal class domination and class exploitation—all in the name of "democracy"—has led this type of "sympathizer" of the proletariat to despair of socialism itself and its ability to liberate and renovate society. The weakness of will, the fear of struggle shown by the way in which the overwhelming majority of the proletariat outside Soviet Russia tolerates this treachery, and under capitalist whips drudges to consolidate its own exploitation and enslavement, has robbed these small and middle bourgeois, as well as the intellectuals, brought into a state of ferment, of their belief in the working class as the mighty agent of a radical social transformation. They have been joined by many proletarian elements who, looking for and demanding action, feel dissatisfied with the behaviour of all political parties. Fascism also attracts the disappointed and declassed, the rootless in every social stratum, particularly ex-officers who have lost their occupation since the end of the war. This is particularly true of the defeated Central Powers, where in consequence fascism has taken on a marked anti-republican character.

Deprived of historical awareness and without political experience, the arrogant fascist group that was made up of extremely disparate social elements expected complete salvation from the "state." The state was their original creature and instrument and purported to be above classes and parties. It was supposed to implement their unclear, contradictory, legal or extralegal program by means of either "democracy" or a dictatorship.

In the period of revolutionary ferment and proletarian risings, fascism to some extent sympathized or at least flirted with proletarian revolutionary demands. The masses which followed fascism vacillated between the two camps in the great and universal class contradictions and class struggles. But with the consolidations of capitalist rule and the general bourgeois offensive they threw themselves definitely on the side of the bourgeoisie, where their leaders had stood from the beginning. The bourgeoisie immediately took fascism into paid service in their fight to defeat and enslave the proletariat. The longer the dissolution and breakdown of the capitalist economy goes on, the more unbearable are the burdens and sufferings imposed on the proletariat. And the less able are the reformist socialists, with their collaborational attitude and pacifist intentions, to protect the bourgeois order against the thrust of the active masses. The bourgeoisie needs an aggressive power to protect itself against the working class. The old, allegedly non-political apparatus of the bourgeois state no longer guarantees the bourgeoisie adequate security. The bourgeoisie have set about creating special class-struggle troops against the proletariat. Fascism provides these troops.

Although fascism by its origins and its exponents also includes revolutionary tendencies, which might turn against capitalism and its State, it is nevertheless becoming a dangerous counterrevolutionary force. That has been shown where it triumphed, in Italy.

Of course, in different countries Fascism reveals varying characteristics according to differing historical circumstances. But everywhere its essence consists of a mixture of the most brutal and terroristic force and an apparently revolutionary jargon that is demagogically made relevant to the needs and sentiments of vast masses of the workers. To date its most mature development has been in Italy. In Italy the door to fascism was opened by the passivity of the socialist party and the reformist trade union leaders; its revolutionary phraseology won over many proletarian elements, which made its victory possible. The evolution of fascism in Italy is the result of the inability of workers' parties and associations to take advantage of the occupation of the factories in 1920 in order to intensify the proletarian class struggle. The result of fascist victory is the use of force to stand in the way of every workers' movement, even apolitical movements for wages. The triumph of Fascism in Italy spurs the bourgeoisie of other countries to take the same course in defeating the proletariat. The working class of the entire world is threatened by the fate of their Italian brothers.

But the development of Fascism in Italy also demonstrates that Fascism has a disharmonious nature and carries within it strong elements of political decomposition and dissolution. Its objective to transform by means of hammer blows the former bourgeois "democratic state" into an authoritarian Fascist state unleashes conflicts between the old bureaucracy and the new Fascist one; between the regular army and its career officers and the new Fascist Militia with its leaders; between despotic and Fascist policies in the economy and the state and the ideology of the remaining liberal and democratic bourgeoisie; between Monarchists and Republicans; between the true black-shirted Fascists and Nationalists welcomed into the party and the Militia; and between the original fascist program that hoodwinks and conquers the masses and the actual Fascist policy that serves the interests of industrial capital and especially an artificially encouraged heavy industry. But behind these and other conflicts there remain insurmountable and irreconcilable economic and social conflicts among the various capitalist strata of society, among the petty, middle and upper bourgeoisie, the small farmers and intellectuals, and, most important of all, the economic and social conflicts—the class struggle between the bourgeoisie and the proletariat. These conflicts spell the ideological failure of Fascism that is also evident in the disparity between the Fascist program and the manner in which it is implemented. It may be that for some time to come unscrupulous use of terror and weapons will mask the revelation of these conflicts and hide the ideological failure. But in the end the conflicts will become apparent even within the Armed Forces and this will mark the demise of Fascism.[46]

With the Fifth Congress of the International, in the summer of 1924, it became increasingly difficult to deviate from the official position. Gradually, as the relation between capitalism and Fascism was defined, reference to the lower middle class as the chief constituent element of Fascism became tantamount to heresy. For the Fifth

Congress, Fascism was "the instrument employed by the upper
middle class in its struggle against the proletariat." The fact that
Fascism was still conceded to have roots in the middle classes that
were "condemned to disappear," in people dislocated by the war,
and among certain disillusioned proletarian elements became a
matter of secondary importance, one that concerned Fascism only
insofar as it constituted an element of both its demagoguery and its
weakness. And in 1928, even this concession had little more than
platonic value.

At the Seventh Congress, Dimitrov did away with it alto-
gether by denying that the lower middle class had constituted an
important element in the original nucleus of Fascism. According to
him, the lower middle class had only been dragged into the wake of
Fascism through a series of demagogic expedients and against its
real interests. Fascism in power is:

> the terroristic open dictatorship of the most reactionary,
> chauvinistic, imperialistic elements of finance Capitalism.
> The most reactionary type of Fascism is the German . . . Fas-
> cism is not a power that is above classes just as it is not the
> power of the petty bourgeoisie or of the *lumpenproletariat*
> over finance Capitalism. It is the organization of terror at
> work over the laboring class and against the revolutionary
> segments of the peasantry and the intellectuals . . . It is
> necessary to stress most forcefully this characteristic of Fas-
> cism because the use of its social demagoguery has allowed
> Fascism in many countries to drag along with it the masses
> of the petty bourgeoisie that have been blown off course as a
> result of the crisis and even some of the more backward ele-
> ments of the proletariat who would never have followed
> Fascism if they had understood its true class nature.[47]

With the adoption of this position, only the Trotskyites in
the International Communist movement recognized the importance
of a fair evaluation of the role of the lower middle classes in the
establishment of Fascism in Italy and Germany (and consequently
the importance the problem had for the establishment of Communist strategy in countries threatened by new inroads of Fascism).
And even their leader, Leon Trotsky, fervently supported the gen-

eral relationship between capitalism and Fascism. His analysis of Fascism, however, was much less schematic and more comprehensive and subtle than that of the Third International. Having made a careful study of events in Italy and the errors committed by the Italian Communists in their evaluation of Fascism, he understood the decisive role of the lower middle class, and he repeatedly warned against falling into the same trap in Germany. According to Trotsky, Fascism, once in power, was anything but the government of the lower middle class; on the contrary, it was the dictatorship of monopoly capitalism, and the lower middle class was subjugated to it. However, in its origins, the lower middle class played an essential role in determining the success of Fascism. Contemporary society, he wrote in 1934,

> is made up of three classes: the upper middle class, the proletariat, and the "middle classes," or petite bourgeoisie. In the final analysis, the relation among the three determines the political situation in the country. The fundamental classes in society are the upper middle class and the proletariat. Only these two can have independent, clear, and relevant policies. The lower middle class is distinguished by its economic dependence and heterogeneity. Its lower levels fuse with the proletariat and descend almost to the status of *lumpenproletariat*. Because of its economic position the lower middle class cannot have an independent policy. It is forever oscillating between the capitalists and the workers. Its upper level pushes it to the right; its oppressed and exploited lower levels, under certain circumstances, abruptly veer to the left.
>
> These contradictory relationships of the middle classes have always determined the confused and absolutely inconsistent policies of the radicals. The radicals are undecided whether to form a bloc with the socialists to satisfy the lower levels or to create a national bloc with the capitalists to save the bourgeoisie. The final disintegration of radicalism begins when the beleaguered middle classes no longer permit this wavering. The lower middle class, made up of the ruined masses from the city and the countryside, become impatient and increasingly hostile toward the stratum above them; they become convinced of the inconsistency and perfidy of its political leadership. The poor peasant, the artisan, and

the small shopkeeper come to believe that an abyss separates them from the mayors, lawyers, and political *arrivistes* of the type of Herriot, Daladier, Chautemps, and others whose life-styles and opinions classify them among the upper middle class.

This very disillusionment of the lower middle class, its impatience, and its desperation are exploited by Fascism. Its agitators stigmatize and curse the parliamentary democracy that supports the climbers and Staviskyites but gives nothing to the lower-class workers. These demagogues shake their fist at bankers, big businessmen, and capitalists. Such words and actions are welcomed by the small owners, who are in a situation with no exit. The Fascists make a show of daring, demonstrate in the public squares, attack the policy, and try forcibly to oust the parliament. This has its effect on the lower-middle-class man who has fallen into despair. He says to himself: "The Radicals, among whom there are too many scoundrels, have definitely sold themselves out to the bankers; the Socialists have long promised to do away with exploitation, but their words are never translated into action; the Communists are incomprehensible, today they are one thing, tomorrow another; perhaps the Fascists represent salvation."[48]

The lower middle class maintains order so long as things are going well, but once it loses hope, it is ready to turn to more extreme solutions. "Otherwise, how would it have been possible to overthrow the democratic state and bring Fascism to power in Italy and Germany? The desperate lower middle class looks to Fascism as a fighting force against big Capital and believes that, contrary to the working-class parties which deal only in words, Fascism will use force to establish greater 'justice.' " For Trotsky this analysis obviously was dictated by the practical and political need to correct the errors of Communist policy toward the lower middle class and prevent the latter from joining the Fascist ranks as it had in Italy and Germany. The same analysis constituted one of the basic reasons, and merits, for Daniel Guérin's attempt—which was not only political but, in part at least, historiographic—to define and provide a historical reconstruction of the Fascist phenomenon. That attempt, although outdated and now unsatisfactory, remains nevertheless a stimulating contribution of Marxist thought because of its emphasis on the relation between the lower middle class and Fascism.[49]

The essay that in my opinion is the most noteworthy contribution Marxist thought has made to the interpretation of Fascism was written in 1935 by Richard Löwenthal, under the pseudonym Paul Sering. Löwenthal stresses particularly the economic conditions that prevailed when Fascism took hold in Italy and Germany. He did not consider the other dictatorships that had arisen in Europe as lying within the Fascist framework. He eliminated schematization and a-priori judgments and, instead, endeavored to pinpoint the most characteristic changes that had occurred in the Italian and German economies and that might occur in other countries. He especially analyzed the changes within classes and noted three processes: (1) a proportional increase in the nonproductive sectors of the population (permanently unemployed, propertyholders, workers in the distribution systems, and administrations); (2) social mobility within the working class (decrease in the number of specialized laborers, coupled with an increase in their indispensability; and development of a new class of technicians); and (3) an economic wasting away of small producers. One of the consequences of these changes was the creation of new interest groups, which led to a series of political repercussions. In particular, according to Löwenthal, these had brought about "within the middle class a basic conflict that was especially felt in the productive sectors, which needed support when a solidarity of interests develops between the bourgeoisie and the proletariat. The mutual interest in the maintenance of an enterprise operates here as a real barrier to the development of class struggle and makes unity with the proletarian class difficult. Within the bourgeoisie and the middle class the differing rates of development of the productive sectors favor the creation of lasting debt relations; the conflict between creditors and debtors in turn provokes a more lasting differentiation." These shifts within the classes and interest groups are characteristic of more recent capitalist development; they burgeon in periods of crisis and tend to make state intervention the only recourse, thus placing all hope in "purely political organization," weakening the working class and its organizations, and provoking a crisis in democracy.

According to Löwenthal, it is at this stage that Fascism comes into being:

> The concentration of those who have abandoned parties and organizations primarily because they have a greater material interest in the State or who temporarily substitute [interest in the State] for productive class interests along with other organizations that can themselves no longer impose class interest; the concentration of agriculture against industry, of the steel trust against the industrial trade union, of debtors against creditors, of the unemployed against the employed, of the supporters of economic self-sufficiency against the supporters of a world economy—all of this is translated into a new mass party that is concerned only with political power: the Fascist party. We have thus explained how this party recruited its members from all the classes and how certain classes gain predominance and form its nucleus; these classes are uncomfortably defined as the middle classes. The bourgeoisie is represented, but it is the indebted bourgeoisie requiring support; the working class is represented, but it is the permanently unemployed who are unable to do battle and who are concentrated in poor neighborhoods; the lower middle class comes flocking, but it is the ruined lower middle class; even propertyholders come running, but primarily those among them who have been dispossessed by inflation; there are officials and intellectuals, but they are officials without jobs and failed intellectuals. These constitute the nucleus of the movement, and it has all the features of a community of failures. It can expand beyond the central nuclei in parallel fashion to the crisis and into all the classes because it has social links with all of them.[50]

Such a party obviously had a leadership of its own elite. This explained why, until its victory, the ranks of Fascism did not include members of the ruling class and "*routiniers* of political leadership," and why the latter did not exert any influence in the "political and technical sense." Bourgeois elements might sympathize with Fascism, but they rarely would allow themselves to be ranked under an elite of "dilettantes and desperadoes," even though their common objectives served as a unifying factor. And the upper middle class had maneuvered for some time between the expanding Fascist bloc and the retreating proletarian bloc. As its internal conflicts became more pronounced, the race to curry favor with the Fascist party—"a race in which the reactionary wing is naturally superior"—was stepped up, until Fascism was forced to enter into a coalition government with the upper middle class. The transition to a "regime" was brief:

> The Fascist party, irregardless of the agreements it had concluded, is by far the strongest participant in this coalition. Based on a mass ideology that carries with it even the reactionary bourgeois wing, uncompromised by its open nature as a representative of determined interests, it increasingly becomes the object on which all hopes are focused. Within the coalition it can always denounce bourgeois interests and vestigial party economics as the reason for the insufficient progress. The Fascist party thus rapidly heads toward a coup d'état and the decisive break with "the system." At this point it completely assumes the apparatus of State, shakes off the bonds of the coalition, and comes into its own in the struggle against the mass organizations of the proletariat. Having accomplished this, the general prohibition of all parties and the formal end of the coalition are but obvious stages along the road to the Totalitarian State.

This, for Löwenthal, did not mean a fundamentally new economic system.

> Both before and after the Fascist upheaval, Capitalism dominates, but it is a Capitalism in which there are certain mutations: it is a Capitalism with restricted limits of accumulation, where economic dead weights abound, where the destruction of capital increases, and where there are more parasitic and reactionary strata. It is a Capitalism, moreover, with highly developed forces of production and organization, and where chaos prompts an increased need for planning. The general result of these Capitalist transformations, particularly in their reactionary aspects, is the transformation of the State into a State which undertakes a policy of subsidizations.[51]

These are in essence the positions that characterized the political thought and interpretation of Fascism by the Third International and the Communist movement during the 1920s and 1930s. Two other studies should be mentioned, however; although they do not directly concern the interpretation of Fascism, they are related to the problem of Fascism and the way it was viewed by Marxist thinkers. I refer to the extensive research of György Lukács, *Die Zerstörung der Vernunft*, and to the brief essay by Herbert Marcuse, "Der Kampf gegen den Liberalismus in der totalitären Staatsauffassung."[52] The former, and unquestionably more important, tackles the problem of "Germany's road to Hitler in the field of philosophy"—that is, the development of irrationalism in the nineteenth and twentieth centuries. Marcuse attempts to show how the creation of the authoritarian and Totalitarian State (Italy, in particular) was accompanied by a new political *Weltanschauung*, or "heroic and popular realism," and how liberalism evolved into the theory of the Totalitarian State.

3

Other Interpretations, 1930s-1960s

The classic interpretations described in the preceding chapter, more or less equally divided, continue to garner the greatest consensus, both on a historiographical level and on the political and ideological level. In Europe especially, they have been largely responsible for the popular definition of Fascism and are the yardstick for measuring the impact of its individual manifestations. There are other interpretations of Fascism, however. These may be defined as minor, not because they are less important, but because their impact on the scholarly world and among the nonspecialized general public has been limited.[1]

The Catholic interpretation
From a historical and chronological point of view, the Catholic view of Fascism is the most important minor interpretation. Conforming to circumstances and trends within the Catholic world and its related interests, Catholics adopted widely divergent attitudes toward Fascism. It is difficult to pin down any single reaction; even the official edicts of the Holy See are of scant assistance. It is nevertheless possible to suggest an interpretation that confronts Fascism in strictly Catholic terms, although it was not adopted by many Catholics and remained confined to the elite.

A cursory investigation might relate this interpretation to that of moral disease, but further study reveals it to be distinct in several noteworthy respects. Its most eloquent proponents are the French Jacques Maritain and the Italian Augusto Del Noce. For Maritain, who wrote between 1934 and 1936, the world since the Renaissance and the Reformation had been increasingly torn "by powerful and truly monstrous energies, where truth and error are strangely commingled and feed upon each other; by truths that lie and 'lies which speak the truth.'" The dislocation of intellectual and spiritual unity within the Christian order occasioned an absolutist reaction designed to salvage them; however, even this absolutist barricade could not hold out for long against the onslaught of rationalism and liberalism. The triumph of the philosophy of freedom rang the death knell for spiritual unity. It "makes of each abstract individual and his opinions the source of all right and truth." But individualistic liberalism was a purely negative force, which "lived by its opposite and because of it"; once the obstacle no longer existed, liberalism crumbled. Maritain ascribed the rise of antiliberal reaction, the birth of Communism and Fascism and their Totalitarian manifestations over the century, to the contemporary profound internal conflict within the capitalist and industrialist system.

> At such a moment it is natural that there should be not only revolutionary explosions which menace the very essence of this individualistic and liberal civilisation, but also reflex actions of defence, anti-liberal reactions, so to speak, of a biological order. It is the final stage of that process of descent of which I have spoken. For these reactions have no other interior source in the life of souls than physical and moral distress and too great suffering. And if they are indubitably capable of rousing heroism, faith and almost religious devotion, it is by the expenditure of an inherited spiritual capital; they have no power to recreate it. Thus the political unity of the commonwealth can only be sought for by external adjustments, by compulsion and political pedagogy, by a use of the State highly resembling in technical character those employed by Soviet communism for its own dictatorship. And since it is well understood that an inner accord of thought and feeling is necessary for the solidarity of the political unity, intellectual and spiritual pseudo-unity will be sought and imposed by the same means. The whole machinery of ruse and violence of politi-

cal machiavellianism is so brought to bear on the universe of the conscience itself and claims to storm this spiritual stronghold to extort the assent and the love of which there is such imperious need. This is a highly characteristic form of violation of invisible sanctuaries.[2]

Historically, Maritain considered Communism and Fascism inseparable:

> By an automatic reflex action, which is not human but mechanical, communism rouses and nourishes defensive reactions of a fascist or racist type, and these in their turn rouse and nourish communist defensive reactions, so that these two multitudinary forces grow in simultaneous opposition: the one and the other make a virtue of hatred, the one and the other are vowed to war, a war of nations or a war of classes, the one and the other claiming for their temporal community that messianic love with which the Kingdom of God should be loved; the one and the other bowing men down before some inhuman humanism, the atheist humanism of Caesar, or the zoological humanism of blood and race.[3]

Maritain endowed Communism and Fascism with identical roots, but he calculated their potential very differently. Communism was an "erroneous system" that also "stimulates and deforms a process given positively in existence: that process of historical 'generation and corruption' by which a new civilisation . . . will be raised outside the—broken—shapes of bourgeois civilisation."

> It is, on the contrary, as a defensive reaction at once against their existential process and against communism that the various forms of "fascism" have primarily been built up; hence they tend, by virtue of their original impulse, to keep the development of history *inside* the forms of capitalist civilisation, while carrying to a point of revolutionary intensity certain defensive reactions aroused by its disturbance, and having recourse to a large measure of State socialism; and they can only nourish their moral and emotional dynamism on a historical retrospect towards certain ideal forms in the past.

He predicted the parallel paths looming before Totalitarian Fascism when he wrote: "On the one hand, to orient their internal evolution in a way which is more and more close to the communist morphology"; on the other, to develop "an ethnic or national imperialism and a policy of prestige which will shake to the roots what remains of a common European civilisation."

> By virtue of this double process the fascist or racist regimes seem destined to lead, inside the forms of capitalist civilisation, not by dissolution and collapse like the liberal-individualist democracies, but by an excess of tension and stiffening, the nations belonging to the old Western culture to the requisite point for some communist or imitation-communist experience, as the product of fascism or racist totalitarianism or in reaction from it,—at least if they do not lead quite simply to mutual destruction which will leave Europe as a field for the conquering enterprises of other continents.

This basic prognosis was repeated in the fifties and sixties by Augusto Del Noce, whose series of stimulating essays is a major contribution of historical research on the interpretation of Fascism.[4] Del Noce's first postulate is similar to Maritain's: Totalitarianism must be viewed as a secular religion. It should be studied in the context of modern Western civilization's moral and religious crisis and with particular reference to the spread of atheism in this century. Del Noce asserts:

> Totalitarianism is not mere dictatorship. It is, rather, a new historical phenomenon that evolves when political values become the supreme consideration, in the light of which all other values must be judged. (It is a total negation, therefore, of liberalism because it allows for no "distinctions.") . . . This [Totalitarianism] can be observed for the first time in the Leninist evolution of Marx's thought. Briefly, we find it in the theory whereby philosophy no longer expresses itself in the form of a system (understanding, self-knowledge, and so on, of an accomplished totality), but instead expresses itself in the *accomplishment of a totality*, such as the building of a classless society in which universality of thought will result from the suppression of

classes. In this dialectical conception of reality the party becomes the philosophical counterpart to what was a system in a static conception of reality (hence the thesis of the reification of the party, *partitarietà*, in philosophy, and so on). Such a thesis evolves naturally from the radical negation of Platonic-Christian philosophy, which is embodied in the Marxist view of social man. (Hostility to Christianity thus becomes an essential element of Totalitarianism.)[5]

Any search for the historical roots of Totalitarianism outside this frame of reference is absurd, for "in each instance Totalitarianism derives its power of persuasion by seeming to embody 'the sense of history.' " A logical rebuttal of this claim will result "in Totalitarianism's definitive rout," even though some nostalgic survivors may remain. Consequently, "the form of life of every Totalitarianism is cyclical." Rather than inquire into the roots of Totalitarianism (which do not exist), the historian should ask why its adversaries put up so little resistance.[6]

Del Noce's second postulate also resembles Maritain's thought: the accepted view of the concept of Totalitarianism normally includes Communism, Nazism, and Fascism. In reality, however, we can speak correctly only of Communism and Nazism as being Totalitarian, and they are so in a completely opposed sense. Nazism is Totalitarian because it is completely subordinate to Communism; it is its irrationalist counterpart. These are the two sides to the Totalitarian coin, "because contrary to Marxist prediction, class struggle has not replaced national struggle."[7] Del Noce agrees with most sociologists that Italian Fascism—and, by extension, other so-called Fascisms as well—cannot be considered authentically Totalitarian. It is a truncated form of Totalitarianism. His third, and most original, postulate begins:

Nazism and Fascism belong to different historical contexts. The former stems from the "German philosophical drama" that Lukács has clarified in many of its extremely important aspects, suggesting themes that are equally valuable to non-Marxist scholars who may, however, view them from a different angle. Broadly speaking, I would say that Nazism is the only possible political response to the Com-

munist challenge issued against the historical primacy of
German immanent and secular thought. Fascism, by contrast, is best understood when it is measured against the
reality of Marxism.[8]

According to Del Noce, Fascism arose "from an extremely
important intuition: that there is a more profound reality underlying the reality of class, one that Communism has ignored—the
reality of nations. This has been proved by the fact that what was
expected to be a worldwide revolution has been halted." This intuition occurred to Mussolini, "according to the categories of revolutionary socialism," that is to say, he detached the idea of revolution
from Marxist materialism and linked it instead "to the *élan vital*
philosophy of the early 1900s." And here we find an explanation
for the irrational aspects and aimless activism of Fascism: "the final
contradiction of activism between the *politicità* [essence of things
political] and the solipsism that are activism's intrinsic components." Hence, on the national level, "political action can only be
viewed as a shattering of established reality," while, on the international plane, it becomes "a nationalist attempt to substitute the
struggle among nations for that among classes."[9]

Fascism as a manifestation of Totalitarianism

The origins of this interpretation can be traced back to the
thirties, most particularly to certain American essays. The theory
came into its own after World War II; although during the Cold
War it was more an object of political argument than scientific discussion.[10] During the 1950s it was interpreted more scientifically,
evolving into a full-blown, precise interpretation that raises interesting points while giving rise to many doubts. Nevertheless, it is
important for the study and historical interpretation of the Fascist
phenomenon.

Two aspects of it should be stressed. First, studies aimed at
proving that Totalitarianism is one of the typical forms of political
organization in modern mass society enable us to make more precise and realistic distinctions among the various forms of Fascism.
Thus, we can distinguish the real Fascism from forms that are
merely authoritarian and conservative movements, parties, and
regimes that are often closely linked to strictly local historical tradi-

tions—Latin American caudillismo, for example.[11] Second, such studies have allowed us to assess the decisive importance in Fascist regimes of technological development. They illustrate the value of using exquisitely modern means to organize the consensus—something totally ignored by previous autocratic regimes. Ever since antiquity, history has recorded the existence of many autocratic regimes that have established total control over a political community. These have nothing in common with modern Totalitarianism, which can be clearly distinguished by its radically different historical context, its objectives, and the technological means used to achieve them. It is, therefore, impossible to compare the two types of autocratic regimes. Fascism can arise only in a mass society and is a strictly modern phenomenon. But studies of Totalitarianism may provide responsible historians with the opportunity to seek out analogies and differences among the various forms of Fascism, especially between the German and Italian varieties.[12]

The most significant and important of the studies devoted to Totalitarianism are *The Origins of Totalitarianism* by Hannah Arendt and *Totalitarian Dictatorship and Autocracy* by Carl J. Friedrich and Zbigniew K. Brzezinski.[13] According to Arendt, the rise of Totalitarianism is closely linked to three indispensable and typical contemporary premises: the weakening of the national State and the rise of Imperialism; the demise of the class system and its values; and the atomization and individualization of modern mass society. The conditions necessary to produce these three factors developed in Europe during the last decades of the nineteenth century. World War I made them fully operative. Arendt devotes some extremely interesting passages to the effect of war on the moral and material disintegration of Europe, particularly in the defeated countries. She describes the establishment of the first Totalitarian movements and regimes. And she clearly proves that on August 4, 1914, a chain reaction was set in motion that has not yet been arrested.[14]

Arendt considers the transition from national State to Imperialism not only for its economic and political implications (the exporting of capital followed by the exporting of state power); she also views the progressive establishment of Imperialism from the standpoint of a series of phenomena that accompanied it. The support the new policy received from the various social levels is studied.

The bureaucracy benefited from it and was strengthened in terms of quantity and power. The "educated classes" and the bourgeoisie were granted a half-century's respite, and "a series of antiquated social and political structures were reinforced that had been threatened by new forces and that without Imperialism's solutions would have disappeared long before the two world wars." The masses of the dispossessed who began to accompany capital in its flight abroad became imbued with the spirit of Imperialism and were influenced by Imperialist policies. Other important phenomena that accompanied the progressive strengthening of Imperialism were the increasing idolatry of the individual personality (arbitrariness crowned by success became a sign of genius; there was a cynical receptiveness on the intellectual level toward any idea that could gain success by any means);[15] the widespread establishment of racism throughout the masses; the political virulence of the pan-movements (pan-Germanism, pan-Slavism, and so on), as countries that were unable to exercise colonial expansion turned on their immediate neighbors; the estrangement of the masses from government and parties; and the gradually increasing popularity of political groups that presented themselves as being above party and class interests.

For Arendt the breakdown of the class system and the atomization and individualization of mass society were not so much related to the growing equality of conditions, the increasingly marked social stratification, and the spread of education with a resulting lowering of intellectual standards and popularization of ideas, as they were attributable to the leveling and disintegration of European society brought about by World War I. This was a process that took place at different rates and under different circumstances in various countries. It was more rapid and dramatic in those countries that suffered the consequences of defeat (inflation and unemployment, refugees and national minorities). In other countries it was slower and progressed through preliminary stages. But everywhere it characterized the period between the two world conflicts and even the years following World War II. Arendt writes:

> Membership in a class . . . was generally by birth, and only extraordinary gifts or luck could change it. Social status was decisive for the individual's participation in

politics, and except in cases of national emergency when he was supposed to act only as a *national*, regardless of his class or party membership, he never was directly responsible for their conduct. The rise of a class to greater importance in the community was always accompanied by the education and training of a certain number of its members for politics as a job, for paid (or if they could afford it, unpaid) service in the government and representation of the class in Parliament. That the majority of the people remained outside all party or other political organization was not important to anyone, and no truer for one particular class than another. In other words, membership in a class, its limited group obligations and traditional attitudes toward government, prevented the growth of a citizenry that felt individually and personally responsible for the rule of the country. This political character of the nation state's population came to light only when the class system broke down and carried with it the whole fabric of visible and invisible threads which bound the people to the body politic.

The breakdown of the class system meant automatically the breakdown of the party system, chiefly because these parties, being interest parties, could no longer represent class interests. Their continuance was of some importance to the members of former classes, who hoped against hope to regain their old social status and who stuck together not because they had common interests any longer but because they hoped to restore them. The parties, consequently, became more and more psychological and ideological in their propaganda, more and more apologetic and nostalgic in their political approach. They had lost, moreover, without being aware of it, those neutral supporters who had never been interested in politics because they felt that parties existed to take care of their interests. So that the first signs of the breakdown of the Continental party system were not the desertion of the old party members, but the failure to recruit members from the younger generation, and the loss of the silent consent and support of the unorganized masses who suddenly shed their apathy and went wherever they saw an opportunity to voice their new violent opposition.

The fall of protecting class walls transformed the slumbering majorities behind all parties into one great unorganized, structureless mass of furious individuals who had

nothing in common except their vague apprehension that the
hopes of party members were doomed, that, consequently,
the most respected, articulate and representative members
of the community were fools and that all powers that be
were not so much evil as they were equally stupid and fraud-
ulent.[16]

Hannah Arendt believes that the atomization and individualization of society were the principal results of the breakdown of
the class system. The loss of traditional class points of reference
forced a wide segment of the population into a state of isolation, devoid of social ties and marked by individualistic egocentrism that
weakened their instinct for self-preservation and left them prey to
more demagogic elements. In other words, the atomization and individualization of society brought about the birth of the masses,
groups of men "who either because of sheer numbers, or indifference, or a combination of both cannot be integrated into any organization based on common interest, into political parties or municipal
governments or professional organizations or trade unions," and
whose behavior was dictated neither by the class to which they belonged nor by the ruling class but by an "inarticulate baggage" of
ideas and suggestions taken from all classes of society. "The truth is
that the masses grew out of the fragments of a highly atomized society whose competitive structure and concomitant loneliness of
the individual had been held in check only through membership in
a class. The chief characteristic of the mass man is not brutality and
backwardness, but his isolation and lack of normal social relationships."

Such was the climate in which Totalitarianism took hold.
This type of movement and regime required the presence of large
masses indifferent or outrightly hostile to traditional parties and to
the social framework that supported them, but who, for one reason
or another, "acquired the appetite for political organization. Masses
are not held together by consciousness of common interest and they
lack that specific class articulateness which is expressed in determined, limited and obtainable goals." In this respect Arendt notes:

It was characteristic of the rise of the Nazi movement in
Germany and of the Communist movement in Europe after

1930 that they recruited their members from this mass of apparently indifferent people whom all other parties had given up as too apathetic or too stupid for their attention. The result was that the majority of their membership consisted of people who never before had appeared on the political scene. This permitted the introduction of entirely new methods into political propaganda, and indifference to the arguments of political opponents; these movements not only placed themselves outside and against the party system as a whole, they found a membership that had never been reached, never been "spoiled" by the party system. Therefore they did not need to refute opposing arguments and consistently preferred methods which ended in death rather than persuasion, which spelled terror rather than conviction. They presented disagreements as invariably originating in deep natural, social or psychological sources beyond the control of the individual and therefore beyond the power of reason. This would have been a shortcoming only if they had sincerely entered into competition with other parties; it was not if they were sure of dealing with people who had reason to be equally hostile to all parties.[17]

As viewed by Hannah Arendt and other scholars who make of Totalitarianism a single political model, the relation between the masses, on the one hand, and Totalitarian parties, movements, and regimes, on the other, explains the basic similarities among all these parties, movements, and regimes in the twentieth century, even though they present very different and contrasting programs and ideologies. A second explanation lies in the types of power these parties, movements, and regimes exercised. They too are always similar: the only difference being the degree of Totalitarianism involved. This degree is determined by the extent of "massification" of individual societies and by the numerical strength of the masses. It explains why, for Arendt and other advocates of this interpretation, Totalitarianism came about in Nazi Germany and Stalinist Russia in particular (and, according to some, in Communist China). Italian Fascism did not achieve Totalitarianism until 1938. Before then it "was not a truly Totalitarian regime, it was a nationalist dictatorship that had resulted from the difficulties experienced by multiparty democracy." Most of the other Fascist parties, movements, and regimes merely had conservative or autocratic natures, although some possessed certain Totalitarian aspects.

Arendt, in *The Origins of Totalitarianism*, and Friedrich and Brzezinski, in *Totalitarian Dictatorship and Autocracy*, have detailed the types of Totalitarian power and the consequences that Totalitarianism had on social organization and relations. The key elements of this approach are the nature of the consensus that is fundamental to Totalitarianism, the scientific use of propaganda and mass terror, the organization of the State and its apparatus, the special role of the leader, the organization of international relations, and the ideological basis underlying all these manifestations of Totalitarianism that absolutely distinguish it from other autocratic regimes—its ends as well as its exquisitely modern means. A detailed study of these points would contribute to a better understanding of the Totalitarian interpretation, and before concluding, I should at least refer to the six characteristics of Totalitarianism elaborated by Friedrich and Brzezinski, which provide a useful point of reference for understanding their premises. Totalitarian dictatorships, they state, all possess:

1. An elaborate ideology, consisting of an official body of doctrine covering all vital aspects of man's existence to which everyone living in that society is supposed to adhere, at least passively; this ideology is characteristically focused and projected toward a perfect final state of mankind—that is to say, it contains a chiliastic claim, based upon a radical rejection of the existing society with conquest of the world for the new one.

2. A single mass party led typically by one man, the "dictator," and consisting of a relatively small percentage of the total population (up to 10 percent) of men and women, a hard core of them passionately and unquestioningly dedicated to the ideology and prepared to assist in every way in promoting its general acceptance, such a party being hierarchically, oligarchically organized and typically either superior to, or completely intertwined with, the governmental bureaucracy.

3. A system of terror, whether physical or psychic, effected through party and secret-police control, supporting

but also supervising the party for its leaders, and characteristically directed not only against demonstrable "enemies" of the regime, but against more or less arbitrarily selected classes of the population; the terror whether of the secret police or of party-directed social pressure systematically exploits modern science, and more especially scientific psychology.

4. A technologically conditioned near-complete monopoly of control, in the hands of the party and of the government, of all means of effective mass communication, such as the press, radio, motion pictures.

5. A similarly technologically conditioned near-complete monopoly of the effective use of all weapons of armed combat.

6. A central control and direction of the entire economy through the bureaucratic coordination of formerly independent corporate entities, typically including most other associations and group activities.[18]

Fascism as a metapolitical phenomenon

In a strict sense, to speak of an interpretation of Fascism as a metapolitical phenomenon is, at the very least, excessive. And, in fact, this interpretation has been advanced only by Ernst Nolte, in his massive study _Der Faschismus in seiner Epoche_ (1963), and continued by him in successive works. From the start it was universally attacked in one degree or another. Only one ranking historian, George L. Mosse, approved of its conceptual structure, and, though he did not demolish the thesis out of hand, he leveled strong criticism at it.[19] Most scholars considered the historical aspects of Nolte's book, rather than the interpretation; this explains the prestige the book has enjoyed, despite its fundamental premise. Nolte's attempt to provide a typology of the Fascist phenomenon has been particularly well received. Looking beyond the classic interpretations, and discarding the Totalitarian interpretation, he has selected that minimal common denominator that enables us to view all the manifestations of Fascism between the two World Wars as the single phenomenon of an "epoch."

This typology is undoubtedly interesting and largely acceptable, although some points are subject to debate.[20] Further, the

purely historical reconstruction of Italian Fascism and National
Socialism is also open to question, and we must ignore the portion
of *Der Faschismus in seiner Epoche* devoted to Action Française,
for it is unacceptable within the context of a history of the Fascist
phenomenon.[21] We must, however, consider Nolte's basic thesis,
particularly because of Augusto Del Noce's agreement with and
criticism of it.

Nolte's specifically declared goal (he was much influenced
by Heidegger and Weber) was to study Fascism not only in the light
of thorough historical analysis but also from a rigorous philosophical point of view. He sought to study its essence and basic significance without being sidetracked by secondary issues. At the end of
his work he reached a dual conclusion: that Fascism can arise "only
within the sphere of the liberal system," and that "Fascism cannot
exist without the Bolshevist challenge." His interpretation of Fascism is based on these two conclusions. In his final book on Fascism, Nolte writes:

> Even if Fascist movements can arise only in the sphere of
> the liberal system, they are not the original expressions of
> the radical protests possible in that sphere. They should be
> interpreted as answers to the protests. When they first arise
> they often declare themselves willing to defend the system
> from frontal attacks before which the State seems unarmed.
> Fascism cannot exist without the Bolshevist challenge. But
> Fascism is not merely anti-Bolshevism. Characteristically,
> every form of Fascism discards out of hand the somewhat
> controversial derivation of Bolshevism from Marxism and
> sets itself up as, above all, anti-Marxist. When groups, even
> those from the extreme Right, have aligned themselves with
> Bolshevism and been inspired by Marxist dialectics, they
> have never referred back to the memory of Hitler and Mus-
> solini; they do not hark back to Fascism. The Bolshevist
> challenge to the liberal system issued in 1919 and 1920, after
> Bolshevism was triumphant in Russia and was becoming or-
> ganized as a worldwide party through the Communist Inter-
> national, constituted the key element in European history
> between the two World Wars. This does not mean that it
> was the only event, or the main event in and of itself. The
> revolutionary attempt failed before it got off the ground in

very important countries. On the one hand, it is the key element because where it left its most indelible traces it gave rise to Fascism. On the other hand, in countries it barely touched it aroused deep sympathy for an opposition that derived its power from the very depths of society and represented itself as a bulwark in defense of the State.

A few pages later, stressing the need to view World War I as another prerequisite—although with reverse significance—of both Bolshevism and Fascism, he raises a problem that is the key to the rest of his argument:

> A distinction absolutely has to be made as to whether "the challenge launched by Bolshevism" was merely an external threat or whether it is an intrinsically vital process of the liberal system itself. It is not the same thing to consider the European party system as an historical accident, a mere disguise of positions of power to be found everywhere, and also to consider it a fundamental factor and the expression of a long historical tradition.[22]

If we want to resolve such a problem, we cannot, Nolte says, use the same means that have been previously used. Sociological, psychological, and socioeconomical analyses of the middle classes, as well as Marxist studies of the economic "background" and types of Fascism and the consequences of its accession to power, have a "strictly limited value." They isolate aspects of no particular importance and provide only a partial notion of particular material interests. They are of no use in establishing the essence of the Fascist phenomenon. According to Nolte, to discover its essence it is necessary to view Fascism as a wider and deeper phenomenon, as a "metapolitical phenomenon" of resistance and opposition to practical transcendence (horizontal transcendence, the social order) and to theoretical transcendence (vertical transcendence that can be summed up as a struggle against nature and in "liberty toward the infinite," which is innate in the individual and real in universal evolution but frightening because it "threatens to destroy what is familiar and beloved"). Concretely, it must be viewed in relation to the peculiar transcendental nature of liberal society and to the threat posed to it by Bolshevism, which Nolte distinguishes from orthodox Marxism. These aspects are fully developed in *Der Faschismus in seiner Epoche*, but it is important to note the three analytic premises. For Nolte, "liberal society is a society of abundance—all forms of theoretical transcendence can develop independently, although not without being affected externally; a self-critical society—the attainment of practical transcendence remains subject to criticism; and an uncertain society—it is continually subject to self-doubts."

Within liberal society there is a commingling of the two types of transcendence and, however delicate, a balance between the two. This balance is destroyed by Bolshevism. Indeed, "Bolshevism signifies the dominating emergence of the element that had remained half-hidden in bourgeois society; it is the most unequivocal affirmation of material production and at the same time of practical transcendence. Society thereby loses its spiritual wealth and the spur of self-criticism and acquires an unshakable complacency and a hitherto unknown enthusiasm in its sense of historical necessity."

There follows Nolte's conclusion of his interpretation of Fascism and of its being subsumed under the general concept of a conservative revolution:

> It is not that resistance to practical transcendence, which is more or less common to all conservative movements. It was only when theoretical transcendence, from which that resistance originally emanated, was likewise denied that fascism made its appearance. Thus, fascism is at the same time resistance to practical transcendence and struggle against theoretical transcendence. But this struggle must needs be concealed, since the original motivations can never be entirely dispensed with. And, insofar as practical transcendence from its most superficial aspect is nothing but the possibility of concentration of power, fascism pursues its resistance to transcendence from within that transcendence and at times in the clear consciousness of a struggle for world hegemony. That is the transcendental expression of the sociological fact that fascism has at its command forces that are born of the emancipation process and then turn against their own origin. If it may be called the despair of the feudal

section of bourgeois society for its traditions, and the bourgeois element's betrayal of its revolution, now it is clear what this tradition and this revolution actually are. Fascism represents the second and gravest crisis of liberal society, for it achieves power on its own soil and, in its radical form, is the most complete and effective denial of that society.[23]

As an interpretation of Fascism, Nolte's theories have not had a real following. Those for whom they have positive value have considered them an invitation to conduct a thorough investigation of the cultural roots of Fascism, its various manifestations, and their development between the two World Wars. They have been useful in refuting the simplistic notion that Fascism had no ideology or culture of its own—that it was nonculture and, when in power, a "rule of wild asses" (onagrocracy). Nolte's work also has been considered an invitation to retrace the paths opened up for Germany (and other countries) by Marcuse, Viereck, and Lukács, while keeping an open mind about the possibility of less exclusive and univocal interpretations—interpretations less apt to consider cultural situations and problems as marginal or deviant when they were not really such, or at most became such only in unusual circumstances. It is interesting to consider the suggestion that, from a Weberian cultural perspective, *Der Faschismus in seiner Epoche* did for all of Europe what several years earlier Lukács had done from a Marxist perspective for German reactionary thought. In the eyes of his supporters Nolte is regarded first and foremost as a historian of Fascist thought and of European conservative thought in general. They rank him with other great scholars of the subject, such as René Rémond and George L. Mosse.[24]

Nolte's interpretation is particularly interesting because of the influence it had on and the stimulus it provided for Augusto Del Noce. Del Noce's earliest writings on the problems of Fascism, as well as certain parts of his introduction to *Il problema dell'ateismo* in 1964, unfolded within the framework of a Catholic perspective inspired by Maritain's *True Humanism*. In two later studies he further developed this position and refined it in several important aspects.[25] He separated his interpretation of Fascism from the immediately Catholic frame of reference, without, however, repudiating any of his strong Catholicism. Though it may seem somewhat deceptive, with respect to this problem it is possible to refer to an early and a later Del Noce. The early Del Noce was still tied to the Catholic interpretation that stressed the growth of atheism in contemporary society. The later Del Noce advocates his own interpretation of what can be defined as "the Fascist moment in the age of secularization." This interpretation, which considers Fascism in its full contemporary historical context, is significant even to scholars who do not study history from a religious perspective.

In discussing Nolte's contentions, Del Noce writes that, in general, "the weight of disagreement" with them "is greater than the agreement."[26] One need only read his last essays to realize the extent of this disagreement. Yet it seems incontestable that Del Noce's thoughts about *Der Faschismus in seiner Epoche* (which he had already read when he wrote his introduction to *Il problema dell'ateismo*), along with more specific published historical research on Fascism, subsequently represent an important stage of the evolution of his position. It provided him with at least one means of surmounting the preeminence he had earlier assigned to the crisis of religious values.

For Del Noce, defining Fascism as a transcendental phenomenon begins with the premise that Fascism, like Nazism and Communism, is a manifestation of the age of secularization. More precisely, it is a product of the age of secularization's first, and "sacred," period, one which is followed by a "profane" period expressed by an opulent society. Having established this first point, with all it implies, the next question is "whether it is possible to group together under the common denominator of counterrevolution (or reaction, or resistance to transcendence, and so on) traditional and nationalist movements such as Fascism and Nazism, all more or less inspired by the doctrinaire aspects of Action Française. It is possible to speak of a single essence that took different forms depending on the cultural and economic circumstances prevailing in the countries where it occurred, or should the emphasis be placed instead on the differences? If the latter, two interpretations are possible: should qualitative distinctions be made between nationalist movements and Fascism and Nazism, nevertheless conceding a single essence to the latter phenomena, or should we refer to Fascism and Nazism as phenomena that are essentially different?"

Del Noce is firm and precise in his answers. Attention must be focused above all on the differences. The difference between nationalist movements and Fascism and Nazism is very clear:

> The distinction between Fascism and Nazism on the one hand and Nationalism can be easily established. Nationalism presents itself as a traditionalism, as an effort to perpetuate a heritage. This heritage is legitimized in relation to transcendental values, even though later the tendency is to view it merely in its function of legitimizing a heritage. (This is why it is possible to see in Nationalism the final outlet of an imprecise notion of tradition.) Fascism, on the other hand, conceives of the nation not as a heritage of values but as a growth of power. History is not viewed as a *loyalty*, as it was under Nationalism, but as a *continuous* creation that has the right to overthrow everything that opposes it.[27]

Given these premises, it is obvious that the answer to the second question is the one provided in *Il problema dell'ateismo:* Italian Fascism and National Socialism, although they may have many superficial similarities, are different at their roots. National Socialism was complete Totalitarianism, born in opposition to and as an irrational translation of Communism. Fascism had quite different origins and different significance. Del Noce explains:

> It follows from what we have said that Fascism occupies a revolutionary position that is of Marxist origin and that became so after it absorbed the criticisms of Marxist theory that took place in Italy at the turn of the century (a development which culminated in the [Gentilian] philosophy of "actualism"). Naturally, this definition concerns only its *form*, which by itself is insufficient to explain its practical realization. Obviously the latter would not have occurred without a series of historical events: the World War, the unusual manner in which Italian intervention took place, the defeat of Caporetto, the transfiguration of the battle of Vittorio Veneto into the myth of a "mutilated victory," the Russian Revolution, the Red Biennium, and so on.
> How does [Fascism] fit into what we have earlier called the age of secularization? In this respect it must be defined as an *alternative to Leninism* (to Leninism, we emphasize, not

to Stalinism; even though Stalinism and the withdrawal of
Russia into herself might seem to confirm the validity of the
Fascist solution). But the term "alternative" ("either they or
we") can be understood in two ways: as an absolute opposition, or as opposition that is developing in a form suitable to
a country whose civilization and culture were superior to
Russia's. (We could say "countries," if we recall that around
1930 Mussolini predicted that the entire world would soon
turn to Fascism.)

To my mind, Mussolini thought about Fascism in the
second way, and this is the difference between Fascism and
Nazism. Around 1920 two men were vying for the title of
real revolutionaries: Lenin and Mussolini. It must be recognized that Mussolini was absolutely sincere in this pretension. It was a failed revolution that found its historical justification in the fact that Marxism-Leninism could not take
place as a worldwide revolution but had to call a halt when
confronted with the reality of nationalisms. But to note that
Fascism failed as a revolution does not mean that it must be
considered a reactionary phenomenon. Nor does it justify
judgments according to which Mussolini had been lying
from the beginning and using revolutionary terminology as
a cover. A judgment of the outcome of a movement cannot
be used as the criterion for defining its origins. For example,
those who maintain that Communism failed because it
created "a new class" that was more oppressive than any
other, certainly do not mean by this that Communism
emerged with a reactionary intention.[28]

Having traced the essential outlines of the metapolitical interpretation, we must now evaluate it. Nolte's version consists of a
praiseworthy attempt to reclaim from history's judgment of Fascism, areas that until now had been considered marginal or had
been too hastily aligned with a facile Benda-style progressive and
moralistic enlightenment. It is especially indicative of developments in the moral-disease interpretation that can take place in an
atmosphere such as has prevailed in the last few years—particularly for existentialism and the difficulties exhibited by idealist as
well as Marxist historicism in updating themselves in order to confront the new "welfare-state ideologies." Del Noce's interpretation,

apart from some specific assertions that can and should be investigated, occupies a very rigorous conceptual level and is potentially
capable of being translated into a concrete historical reconstruction. To speak, as Del Noce does, of contemporary history as philosophical history—"history of philosophy that becomes the world"
—is suggestive and theoretically correct. But Huizinga's bitter statement is just as correct: "a sincere view of recent history" may be
"one of the prerequisites for restoring health of civilization," but it
seems impossible "to bring man to a single conception of events."
The most important aspect of Del Noce's version, as a point of arrival of the moral-disease theme and as a point beyond which one
may proceed to find other areas of agreement, seems to be the concept of the "era of secularization." If they accept this concept, historians will have to establish the limits, nature, weight, and influence of the "Fascist moment" in this era—even though it be, as Del
Noce suggests, under the guise of apparent rejection.

4

Interpretations
by Social
Scientists

The interpretations of Fascism described in the two preceding chapters have very few elements in common. For the most part they inspire divergent evaluations and conclusions. They provide scant satisfaction to the historian who examines them individually in search of a systematic and comparative analysis of Fascist movements, parties, and regimes. However, all of these interpretations share a common historicity. Although the Totalitarian interpretation, as well as several others, contains sociological suggestions and proclivities, these elements are subordinated to a historicist conception of reality. By contrast, the interpretations discussed in this chapter are either completely or in large part devoid of historicist connotations. They are not formulated by historians, nor do they stem from predominantly political considerations. They have been elaborated by social scientists on the basis of theories, hypotheses, and methodologies derived from modern psychology and sociology.

For almost a half-century the contribution of the social sciences to the analysis and interpretation of Fascism has been extensive and thought-provoking, especially where the study of mass society is concerned. Since World War II the various approaches to Fascism proposed by the social scientists in the United States have gradually been disseminated throughout the Anglo-Saxon world and to the European continent.[1] In certain instances they have even "infiltrated" the people's democracies. Today we can confidently say that such interpretations dominate the social sciences. More-over, as Fascism is transformed from a political event into a histori-cal fact, these approaches exercise increasing influence not only on the thinking of the average person in many countries but also among historians.

An evaluation of the contribution of the social scientists to the historical understanding of the Fascist phenomenon leads to certain conclusions. First, it is difficult to accept their tendency (in certain instances, pretension) to view their contributions as full-blown interpretations of Fascism. As historical reconstructions and evaluations these analyses and explanations (including those least inspired by a historical approach) are individually unsatisfactory because they are narrow and incomplete. They are distortions, re-verting to schematic and unilateral interpretations based on the exaggeration of a single aspect of the phenomenon and the denial (or, in better examples, underestimation) of other aspects. In cer-tain cases the problem is stated in terms so general that abstract models are created. To justify these models requires so many excep-tions and variants that the interpretation is undermined. Worst of all, these generalizations, which greatly diffuse the geographical and chronological scope of the Fascist phenomenon, lead some social scientists to apply the Fascist label to a whole series of single-party African, Asian, and Latin American countries. In so doing, they overlook one of the fundamental characteristics of Fascism: its intrinsic relation to the moral, economic, social, and political crisis of European society in the aftermath of World War I.

This negative appraisal is counterbalanced by positive con-siderations. Although I deny that the theories, hypotheses, and methodologies of the social sciences allow us completely to resolve the historical problems of Fascism, we must acknowledge the sig-nificant contributions made by experts in the fields of social psy-chology, sociology, economic development, and "modernization" to the critical reexamination of several interpretations of Fascism. Not only have the social sciences demonstrated beyond any doubt the narrowness and deficiency of these interpretations, but they have defined and focused on yet another fundamental characteris-tic of the Fascist phenomenon: the undeniable link between Fascism and mass society at a time when the latter is most vulnerable to inherent tensions and contradictions—in its incipient stages. Their study of social mobility has enabled the social scientists to clarify the nature and limits of the contribution made to Fascism by the various classes as a whole and the decisive role of the middle classes and elites. The social sciences have stressed that to understand a revolutionary process—which Fascism certainly was—one must take into account not only the relation of class structure to the system of production, but also the normative or guiding force of a system of institutionalized values, as well as a variety of other psychosocial motivations.[2]

With certain exceptions, all the social sciences have contributed in some degree to the formulation of the interpretations we shall examine. For this reason, perhaps these interpretations should be studied as a more or less single group. However, because this book attempts to analyze the characteristics of the debate over the meaning of the Fascist phenomenon, I have divided the interpretations into three subgroups according to the preponderance of psychosocial (that is, sociopsychology of collective behavior) aspects over sociological and socioeconomic aspects. This permits a clearer understanding of the individual aspects of the Fascist phenomenon stressed by various scholars in interpreting the phenomenon as a whole. It also makes it easier to evaluate the contribution made by these interpretations to research of a more purely historical nature.

The psychosocial interpretation

The sources of this interpretation are numerous. Besides scientific studies dating back to the 1930s and 1940s we must consider other works (which tended to view Fascism in general, and National Socialism in particular, as mere insanity and demonism) conceived as a means of combating Fascist propaganda with democratic counterpropaganda. Some of them are relatively remote, such as the essays by Harold Lasswell, "The Psychology of Hitlerism," published in 1933 in *The Political Quarterly* and Wilhelm Reich's *Massenpsychologie des Faschismus* (*Mass Psychology of Fascism*), published the same year in Copenhagen.

Elaborating on Freudian themes, Reich attempted to explain Fascism in terms of sex and economics, defining it as an international political psychology of the masses who were frustrated in their attempts at rational solidaristic action and thus unable to attain the democratization of society.[3] He blamed this frustration on masochism and age-old repression of the natural laws governing life and love. World War I destroyed many authoritarian institutions and launched an attempt on the part of democracies to "lead humanity toward freedom."

However, this European universe, in its efforts directed toward freedom, committed a grave error in calculation. It overlooked the fact that the destruction of man's vital function that had taken place over thousands of years had profoundly rooted a character neurosis. It was at this point that the great catastrophe constituted by the "psychic plague" irrupted. This was the disastrous predominance of the irrational human nature which took the form of a triumphant dictatorship. Forces that had been too long repressed by the superficial layer of good manners and the domination of an artificial Ego, which were carried by the same multitudes that searched for freedom, cleared a path toward action.[4]

Fascism, and especially Nazism, did not, in Reich's view, attain power by means of economic or political programs but through an "appeal to obscure mystical sentiments and nebulous desires that remained unidentified but strong," an appeal to the tragic conflict that characterized the human masses—"the conflict between the desire for freedom and the real fear of freedom." In contrast to "liberalism, which represents the surface layer of character" (its repressed and manipulated aspects), and "in contrast to genuine revolution, which embodies the deepest layer" (man's biological center), Fascism represents the intermediate layer of the real personality: its secondary drives (cruelty, sadism, lasciviousness, envy, and so on). Thus, Fascism is but "the organized political expression of the structure of the average man's character" and "the basic emotional attitude of the suppressed individual of our authoritarian machine civilization and its mechanistic-mystical conception of life." The "mechanistic-mystical character of modern man produces Fascist parties, not vice-versa." Here are the conclusions Reich reached in the preface to the third edition of *Mass Psychology of Fascism:*

To the detriment of genuine efforts to achieve freedom, fascism was and is still conceived as the dictatorship of a small reactionary clique. The tenacity with which this error persists is to be ascribed to our fear of recognizing the true state of affairs: fascism is an *international* phenomenon, which pervades all bodies of human society of *all* nations . . . My character-analytic experiences have convinced me that there is not a single individual who does not bear the elements of fascist feeling and thinking in his structure. As a political movement fascism differs from other reactionary parties inasmuch as it is *borne and championed by masses of people* . . . Since fascism, whenever and wherever it makes its appearance, is a movement borne by masses of people, it betrays all the characteristics and contradictions present in the character structure of the mass individual. It is not, as is commonly believed, a purely reactionary movement—it represents an amalgam between *rebellious* emotions and reactionary social ideas . . . Fascist mentality is the mentality of the "little man," who is enslaved and craves authority and is at the same time rebellious.

Several studies and research projects influenced the development of this interpretation. One of the most famous is *The Authoritarian Personality*, by T. W. Adorno, Else Frenkel-Brunswik, Daniel J. Levinson, and R. Nevitt Sanford.[5] It is based on the hypothesis that the political, social, and economic convictions of an individual often create a wide organic scheme, as though they were held together by a "mentality" or a "unifying spirit," and this scheme expresses tendencies deeply rooted in the personality. It is possible to distinguish various personality types and syndromes. The "authoritarian syndrome," makes the "potentially fascistic" individual particularly susceptible to antidemocratic propaganda because his sadomasochistic character induces him to repress his superego and orient his social adaptation toward obedience, subordination, and love of an "authoritarian figure" and to unload part of his aggressions outside the family.

Among this vast body of literature, for our purposes it will suffice to focus on only the most important works, particularly those in which the Fascist phenomenon is viewed and interpreted in its more general and characteristic terms: the works of Erich Fromm and Talcott Parsons.

The most significant work of Fromm in this respect is *Escape from Freedom*, written in 1941, where he investigates the case of the authoritarian personality later studied by the Adorno group. *The Sane Society*, written in 1955, is also extremely useful, especially insofar as it views Fascism in a wider context and with additional nuances. In the case of Talcott Parsons, I refer primarily to his essay written in 1942, "Some Sociological Aspects of the Fascist Movements."

Two levels can be distinguished in Fromm's treatment of Fascism. The general level concerns the condition of the individual in modern capitalist society. The specific level deals with the psychological mechanism that led millions of individuals to support Fascism. Insofar as the individual's condition in modern capitalist society is concerned, Fromm maintains that the essential characteristic is the dissolution of primary ties to the outer world. These previously had enabled the individual to feel that he belonged to a community and that, even in times of suffering and pain, he had his own place in society and could safely and freely express his own personality in his work and in his sentiments.

Capitalism freed man from his traditional bonds and became a strong influence in the increase of positive freedom and the development of an active critical and responsible personality:

> However, while this was *one* effect capitalism had on the process of growing freedom, at the same time it made the individual more alone and isolated and imbued him with a feeling of insignificance and powerlessness . . .
>
> Modern man's feeling of isolation and powerlessness is increased still further by the character which all his human relationships have assumed. The concrete relationship of one individual to another has lost its direct and human character and has assumed a spirit of manipulation and instrumentality. In all social and personal relations the laws of the market are the rule . . .
>
> Not only the economic, but also the personal relations between men have this character of alienation; instead of relations between human beings, they assume the character

of relations between things. But perhaps the most important and the most devastating instance of this spirit of instrumentality and alienation is the individual's relationship to his own self. Man does not only sell commodities, he sells himself and feels himself to be a commodity. The manual laborer sells his physical energy; the businessman, the physician, the clerical employee, sell their "personality."[6]

The individual's sense of impotence is sharpened by several other aspects of modern capitalism. The expansion of the economic and political scene renders an understanding of problems increasingly difficult. The threat of annihilating wars has become a nightmare for mankind. In these circumstances, modern man's isolation, insecurity, and impotence bring into play "mechanisms of escape" or defense by means of which the individual alone or in groups reacts to his plight.

Once the primary bonds which gave security to the individual are severed, once the individual faces the world outside himself as a completely separate entity, two courses are open to him since he has to overcome the unbearable state of powerlessness and aloneness. By one course he can progress to "positive freedom"; he can relate himself spontaneously to the world in love and work, in the genuine expression of his emotional, sensuous, and intellectual capacities; he can thus become one again with man, nature, and himself, without giving up the independence and integrity of his individual self. The other course open to him is to fall back, to give up his freedom, and to try to overcome his aloneness by eliminating the gap that has arisen between his individual self and the world. This second course never reunites him with the world in the way he was related to it before he emerged as an "individual," for the fact of his separateness cannot be reversed; it is an escape from an unbearable situation which would make life impossible if it were prolonged. This course of escape, therefore, is characterized by its compulsive character, like every escape from threatening panic; it is also characterized by the more or less complete surrender of individuality and the integrity of the self. Thus it is not a solution which leads to happiness and positive freedom; it is, in principle, a solution which is to be found in all neurotic phenomena. It assuages an unbearable anxiety and makes life possible by avoiding panic; yet it does not *solve* the underlying problem and is paid for by a kind of life that often consists only of automatic or compulsive activities.[7]

Certain mechanisms of escape have but little social relevance. Others, Fromm thought, exerted an important influence; a knowledge of them was necessary to an understanding of modern political and social phenomena.

In *Escape from Freedom* Fromm discusses the mechanisms of escape that are the basis of Fascism. Here his argument makes the transition from the general to the specific. These mechanisms of escape are "authoritarianism" (sadomasochistic in origin), "destructiveness," and "automaton conformity." He also discusses the problem of Fascism itself, concluding that it cannot be explained merely in terms of politics or economics. Although the latter are important, the psychological factors are equally so. Fascism is indeed an economic and political problem, but the reasons for its success and attraction for millions of individuals can only be explained from a psychological point of view. Any such explanation must take into account two factors: "the character structure of those people to whom it appealed, and the psychological characteristics of the ideology that made it such an effective instrument with regard to those very people."[8]

The second of these factors is of little significance for our purposes. It centers around a study of *Mein Kampf* and the most important postures adopted by Hitler and some of his closest associates (Goebbels and Ley, in particular), exposing their "sadistic aspects" and "authoritarian" elements (an urge for power over mankind and a desire for submission to an irresistibly strong external power). But Fromm's discussion of the first of these points is of great interest. He attempts to couch his psychological examination on several different levels so as to explain the behavior of that portion of the German population that "bowed to the Nazi regime without any strong resistance, but also without becoming admirers of the Nazi ideology and political practice"; this included the working class and the liberal and Catholic bourgeoisie. It also explains the behavior of those (the lower levels of the middle class, small shop-keepers, artisans, employees, and so on) who had enthusiastically backed National Socialism. The former, he says, generally had not given evidence of the "inner resistance one might have expected as the outcome of their political convictions."

Psychologically, this readiness to submit to the Nazi re-gime seems to be due mainly to a state of inner tiredness and resignation, which . . . is characteristic of the individual in the present era even in democratic countries. In Germany one additional condition was present as far as the working class was concerned: the defeat it suffered after the first vic-tories in the revolution of 1918. The working class had en-tered the postwar period with strong hopes for the realiza-tion of socialism or at least for a definite rise in its political, economic, and social position; but, whatever the reasons, it had witnessed an unbroken succession of defeats, which brought about the complete disappointment of all its hopes. By the beginning of 1930 the fruits of its initial victories were almost completely destroyed and the result was a deep feel-ing of resignation, of disbelief in their leaders, of doubt about the value of any kind of political organization and po-litical activity.

The behavior of the latter, on the other hand, especially the youngest, who were the strength of the militant National Socialists, should be explained in terms of the social characteristics of the petty bourgeoisie: its love for the strong, hatred of the weak, petti-ness, and "thriftiness with feelings as well as with money."

Although it is true that the social character of the lower middle class had been the same long before the war of 1914, it is also true that the events after the war intensified the very traits to which the Nazi ideology had its strong appeal: its craving for submission and its lust for power . . .

It was not only the economic position of the lower middle class that declined more rapidly after the war, but its social prestige as well . . .

In addition to these factors the last stronghold of middle-class security had been shattered too: the family. The postwar development, in Germany perhaps more than in other countries, had shaken the authority of the father and the old middle-class morality. The younger generation acted as they pleased and cared no longer whether their actions were approved by their parents or not . . .

The increasing social frustration led to a projection which became an important source for National Socialism: instead of being aware of the economic and social fate of the old middle class, its members consciously thought of their fate in terms of the nation. The national defeat and the Treaty of Versailles became the symbols to which the actual frustration—the social one—was shifted.[9]

In sum, for Fromm, Fascism can only be completely explained on the basis of the interdependence of economic, psychological, and ideological forces and of the pivotal role played by social character in this interdependence. In the case of the Nazis this process was particularly clear: "the lower middle class reacted to certain economic changes, such as the growing power of monopolies and postwar inflation, with an intensification of certain character traits, namely, sadistic and masochistic strivings; the Nazi ideology appealed to and intensified these traits; and the new character traits then became effective forces in supporting the expansion of German imperialism."[10] From this point of view Fromm also thought that, despite their important differences, Fascism and Stalinism had something in common: both "offered the atomized individual a new refuge and security." Both systems, he wrote in *The Sane Society*,

are the culmination of alienation. The individual is made to feel powerless and insignificant, but taught to project all his human powers into the figure of his leader, the state, the "fatherland," to whom he has to submit and whom he has to worship. He escapes from freedom into a new idolatry. All the achievements of individuality and reason, from the late Middle Ages to the nineteenth century, are sacrificed on the altars of the new idols. The new systems were built on the most flagrant lies, both with regard to their programs and to their leaders. In their program they claimed to fulfill some

sort of Socialism, when what they were doing was the negation of everything that was meant by this word in the socialist tradition. The figures of their leaders only emphasize the
great deception. Mussolini, a cowardly braggart, became a
symbol for maleness and courage. Hitler, a maniac of destruction, was praised as the builder of a new Germany.
Stalin, a cold-blooded, ambitious schemer, was painted as
the loving father of his people.[11]

These are the most important aspects of Fromm's position. It
is a position that certainly has merits, and Fromm sought to emphasize them by turning to German postwar society for confirmation
of his basic thesis. Notwithstanding, the historian must remain
skeptical when confronted with the difficult task of applying to
large groups of individuals a psychological mold that is chiefly theoretical, corroborated only by research on limited samplings, and
elaborated according to methods that have on occasion perplexed
the social psychologists themselves. The historian finds it difficult
to accept a reconstruction of the personality and behavior of a Hitler or a Mussolini if such a reconstruction is based largely on a psychoanalytic evaluation of their public statements and on the attempt to deduce from such public statements characteristic traits of
a frenzied authoritarian personality.

  These difficulties explain why the position of Fromm and his
disciples has not made further inroads among historians.[12] They
also explain why, even within the realm of the social sciences, they
have been outflanked by positions that may stem from the same
psychological premises but that provide better definitions of the
isolation, insecurity, and impotence of "potentially Fascistic" individuals and groups, of the particular conditions of the society in
which they operate, and especially of their elevation to the ideological level.

  In this respect, Parsons' position is significant, as it is stated
in the essay already cited and in others where he has dealt with Fascism.[13] Parsons operates from the same premises as Fromm, but his
argument is more circumspect and better articulated. He views
insecurity and lack of integration as the explanation of a particular
psychological situation that causes many sectors to be susceptible
to the Fascist appeal. Individually, however, they do not in themselves explain the origins of such movements, nor, more specifi-

cally, do they explain their political structure. Thus, Parsons' aim is to probe the latter aspect. He does so in terms that are substantially more sociological than psychological.

The sociological approach

This interpretation should be studied within the wider framework of the attempts made by sociologists to examine the interrelation of ideas, doctrines, and sociohistorical situations, and their efforts to define various aspects of historical and political thought within the context of the structural transformation of society. Here, too, confronted with a vast amount of published material, we shall limit ourselves to consideration of the most important positions.

A view that continues to attract many supporters was developed by Karl Mannheim in his famous *Ideology and Utopia*, published in 1929. According to Mannheim, thought that exists concretely cannot be separated from the context of the situation nor from collective action. It is not men "in general" or men as individuals who think, "but men in certain groups who have developed a particular style of thought in an endless series of responses to certain typical situations characterizing their common position." Just as men act differently depending on the groups in which they live, men think differently; "in accord with the particular context of collective activity in which they participate, men always tend to see the world which surrounds them differently." "But in addition to the general dynamics of the historical process," there are several other factors at the base of this thinking process. Most important among them is the intensification of social mobility in either a horizontal direction ("movement from one position to another, or from one country to another without changing social status"), or, more significantly, in a vertical direction ("movement between strata in the sense of social ascent and descent").[14]

Within the framework of this process, Mannheim detects five very important representative ideal-types in the nineteenth and twentieth centuries. They correspond to the various currents of contemporary political and historical thought and to as many political movements. They are bureaucratic conservatism, conservative historicism, liberal-democratic bourgeois thought, the socialist-communist conception, and Fascism. Each reflects a particular social group and its "sphere of knowledge" of society. As has been noted, "Democratic bourgeois thought fused the rationalism of the officials with the political conscience of the conservatives, acknowledging the possibility of instituting controls over organized reality: thus, socialist doctrine reveals not only liberalism's intellectual limits but also the economic and social conditioning of political thought. It produces the integration of a rational element with a historical element of conservative origin."[15]

Mannheim views Fascism as an entirely new disruptive element in the system that is characteristic of our century. It is the irruption on the political scene of those irrational masses who have been least integrated into the existing social order and who are guided by intellectuals who have not been socially integrated. For him, Fascism as a concept is "activistic and irrational":

> It couples itself, by preference, with the irrationalist philosophies and political theories of the modern period. It is especially Bergson, Sorel, and Pareto who, after suitable modification of course, have been incorporated into its *Weltanschauung*. At the very heart of its theory and its practice lies the apotheosis of direct action, the belief in the decisive *deed*, and in the significance attributed to the initiative of a leading *elite*. The essence of politics is to recognize and to grapple with the demands of the hour. Not programmes are important, but unconditional subordination to a leader. History is made neither by the masses, nor by ideas, nor by "silently working" forces, but by the *elites* who from time to time assert themselves. This is a complete irrationalism but characteristically enough not the kind of irrationalism known to the conservatives, not the irrational which is at the same time the super-rational, not the folk spirit (*Volksgeist*), not silently working forces, not the mystical belief in the creativeness of long stretches of time, but the irrationalism of the deed which negates even interpretation of history . . . However different the picture which conservatives, liberals, and socialists have derived from history, they all agree that history is made up of a set of intelligible interrelations . . . Fascism [on the other hand] regards every interpretation of history as a mere fictive construction destined to disappear before the deed of the moment as it breaks through the temporal pattern of history. That we are dealing here with a

theory which holds that history is meaningless is not changed by the fact that in fascist ideology, especially since its turn to the right, there are found the ideas of the "national war" and the ideology of the "Roman Empire." Apart from the fact that these ideas were, from the very first, consciously experienced as myths, i.e. fictions, it should be understood that historically oriented thought and activity do not mean the romantic idealization of some past epoch or event, but consist rather in the awareness of one's place in the historical process which has a clearly articulated structure. It is this clear articulation of the structure which makes one's own participation in the process intelligible. The intellectual value of all political and historical knowledge *qua* knowledge, disappears in the face of this purely intuitional approach, which appreciates only its ideological and mythological aspect. Thought is significant here only in so far as it exposes the illusory character of these fruitless theories of history and unmasks them as self-deceptions. For this activistic intuitionism, thought only clears the way for the pure deed free from illusions. The superior person, the leader, knows that all political and historical ideas are myths. He himself is entirely emancipated from them, but he values them—and this is the obverse side of his attitude—because they are "derivations" (in Pareto's sense) which stimulate enthusiastic feelings and set in motion irrational "residues" in men, and are the only forces that lead to political activity.[16]

With regard to the social forces, Fascism reflects "the ideology of 'putschist' groups led by intellectuals who are outsiders to the liberal-bourgeois and socialist stratum of leaders, and who hope to seize power by exploiting the crises which constantly beset modern society." In other words, Fascism reflects the psychological and social situation of groups for whom the development of society appears irrational and disorderly because they lack the vision of structural process and social organization. This explains Mannheim's belief that:

The chances for a fascist victory as well as for the justification of its historical theory depend upon the arrival of junctures in which a crisis so profoundly disorganizes the capitalist-bourgeois order, that the more evolutionary means of carrying on the conflict of interests no longer suffice. At moments like these, the chances for power are with him who knows how to utilize the moment with the necessary energy by stimulating active minorities to attack, thus seizing power.[17]

In the long run, however, "with the restoration of equilibrium following the crisis, the organized, historical-social forces again become effective"; even though the Fascist elite is able to adapt to the new situation, "the dynamic forces of social life nevertheless reassert themselves in the old way"; in the final analysis, what transpires is not a transformation of the social structure "but rather . . . a shift in personnel among the various social classes within the frame of the social process which continues to evolve." Mannheim finds confirmation of this process in the development of Italian Fascism:

> In the history of fascism, two periods may be distinguished, each of which has had distinct ideological repercussions. The first phase, about two years in length, during which fascism was a mere movement, was marked by the infiltration of activistic-intuitive elements into its intellectual-spiritual outlook. This was the period during which the syndicalist theories found entrance into fascism. The first "fasci" were syndicalist, and Mussolini at that time was said to be a disciple of Sorel. In the second phase, beginning in November, 1921, fascism becomes stabilized and takes a decisive turn towards the right.[18]

An argument similar to Mannheim's—at least in the fundamental elements that constitute the interpretative premise—is propounded by other sociologists. Georges Gurvitch's interpretation, for example, is also based on the framework of "spheres of knowledge" of society. Gurvitch, however, views Fascism from a different perspective. His theory is not limited to the fascisms that developed between the two World Wars. It encompasses the Peronista movement and even some current Third World regimes, such as those of Egypt and Algeria. Its scope is wider and considerably more abstract. Gurvitch bases his reasoning not so much on the genesis of Fascism as on its fulfillment as a political and social regime. Fascism is, above all, the expression of "technical and bureaucratic" modern society. On the political level, it is essentially translated as "the total fusion of the Totalitarian State with economic planning agencies and the army organization, overseen by technocratic groups" that have risen from the ranks of the army, the upper levels of bureaucracy, and even the trusts, banks, and "veterans" of the "revolution." The "semi-charismatic" leader is an essential but secondary element. His personality varies with the different forms of Fascism. He can be the straw man of technocrats or of foreign economic interests (Franco and Salazar) or a demagogic agitator (Hitler and Mussolini), or he might base his programs on the haste exhibited by "young nations" to rush through all the stages of capitalism regardless of the means (Nasser and Ben Bella).[19]

Once the basic configuration of the sociological interpretation has been described, a listing of the "spheres of knowledge" elaborated by sociologists with reference to Fascism is of little value.[20] Because no sociologist has projected a thesis more convincing than that of Mannheim, it is more productive to study the significant ramifications of his interpretation. These ramifications should be analyzed with particular reference to "the irrational masses that have least been integrated into the existing social order" to which Mannheim refers. Here again, although a considerable body of sociological literature exists, our discussion can be limited to works that have drawn the most on past research and have become the most significant sociological interpretations of Fascism.

Mannheim's interpretation placed great emphasis on social mobility. Many other authors, including some who were not sociologists, focused on the middle classes and the petty bourgeoisie. These are the directions taken by scholars who wish to determine which masses were acted upon by Fascism and constituted its base, at least in the initial stages. This dual course of sociological research has produced the most concrete and persuasive results. They are the same as those attained simultaneously by the best efforts of historiography.

One of the earliest exponents of the social sciences to emphasize the role of the middle classes in Fascism was Harold Dwight

Lasswell. He considered National Socialism "a desperate reaction of the lower middle classes," who were psychologically overshadowed by the increasing strength of the workers and the upper bourgeoisie and wished to gain revenge. Two years later David J. Saposs echoed Lasswell's thesis, asserting that Fascism is "the extreme expression of middle-classism or populism." He stated: "The basic ideology of the middle class is populism . . . Their ideal was an independent small property-owning class consisting of merchants, mechanics, and farmers. This element . . . now designated as middle class, sponsored a system of private property, profit, and competition on an entirely different basis from that conceived by capitalism."[21]

This line of thought was adopted by Svend Ranulf, Fromm and Parsons, and subsequently by a number of authors who developed and plumbed the depths of the relation between the middle classes and Fascism. Chronologically, the last of these is Nathaniel Stone Preston, who, in a study of the ideology and reality of capitalism, socialism, communism, and Fascism, defined the last-named as "a revolutionary nationalistic" movement of the economically deprived middle classes. Preston believed this movement was directed against Marxist collectivism and internationalism as well as against capitalist society's tendencies toward concentration.[22] As we shall observe later in this book, this definition was quite analogous to that propounded in 1923 by Luigi Salvatorelli.

The best synthesis of the relation between the middle classes and Fascism is, in my opinion, Seymour Martin Lipset's *Political Man: The Social Bases of Politics.* Lipset, too, considers Fascism "a middle class movement representing a protest against both capitalism *and* socialism, big business *and* big unions." But his argument goes beyond this conclusion. Political and sociological examination of the various movements, parties, and regimes generally defined as Fascist leads Lipset to doubt the validity of this label's being applied to many of them.

According to him, since the French Revolution parties of the Right, Center, and Left have existed, possessing clearly defined ideological and class characteristics.

If we look at the supporters of the three major positions in most democratic countries, we find a fairly logical relationship between ideology and social base. The Socialist left derives its strength from manual workers and the poorer rural strata; the conservative right is backed by the rather well-to-do elements—owners of large industry and farms, the managerial and free professional strata—and those segments of the less privileged groups who have remained involved in traditionalist institutions, particularly the Church. The democratic center is backed by the middle classes, especially small businessmen, white-collar workers, and the anticlerical sections of the professional classes.[23]

Nevertheless, "a study of the social bases of different modern mass movements suggests that each major social stratum has both democratic and extremist political expressions" and that "extremist ideologies and groups can be classified and analyzed in the same terms as democratic groups." The extremists are characterized by their rejection of the democratic method and their tendency to set up totalitarian systems based on the takeover of power by elites from the various social strata.

When Lipset passes from the general to the specific, it becomes evident that even Fascism is subject to this rule. This is the crucial point of his thesis. A close study of what he calls individual manifestations in various countries requires the concession that while all of them are "extremist," they represent three different social strata and their corresponding ideologies. Were we to continue to refer to a single Fascist phenomenon, we would have to maintain that there is a Fascist extremism of the Right (Horthy, Dollfuss, Salazar, the pre-Nazi nationalist movements of the Weimar Republic), a Fascist extremism of the Center (especially National Socialism, since Lipset regards Fascism and Falangism as being a mixture of fascisms of the Right and Center), and an extremism of the Left (Peronism). But this is patently absurd, and Lipset is inclined to consider as truly Fascist only those extremist parties and regimes of the Center and the bourgeois middle class. All others, with the single exception of Peronism, he wisely reduces to being conservative or extremist movements of the Right. Peronism, alone among the presumed fascisms of the twenties, thirties, and forties, is placed among the extremist movements of the Left. On this subject Lipset writes:

This form, Peronism, largely found in poorer under-developed countries, appeals to the lower strata against the middle and upper classes. It differs from Communism in being nationalistic, and has usually been the creation of nationalist army officers seeking to create a more vital society by destroying the corrupt privileged strata which they believe have kept the masses in poverty, the economy underdeveloped, and the army demoralized and underpaid.[24]

After Lipset the sociological interpretation of Fascism arrives at a crucial point and confronts an unavoidable alternative: either we accept Lipset's analysis and cease to refer to a single Fascist *phenomenon* (thereby opening our discussion to as many individual arguments as there are imprecisely defined "fascisms"); or we remain convinced that, despite national characteristics, there exists a minimal common denominator among the various "fascisms." In the latter event, sociologists must define the masses to which Mannheim referred, other than by their identification with the middle classes and the petty bourgeoisie. They must study the relation between the masses and the rest of society and the respective mechanisms for integration. This is precisely what the Italo-American sociologist Gino Germani has attempted to do by developing a more general and comprehensive argument of social mobility and integration than those limited exclusively to the middle classes.

Germani's studies are numerous and important. In general they are based on an examination of Argentine society, the characteristics of Peronism, and a comparison to the European situation and the classic fascisms. As early as 1956 this author indicated the future direction of his studies in the lucid essay "Integración política de las masas y el totalitarismo," where the differences between Peronism and European fascisms are clarified in terms of social bases (the popular classes in the case of Peronism, and the petty bourgeoisie in the case of Europe) and with respect to their ideologies.

For our purposes the most important contribution is Germani's paper "Fascism and Social Class," presented at the international seminar on Fascism at Reading, England, in 1967.[25] The paper is divided into two parts. In the first the author traces concisely the interpretations of Fascism seen from the point of view of class basis and briefly discusses the essential points of each. Despite its broad outlines, even this section contains some critical observations that, coming from a sociologist, are particularly interesting. They indicate that even experts in the social sciences acknowledge the inadequacy of certain arguments that have prevailed in their field for several years. The most substantive aspects of Germani's interpretation, however, are presented in the second part of his paper, where he discusses the problem of "the role of 'classes' and of 'mass society' as general explanatory factors in the emergence of Fascism and Totalitarianism."

Germani, too, detects in modern mass society a process of atomization, depersonalization, and loss of identity of the individual (caused by alienation, isolation, the destruction of primary bonds, and the increasing deterioration of intermediary structures).[26] For him the "psychosocial hypothesis" retains its validity and explains why mass society leads to the negation of values such as reason, liberty, and individuality. However, he hastens to add, this is not an adequate explanation for the birth of Totalitarianism, and of Fascism in particular. Just as important as the psychosocial factors are the "growing participation of the masses and the growing isolation of the elites," both intimately connected with the process of mobilization and social integration.[27] There is no such thing as a perfectly integrated society, Germani writes; "change is permanent and universal and reintegration always carries with it a certain degree of structural change." However, when the changes are significant and "the rates of objective mobilization are very high or the channels of integration are inadequate," and social mobilization is accompanied by the availability of adequate ideologies (that is, the availability of a corresponding elite), then there may take place "that type of displacement associated with the birth of explosive or excessively extremist political and social movements." In this event, reintegration will take place by means of mass disturbances and radical changes in the political or social structures or in both ways at once." According to Germani,

> The creation of mass movements will thus be characterized by a pronounced "displacement" situation and by the presence of the following elements: available masses, available elites, and available ideologies. We have already spoken

of the masses. As to the "availability" of the elites, the mechanisms are the same as those described for the masses. The
elite must, moreover, be in a condition of intense "displacement"; it is, in fact, recognized that a stable and consolidated
elite will not be able to assume the leadership of an extremist
mass movement. The combination of a stable elite with rapidly mobilized masses can produce ideologies that are "superficially" extremist, but it will not be able to translate them
into revolutionary action.

The nature of the mass movements that will thus be created
will be determined by whether the mobilization is "primary" or
"secondary," whether the mobilization is to be explained in "traditional, or nonindustrial structures" (primary) or in "a *more* modern
industrial society" (secondary):

> In the case of primary mobilization, the mobilized groups
> are groups that do not participate in modern society and
> their marginality precedes their insertion into the modern
> structure. Secondary mobilization, on the other hand, takes
> place in groups that are *already participating* in many as-
> pects, and that are nevertheless "displaced" or made mar-
> ginal by factors such as inflation, loss of status, unemploy-
> ment, and so on.

With this formula Germani attempts to explain the difference between Italian Fascism and Argentine Peronism. In Italy, he
says, Fascism resulted from the commingling of primary and secondary mobilizations brought into play by World War I. The primary mobilization had in fact already come into being during the
last decade of the nineteenth century, but until the war it had found
"legitimate or tolerated" channels. The war accelerated its rhythm
and scope, but the organized working class failed to attain power
"because the 'shift' caused by the war and the resulting mobilization
did not find an available elite." Moreover, "the desires for new
forms of participation and consumption had been partially satisfied
by the extension of social rights and increased wages." This explains the decline in tension among the working classes. It was followed by the Fascist violence that interrupted "a process of integra-

tion analogous to that which had taken place in other Western European countries, and which was then taken up anew and successfully after World War II."

The secondary mobilization involved the middle class and experienced a substantially different fate:

> in the first place it had no channels for political expression. In the second place, a new balance could only have been attained by means of the "demobilization" of the lower strata. This would have been a source of considerable satisfaction for the middle class, for it is widely acknowledged that the postwar imbalance had resulted in a loss of status in terms of prestige, power, and wealth for the urban middle class. This loss of status occurred both in relative and in absolute terms: On the relative level the breach with the rising working classes was closed. In absolute terms there was decreased mobility resulting from unemployment, inflation, loss of income, and political influence. But the loss of status in relative terms was particularly important because of the "elitist" nature of the system of social stratification. Thus, the advances of the working classes were viewed as "usurpation" of status. Thirdly, a "displaced" elite was available; moreover, the adopted ideology adequately satisfied the motivation of the mobilized groups. Indeed, it met their demands for "reequilibrium" by stressing concepts of "order, discipline, hierarchy," and the demobilization of the lower classes. Moreover, it transferred frustrations from an individual or class to a national level with territorial claims, dreams of imperial power, and so on. But its success and transformation into a totalitarian state were facilitated by additional elements. Chief among the latter were the predominant interests of the ruling class. In addition, the responsibility of the establishment (political ruling class, monarchy, economic and military elites) in the active or passive support of Fascism was no longer seriously denied.

In Argentina events similar to those that had occurred in Italy brought Perón to power. Certain differences, however, "explain the repeated failure to establish a 'classical' Fascist regime, as well as the success of Peronism." As Germani writes, concluding a systematic recapitulation of the most important social, economic, and political events in Argentina from the second half of the nineteenth century to the present:

> the chief difference between Peronism and Italian Fascism consists in the class from which the masses were mobilized and in the kind of mobilization. Mobilization in Argentina was primary, and the mobilized class was the lower class. Peronism was a "national and popular" mobilization and was probably typical of this kind of primary mobilization. Although Peronism had many totalitarian characteristics, it was not very different from the Radical Party, the liberal-popular movement that had provided political expression to the first stage of the primary mobilization.

Within the sociological interpretation of Fascism, a special place is reserved for Jules Monnerot's book *Sociologie de la révolution.* The author's intention is to emphasize two characteristic aspects of Fascism, and in so doing he refers to arguments set forth in 1933 and 1934 by Georges Bataille. He distinguishes two processes in Fascism:

> A change in the dominant nature of the political class, or in the determining elements within this class. A process of the creation of power: a crisis [*détresse*] situation drawing in its wake a movement of social destruction is translated by means of fear and aversion of chaos in the psyche of the more "homogenous" elements into a growing sense of apprehension when confronted with the advance of chaos, both real and imaginary . . . [and] it arouses in the society in which it occurs a need, a *demand* for power.

According to Monnerot, at the end of World War I, countries with an advanced stage of development from an industrial, cultural, and civic point of view experienced a mobilization of the masses. This was accompanied by a politicization of social categories that had previously been conformist and only slightly interested in public affairs. (They had preferred to acquiesce to the State until such time as it appeared to them that the oligarchy had failed.)

This politicization, in turn, was translated into revolutionary movements, "that aimed not at the destruction of the detested power, but at the foundation of a power whose absence signified a mortal threat to values, goods, and persons and an oppressive vacuum." Those who were marginal, irregular, or "heterogenously subversive" contributed to giving these movements a disruptive force. After its initial stages, however, the characteristic feature of Fascism was, in Monnerot's view, the reconstruction of the State and the elaboration of its myth. In this respect he writes:

> As opposed to Communism, Fascism destroys neither the preexisting social cadres nor the basic institutions on which these are founded . . . but it subordinates them. Fascism brings into contemporary focus the principle of social solidarity for a historical collectivity that Mussolini defined in national terms and Hitler spoke of in racial terms; from this point of view Fascism is socialist in the etymological sense.[28]

The socioeconomic interpretation

Chronologically this is the most recent interpretation of Fascism. Nevertheless, its general terms have already been clearly defined, and it is easy to retrace the influences that led to its conception. All of the authors who propound this interpretation do so within the framework of recent social and economic references to development and industrialization. This tendency may be attributed to the fact that they regard Fascism as one among several efforts to overcome the increasing difficulties, social inadequacy, disorders, and crises that afflict modern laissez-faire economy. It may also be linked to Walt Whitman Rostow's well-known theory explaining the relation between the stages of economic development and the forms of political organization.[29] Finally, this tendency may be the result of the social economists' interest in the specific problems of delayed industrialization.

The most significant expression of this school of interpretation is found in the studies of the Russian-American A. F. Kenneth Organski. He has at least two stimuli, suggestions, preoccupations —call them what you will—that are extremely relevant. No one, however, including the scholars in question, has succeeded in providing truly satisfactory responses to Organski's theories. On the one hand, we find Organski's dissatisfaction with earlier interpretations that he dismisses as partial and, to a lesser or greater degree, incapable of providing a sufficiently cohesive explanation of the Fascist phenomenon. On the other hand, Organski tends to seek similarities between Fascism as it flourished in Europe between the two World Wars and movements and regimes that have arisen in recent years in Latin America and the Third World. This tendency has the merit of inciting researchers to search for an objective explanation for these similarities and to seek a common denominator among such diverse events.

The Stages of Political Development, published in 1965, provides the framework in which Organski locates and explains Fascism. The book concentrates on modern economic development and the relation between it and the political nature of things. According to its thesis, modern political development (for Europe, the beginning of the sixteenth century; for other countries, from the eighteenth, nineteenth, and twentieth centuries, depending on the case in point) is closely related to economic development and undergoes four successive stages: primitive unification, industrialization, national welfare, and abundance (or opulence).

The first stage (prior to the process of industrialization) focuses the center of political life on the problems of national unity, the centralization of power, and, in Europe, the birth and infancy of the nation-states. On the other hand, the second stage corresponds to the coming to power of a new class, closely linked to the new type of economy that followed the "takeoff," and the integration into the nation of the masses that previously had been substantially excluded therefrom. In this stage, the mutual dependence of the people and the government increases at a proportional rate. In the third stage, that of full industrialization, this process is essentially complete. This means that, whereas in the previous stage the principal function of government was to protect capital from the people, its function now becomes quite the contrary: to protect the people from capital by guaranteeing the former even higher standards of living. It is in this stage that mass democracy becomes a reality. In the fourth stage, automation brings about the new industrial revolution.

The first and the last of these stages have nothing to do with so-called Fascism. Indeed, for Organski, Fascism can occur only in the second stage, while the third stage can produce National Socialism (which he does not consider Fascism). In this respect he writes:

> *Fascism* will be used in this book to refer to one of the varieties of the politics of industrialization: a system that arises only in stage two, that springs from fundamentally similar social and economic conditions in each case; that represents . . . a peculiar compromise between two ruling elites; and that contributes in recognizably similar ways to the shape and the pace of industrialization. Viewed in this light, Hitler was an authoritarian dictator, a nationalist, an aggressor, a represser, and a madman, but he was not a fascist, for Germany was fully industrial when Hitler came to power. In terms of the stages of political development . . . the Nazi system was not a form of the politics of national welfare.[30]

Up to the present three forms of power have come to the fore during the second stage: Western bourgeois democracy, Stalinism, and Fascism. In this stage the primary function of the government is to assist in economic modernization, industrial development, and especially in the accumulation of capital by means of a system of low mass consumption that allows capital to be concentrated in the hands of those who reinvest it in the means of production. All three forms of power that developed have pursued these objectives. The difference among them is found especially in the rhythm and speed of industrialization (more rapid in Stalinism, slower in the bourgeois democracy, and slowest of all in a Fascist regime), as well as in the type of elite or alliance of elites that constitute the government. In fact, during the second stage the nation gradually undergoes a process of expansion that includes the industrial elite in the first instance and then, more slowly, the masses that have now become sensitive to public interests.

More specifically, Fascism is a form of power that comes about during the first phase of the second stage. It is the result of the blending of a strong but declining traditional (agricultural) elite and of a modern (industrial) elite that is on the ascendant but is not yet at its fullest strength. A relation of momentary substantial advantage for the first type of elite with respect to the second results. This alliance is in turn dictated by mutual desire to avoid a substantially uncertain confrontation between the traditional and modern elites, and by mutual interest in impeding an excessively rapid affirmation of the masses.

For Organski several consequences result from this premise. One is the refusal to consider Fascism a movement of the petty bourgeoisie. Another is the need to expand the Fascist context beyond its Italian, Spanish, and Argentine manifestations in order to render it applicable to other countries. The Italian, Spanish, and Argentine forms of Fascism are the only ones Organski considers; he relegates other presumed forms of Fascism, such as the German, to the third stage, and other instances to the first stage. Therefore, these cannot be considered true Fascisms. Organski is explicit in seeking to avoid any misunderstanding and moralistic or political judgments. He refers to "syncratic regimes" and "syncratic politics," of which Fascism is merely one manifestation or variant. In this respect he writes:

> It is also necessary to broaden the fascist category to include current and future examples of political systems that resemble the earlier fascist states in some regards but not in others. It appears likely, for example, that a considerable number of the industrializing nations will adopt political systems that are neither bourgeois nor stalinist and certainly not socialist, despite their occasional claims. Some of these governments will closely resemble fascist governments in their structure, in their support, and their handling of industrialization, but they may embrace ideologies which differ considerably from the old model.[31]

The true nature of Fascism-syncratism should not be sought in a presumed classist origin, specific ideology, or in a specific form of organization of the State, but in the rhythm that Fascism imposes on industrial development, especially in its "takeoff" stage. The conclusion to his chapter on "syncratic politics" is characteristic of Organski's thought:

> Marxists are wrong when they claim that fascism is a creature of the bourgeoisie. As we have seen, syncratic systems represent an attempt by the agricultural elite to slow the

pace of industrialization and to control its consequences. Syncratic government is a last victory for the landed aristocracy. Faced with certain defeat, they nevertheless manage to maximize their power and postpone its final shift into other hands.

The effect of syncratic government is not, however, to stop the process of economic modernization. Industrialization continues, though probably at a somewhat slower pace. The main effect of syncratic government is typically to exempt the agricultural elite from paying the economic and social cost of industrialization and to lessen the cost paid by the peasantry. Though their life remains hard and their exploitation at the hands of their landlords is often great, the peasants do not suffer the brutal displacement and abrupt change that afflicted their brothers in bourgeois Europe or in stalinist Russia and China. The burden of paying the price for economic progress is shifted almost entirely onto the backs of the industrial workers, whose lot is harder than it would have been in the absence of a syncratic regime.

It does not follow, nevertheless, that the industrial workers of the syncratic countries have suffered more than those of bourgeois or stalinist countries. Industrialization in the nineteenth century was necessarily a more difficult business than it is today in nations that can take advantage both of the technology and of the social experience of those who preceded them, and industrialization at breakneck speed is more painful than modernization spread over many years. Syncratic industrialization has the advantages of taking place in the twentieth century and of proceeding at a relatively slow pace. Also, it is only fair to note that syncratic systems occur in relatively advanced countries, where the difficult early accumulation of capital has already taken place. Thus it is pointless to compare the lot of workers under early bourgeois or early stalinist systems. The comparison must be made at the comparable stage of economic advance.

Syncratic politics, indeed, is a temporary phenomenon. Unlike bourgeois and stalinist politics, which see the industrialization process through from start to finish, syncratic politics emerges in the middle of the process and disappears once the nation has become industrial. In this sense, and in this sense only, the syncratic system is a variant of the bourgeois pattern, for syncratic politics is preceded by a period of bourgeois development and is followed by a resumption of the bourgeois pattern.

At this point, however, the nation enters a new stage of political growth, and it is no longer appropriate to refer to bourgeois politics. With industrialization achieved, the politics of national welfare begins, bringing great changes to all the developed nations—by whatever path they have reached that position.[32]

In addition to *The Stages of Political Development*, Organski examined the nature of Fascism in his paper "Fascism and Modernization," also presented at the international seminar in Reading in 1967. Although the paper presents no new elements in the position he had evolved two years earlier, two points should be noted: an insistence that Fascism is a contrast between the modern and conventional sectors of the economy, and, more specifically, an attempt to locate Fascism—or its potential expression—at a specific moment within the industrialization process when the modern (nonagricultural) sector constitutes 40 to 55 percent of the national economic complex.[33]

Social Origins of Dictatorship and Democracy by Barrington Moore, Jr., partially shares the interpretative approach of Organski's works. After studying the German, Japanese, and Italian varieties, Moore concludes that Fascism is one of either three or four avenues leading from preindustrial society to modern society. (The exact number depends on whether or not the Indian variety, characterized by a weak impulse toward industrialization, is included with the capitalist-democratic, Fascist, and Communist forms of government.) This road to modernization is the capitalist-reactionary way, along which the moderate-conservative-agrarian attempt was made to counter impending industrialization and massification with a "revolution from above" that modernized and rationalized the old political order without, however, changing the social system. From this point of view, Fascism is characterized by certain basic elements that Moore defines as follows:

Though it might be equally profitable to undertake a parallel consideration of democratic failures that preceded fascism in Germany, Japan, and Italy, it is enough for present purposes to notice that fascism is inconceivable without democracy or what is sometimes more turgidly called the entrance of the masses onto the historical stage. Fascism was an attempt to make reaction and conservatism popular and plebeian, through which conservatism, of course, lost the substantial connection it did have with freedom . . .

The conception of objective law vanished under fascism. Among its most significant features was a violent rejection of humanitarian ideals, including any notion of potential human equality . . . Another feature was the stress on violence . . . Blood and death often acquire overtones of erotic attraction, though in its less exalted moments fascism was thoroughly "healthy" and "normal," "promising return to a cosy bourgeois, and even prebourgeois peasant, womb."

Plebeian anticapitalism thus appears as the feature that most clearly distinguishes twentieth-century fascism from its predecessors, the nineteenth-century conservative and semi-parliamentary regimes. It is a product of both the intrusion of capitalism into the rural economy and of strains arising in the postcompetitive phase of capitalist industry. Hence fascism developed most fully in Germany where capitalist industrial growth had gone the furthest within the framework of a conservative revolution from above . . . though one should not make the opposite error of regarding fascist leaders as merely the agents of big business. The attraction of fascism for the lower middle class in the cities, threatened by capitalism, has often been pointed out . . .

In Japan, as in Germany, pseudoradical anticapitalism gained a considerable foothold among the Japanese peasantry . . .

Italian fascism displays the same pseudoradical and propeasant features found in Germany and Japan. In Italy, on the other hand, these notions were more of an opportunistic growth, a cynical decoration put on to take advantage of circumstances.[34]

Ludovico Garruccio's *L'industrializzazione tra nazionalismo e rivoluzione: Le ideologie politiche dei paesi in via di sviluppo* is more explicitly linked to delayed industrialization.[35] For this author, Fascism is none other than a nationalist-totalitarian ideol-

ogy of transition expressed by the processes of delayed industrialization and by the dichotomy between the traditional and modern
sectors of society. These processes are violently negated as an
"unnecessary luxury" in the name of a higher and more efficient
social and national unity. Thus, Nasserism and Peronism qualify as
fascisms, but Sukarno's "guided democracy" was a "subproduct of
fascism on the subproletarian level," and Nkrumah's regime is a
"caricatural and obscene imitation" of European fascism. Moreover, fascist elements are to be found in the "pluralist variants" of
the political ideologies of several developing countries. According
to Garruccio, in order to understand the main ideological trends of
development, either totalitarian or pluralistic, one must keep in
mind two factors: the predisposing conditions—dualism, national
humiliation, delayed industrialization, national disintegration, and
the "event"—and the particular manifestations of such ideologies—
"unitarian requirements; ascension to power of a new generation,
of a charismatic personality and a new ruling class; attempts to
integrate the masses; doctrinaire eclecticism; promotion of industrial development; adoption of formulas for a guided economy;
adoption of economic and psychological autarchy (radical protectionism); proposal of a particular life style; and recourse to violence against any centrifugal or conflicting national force."[36]

Part Two

Italian Interpretations of Italian Fascism

5

Stages in the History of Fascism and the Problem of Its Origins

Before discussing Fascism and the reasons for its gradual incarnation as the complex political and social phenomenon that characterized Italian life for close to twenty years, a time period for its rise, development, and consolidation must be established. On first examination, journalists, politicians, and scholars appear to agree as to the event that provided the impetus for Fascism: World War I was the great midwife that presided over its birth. Upon closer scrutiny this agreement is less unanimous; there is disagreement as to the precise time of birth during that war.[1]

The effect of World War I
According to Luigi Salvatorelli, who expressed his opinion in *Resto del Carlino* on 18 October 1920 and has since often repeated and clarified it, the sources of Fascism are found in World War I. However, they should not be ascribed so much to the war itself as to the crisis (*radiosomaggismo*, "radiant days of May") that was at the heart of Italian intervention:

> In searching to attribute responsibility, one should focus not so much on the three-year-long skirmishes on the Corso

but rather on the demonstrations of May 1915. When it became acceptable and glorious to assault Parliament and do violence to the decisions taken by the national electorate, to calumniate atrociously the former President of the Council, a cousin of the King, to boast of planning his assassination, to impose decisions involving life and death on the authorities through street demonstrations, the anarchic tendencies that had tenacious roots in the depths of the Italian soul were suddenly brought to the fore, paraded in triumph in the light of day, and officially consecrated as a means of political struggle and an instrument of government. The violence and rebellion of the extremists was ten times weaker than the forces unleashed by the violence and rebellion of the reactionary patriots. Moreover, those May days were not an isolated incident or a passing phenomenon; they generated a tradition that survived the war and that inspired and continues to inspire the political action of the Italian conservatives which Fascism approved and encouraged.[2]

The crisis of May 1915 signaled the demise of "all political and parliamentary situations that had developed since 1900" and marked the assumption of power of "that mixture of nationalism and Mussolinism that is Fascism."[3]

Angelo Tasca and Federico Chabod also ascribed the origins of Fascism to World War I, although they did not place much emphasis on the May crisis (radiosomaggismo). They considered Fascism the result of postwar experience, closely linked to the war and incomprehensible in any other context. The war had created the necessary premises, had given rise to unfavorable economic and social consequences, disillusionment with the undistinguished Italian victory on the part of a large portion of the bourgeoisie, and the rise of the proletarian movement. The rise of the proletarian movement, noteworthy in itself, assumed even greater psychological significance when viewed in the light of the Russian Revolution that threatened for a while to spread to the rest of Europe at the time of the Hungarian and Bavarian uprisings. Although, for Tasca, radiosomaggismo marked the beginning of the crisis of the "new and fragile democratic institutions," he is explicit:

Fascism is a post-war phenomenon . . . Foremost among the conditions that made fascism possible was the economic crisis. No crisis, no fascism; and this refers not to any economic crisis, but specifically to the one that settled permanently over the world after the war . . .

In every country the end of the war and the beginning of the depression saw fairly considerable alterations in social status. The creation of a mass of *nouveaux riches*, and distinct changes in the traditional forms of capitalism resulted in the emergence of a new *bourgeoisie* [for whom the seizure of the state] by any possible means became . . . a matter of life-and-death importance.

On the other hand, the war had set the popular masses in movement, and after the war this movement was accelerated . . .

With the coming of peace the long pent-up demands of the masses were released, at a time when, as a result of the war, there was less than ever to satisfy them. A tendency to hoard available resources rather than find better ways of sharing them brought the problem of power into the foreground.

Nor should a third general condition be underestimated: "Fascism cannot be dismissed as mere war psychosis." But we cannot discount the psychological role played by war-caused "excitement" and "delirium." Viewed within this context, Fascism was the product of the intensification of the class struggle, its increasingly political character, and the relative equality of the opposing forces.

Given the first two, the third is of crucial importance. Such equality is paralysing to any form of government, whether it be a national coalition, a combination of left-wing parties, or a social democratic majority. So long as it continues and no better form of government is found, the state is at the mercy of blind upheavals caused by some instinct of self-preservation, by the defence of threatened privileges, and by the aspirations of classes that have been upset and thrown out of gear by the depression. By abandoning the attempt to gain a solution by legal methods, the working classes turn to the creation of a "second power," within the state and opposed to it; the *bourgeoisie* then has recourse either to "reactionary transformation of the state" or to fascist violence.[4]

Tasca and Chabod in large part adopt the views of Pietro Nenni and Gaetano Salvemini. This, in my opinion the most correct definition of the periodization of Fascism, has led to the most satisfactory consideration of new elements. Unquestionably, precursors of Fascism can be detected in prewar Italy, its economic and social development, political life, psychological and cultural trends, and even in certain practical manifestations. (During the 1908 upheavals in the Parma region, and during the "Red Week" in 1914, there occurred instances of protest against the absenteeism of the State and even cases of self-defense against proletarian violence.) However, one cannot view them absolutely as "Fascist seeds predestined to germinate in the postwar period," as some foreign writers have attempted to do. There is no proof that had there been no war these seeds would have germinated. Indeed, there is much to favor an assumption to the contrary. Salvemini's criticism of the radiosomaggismo appears more consistent, though I shall not attribute undue weight to it (nor reduce it to a simple condemnation of the intervention or to a mere moralistic argument).[5]

The crisis of May 1915 contributed to the wider crisis that led to Fascism, just as the war was followed by a postwar period. This postwar period was not unique to the Italian situation and, upon closer inspection, was not so much related to the manner in which Italy entered the conflict as it was connected to the economic, social, political, and psychological transformations produced by the war in Italy and elsewhere. Because of the decisive nature of the 1914-1918 war (historically a dividing point for the world not unlike the French Revolution), the postwar crisis must be viewed as the point of departure for Fascism.[6] Eloquent confirmation of this position can be found in the fact that if Fascism came into being right after the war (March 1919), it became an important political factor and assumed its basic characteristics and individual identity only at the end of 1920, coinciding with the termination of the first phase of the postwar crisis (the so-called Red biennium). Until that time it had remained a negligible political and social phenomenon that was difficult to define and, despite certain eloquent and involuted symptoms, was linked more to the familiar traditions of subversiveness than to the trends prevailing among the bourgeoisie that had survived the war and become transformed in the sense described by Tasca.

The March on Rome and the coup d'état of 3 January 1925

It is more difficult to establish in the history of Fascism the transition from the period of origins to that in which Fascism assumed the physiognomy and characteristics of a political regime. There are two commonly mentioned points of reference. The first, more external and immediate, was the March on Rome and Mussolini's subsequent rise to power. The second, a more complex event, was the coup d'état of 3 January 1925.

Insofar as Fascism's internal history is concerned, October 1922 has only slight importance. Mussolini's accession to power represented only a moment—important though it was—in the life of Fascism and its revolution. In fact, as of October 1922 there was a new and intense examination of the Fascist situation, encompassing political and personal differences of opinion as to objectives, the nature of the State, the content, forms, and institutions of Fascism, and the forms of power and means of attaining them. Moreover, it cannot be claimed that as of October 1922 the majority of the country or even the political forces gained a real understanding of the Fascist thrust. It is clear today that this thrust had not yet achieved its definitive form and that the Italian situation was still potentially open to alternatives other than the by no means fatal transformation of the Mussolini government into a Fascist regime.

A more significant date is 3 January 1925, many political and juridical scholars maintain, because on that day Mussolini's speech abrogated the legality of the constitution. However, as Livio Paladin emphasized, "the extreme gradualness with which Fascism built its own juridical edifice" makes it difficult to establish a date on which this abrogation took place.[7] Some scholars insist it occurred on 3 January 1925; others attribute it to the period between the end of 1925 and the beginning of 1926 (the transformation of the form of government and elimination of the separation of powers), or to 1928 (the end of representativeness of the Chamber of Deputies, and "constitutionalization" of the Grand Council of Fascism), or even later. (Vezio Crisafulli sets it at the time of the introduction of the racist legislation.) But the date of 3 January 1925 is important for two other reasons, historically more consistent and easier to define. The first, perceptively pointed out by Gabriele De Rosa, is that:

> militant anti-Fascism began to exhibit united characteristics, even with regard to the definition of its various political goals, much later than the March on Rome. The premises of this united anti-Fascism were established . . . only after the Matteotti crime, and not always with the same degree of clarity in all the parties . . . Thus, a history of anti-Fascism must distinguish two phases in the formulation of a united anti-Fascist conscience. One phase preceded the March on Rome, when anti-Fascism existed in the political and cultural individuality of the democratic and Popular parties, but was not yet a dynamic, secure opposition that was immune to Fascism's "normalizing" tendencies. The second phase, which extends to the period of the Aventine opposition, saw the progressive dissipation of all illusions regarding the "normalization" of Fascism, and at the same time saw the move toward a common policy of opposition to Fascism.[8]

The political isolation of Fascism dates from this establishment of a united anti-Fascist conscience. It also marks the end of all collaboration with Fascism by the other parties. Both events were necessary for the establishment of—or rather for the attempt to establish—a true Fascist State and hence for the transition of Fascism from its original phase to its period of maturity.[9] In this new climate the second historically relevant fact was Mussolini's speech of 3 January 1925. Although it is my opinion that from the constitutional point of view this speech did not represent a true break in the Italian liberal regime, and that, on the constitutional level, the Fascist regime was born between December 1925 and January 1926 and perfected at the end of 1926, there is no doubt that from the political standpoint the third of January was the moment of decisive rupture. For this break to become complete, one had to wait until 1926 (with respect to the constitution) and until 1929 (with respect to political transformation). However, it was on 3 January 1925, when all possible political and general alternatives within

Fascism were eliminated, that Fascism took on the unique and unprecedented characteristics of a political regime.

After 25 July 1943

In order to impose a periodization that may help make more intelligible the history of Fascism and its problems, we must also consider a third and final phase: the period following 25 July 1943 that saw the establishment of the Italian Social Republic.

In addition to its numerous and important links between this period and the two preceding phases of Fascism, this stage exhibited peculiarities of its own, both of a subjective type and especially of an objective type. These included the insignificant autonomy the Salò regime had compared to that of Berlin and the German military authorities in Italy, and the noteworthy decline in the role of *Duce* that Mussolini suffered at this time. These objective characteristics justify considering this phase as the third period of Fascism.

6

Interpretations prior to the Matteotti Assassination

The nature of Fascism prior to the March on Rome in October 1922 and until the Matteotti assassination in June 1924 is becoming increasingly clear. Today we can determine the stages of its development and detect its basic characteristics, dynamic elements, purely demagogic elements, and elements destined to fall by the wayside in either the short or the long run. Also, we can identify the aspects and manifestations of Fascism that contained the seeds of future developments. Thus, it is relatively simple now to establish the limits and errors contained in the attitude toward Fascism of the liberal ruling class, the mass parties (Socialist and Popular), and the Communists. However, to evaluate correctly these limits and errors on a historiographic level we must understand how Fascism was viewed by its contemporaries, what opinion they had of it, and where they thought it would lead.

Contemporary writings, 1921-1923

Contemporary writings about Fascism were plentiful: books, essays, pamphlets, magazine and newspaper articles by the dozens, by the hundreds. It is impossible to study them all; and such an examination would be useless, for there are relatively few central themes and the majority of the writings are but repetitions of and variations on these themes. I shall consider only the most important writings, noting that most were published between 1921

Maximalist

Maximalist Fiume

and 1923 in the Biblioteca di Studi Sociali series.[1] An early, convincing evaluation of a good part of these writings (with the exception of the Communist view), which vary greatly in their value and intent as well as in their ideological and political premises, was included in Luigi Salvatorelli's introduction to *Nazionalfascismo* (1923).[2]

All of these writings agreed that a distinction should be made between the Fascism of 1919 through 1920 (often directly linked to the revolutionary interventionism of 1914-15) and that which developed after 1920 (the explosion of agrarian Fascism in Emilia and Romagna). All considered the latter the only significant Fascism. For the Socialist Giovanni Zibordi this was "the true, great Fascism." For the Communist newspaper *L'Ordine Nuovo*, "Fascism as a general and generic organization of war veterans was of no interest; the significance of Fascism stems from the time of its development as the antiproletarian weapon of the farmers of Emilia."[3] And, from an entirely different political point of view, Ivanoe Bonomi echoed these sentiments and provided a lucid explanation of the significance of the transition of Fascism in 1920-21. For him, this transition was linked to the change in attitude that took place at the end of 1920 in Italy, particularly in areas where Maximalist pressure had been strongest. Until that time they had endured the Red offensive; now they were spontaneously on the counteroffensive, though without a predetermined plan of attack. Prior to 1920 Fascism had scarcely existed; it had been ignored. It flourished in this new climate and became a social and political reality. But, as Bonomi observes, its configuration changed:

> The fighting fascists, who scarcely existed before then, or at most as small and unknown groups, increased and spread in the spring of 1921 with bewildering rapidity. Fascism, which had been little known outside Milan, became at last a national movement. Ex-soldiers, intellectuals, students, professional men, and the lower middle classes rushed to join it, inspired by love of liberty and patriotism to combat the arrogance of the deluded mob. The survivors of the Fiume movement rallied to it, and brought it their military organisation, their Roman nomenclature, and their pealing war-

cry. Employers and farmers joined it in crowds as a sure means of overwhelming the extremists and of re-establishing discipline in work. But it was only its fight against Bolshevism that enabled Fascism to draw support from so many different quarters. Its original characteristics, its hostility to the bourgeoisie, its proletarian sympathies and its ambitious radicalism, were suppressed and forgotten in its crusade against Bolshevism. Public opinion saw in the youthful fascists only the vanguard of forces destined to rout the revolutionaries who had threatened for two years, but had never dared to act.[4]

A second area of agreement is found in the evaluation of Fascism as the product of bourgeois reaction against the so-called Red biennium. *Il fascismo milizia di classe: commenti alla cronaca* (Fascism, a class militia: Comments on the news) is a work written in 1921 by Giuseppe De Falco. Its title illustrates a widely held opinion. There is great diversity between those for whom this reaction was a highly patriotic and positive attitude that had been provoked by "Bolshevik" and "anti-national" violence and by the government's inability (not to say lack of inclination) to oppose it, and those—including a range of intermediate opinions—for whom this reaction was the manifestation of the most selfish and unrestrained interests of the bourgeoisie.[5] As Luigi Fabbri states, it was a "preventive counterrevolution," unleashed after the failure of the occupation of the factories, at which time the Socialist movement shifted from the offensive to the defensive.[6]

This range of individual evaluations in no way diminishes the significance of the underlying judgment. On the contrary, it raises the most historically relevant central problem: a class reaction, but by whom and against whom? Today this may seem an idle question. Marxist schematization may well prove inadequate as a sole explanation of Fascism, either because it fails to take into account the ideological element (nationalist patriotism) or because it presumes a monolithic quality in the classes and attributes to them relationships that they in fact did not have. Nevertheless, it is a fact that Fascism encompasses certain aspects, and by no means the least important ones, of class struggle. This is easy for us to say now, with hindsight on the vicissitudes of Fascist development and the role it played in Italian life for twenty or more years. It was far less obvious to Italians between 1920 and 1924. For the majority of them Fascism was as yet an enigma that was fraught with questions. Beyond immediately political (and occasionally moralistic, literary, and stylistic) evaluations, it was difficult to judge the phenomenon and predict the course of its development. Even in 1923 a writer of the stature of Pietro Gobetti could state that "it is not yet possible to speak objectively and culturally about Fascism because it has resolved the problem of government before that of its own identity." He observed:

> The common interpretation (that it is a reaction to anti-patriotic myths and to revolutionary intoxication) has a practical value and appeared to be making headway until the present time. But it has no significance in the political realm, where interests and rhetoric must transform themselves into historical situations. Even the Marxist interpretation (that it is a bourgeois reaction) is inadequate and explains only a few local situations.[7]

Contemporaries, although they witnessed the results of Fascism's armed acts against the political and trade union organizations, could not ignore its revolutionary objectives and claims. (These often jibed, directly or indirectly, with the criticisms these contemporaries themselves aimed at the democratic ruling class and at the mass parties.) Concrete and specific facts, such as the extremely violent internal Fascist disputes on the occasion of the Pacification Pact of 1921, precluded the notion that these objectives and claims were mere demagogic expedients brought into play to mask a reaction. As Salvatorelli correctly indicated, proof of this is found in the fact that, although the results of Fascist action were obviously conservative and reactionary, Fascism remained an enigma to many of its contemporaries, most of whom resorted to references to the "two faces" or "two souls" of Fascism—or even to "two Fascisms."[8] The result, on a practical political level, was the absence of a clear-cut view, an underestimation of Fascism, and delaying tactics in the expectation that Fascism would soon emerge from its equivocation and reveal its true nature.

The view from the Left

We thus return to the initial question: whose reaction, and against whom? On the extreme Left the answer was easy: reaction of the bourgeoisie (viewed generically and as a bloc) against the proletariat. The position of the anarchist Luigi Fabbri was typical:

> The proletarian threat has welded the ruling class into a mass, and today Fascism is its militia and rallying point. And the ruling class is not only comprised of the bourgeoisie in the strictest sense of the word . . . To a greater or lesser extent, Fascism is everybody's standard-bearer; it is well received and sought after everywhere: in the barracks and in the university, in the police stations and in the courts, in the offices of the powerful industrialists as well as in the land-owners' banks. Nor does it lack admiring though half-concealed glances from the caryatids of the Republican and clerical parties, despite the fact that they are in basic opposition to it since they too receive their support from the masses.[9]

Republicans such as Guido Bergamo thought along essentially the same lines: "Fascism is a movement in defense of wounded interests; it is not motivated by moral considerations; and it uses aggressive, violent action as both its means and its goal."[10] Socialists such as Giuseppe De Falco also shared this point of view: "a militia that is not at all disinterested and that is at the disposal of one class against another . . . a conservative movement, a reflection of conservative interests."[11] The vast majority of Communists were of the same opinion. Antonio Gramsci was an exception, though he, too, reconsidered this position several times.

For the prevailing interpretation of the Italian Communist party, we should study the speeches of Amadeo Bordiga at the Fourth and Fifth Congresses of the Communist International, November-December 1922 and June-July 1924.[12] These speeches should be compared to the less schematic opinions adopted during the same period by the International, as well as with the positions of the three principal groups into which the leadership of the Italian Communist party was divided during the first half of 1924.[13] One should also consider the report on Fascism prepared by Palmiro Togliatti for the Fourth Congress. (It was not presented and was replaced by

Bordiga's speech.) Its analysis is subtler and closer to Gramsci's position.[14] A position closer to the prevailing Italian Communist view is represented by the essay "Der Faschismus in Italien," by the Hungarian Djula Šaš, a longtime resident in Italy; it was published in Hamburg in 1923 and subsequently translated into several languages, including Russian and Japanese.[15]

Gramsci's interesting interpretation of the Fascism that existed between 1920 and 1924 reflects several changes of orientation.[16] For him, at the end of 1920 Fascism represented the private sector's reaction and attempt to pass over into the public sector and "become the State." Fascism was the preparatory stage for the restoration of the State, that is, the aggravation of capitalist reaction, the exacerbation of the capitalist struggle against the most vital demands of the proletarian class. But Fascism was not merely an Italian reaction. It was international in nature, "because capitalism, not only in Italy, but elsewhere in the world, has become unable to dominate the productive forces."[17] Toward the middle of 1921 Gramsci arrived at the point where he wrote: "A coalition of all the reactionary elements, from the Fascists and Populars to the Socialists, will take place against the advance of the working class."[18]

In 1921 Gramsci increasingly stressed the interpretation of Fascism as the "final political incarnation of the petty bourgeoisie," a "slave to capitalism and landowners," and an "agent of the counterrevolution." In this sense, his clearest definition is found in an article published on May 25, 1921. "What is Fascism? It is the insurrection of the lowest stratum of the Italian bourgeoisie, the stratum of the ne'er-do-wells, the ignorant, the adventurers, for whom the war provided the illusion that they were good for something and counted for something. Political deterioration has propelled these people to the fore, and their widespread cowardice has come to seem like courage."[19]

The crisis caused by the Pacification Pact led Gramsci to modify this interpretation and refer to "two Fascisms." The first of these was Mussolinian, parliamentary, and reliant on the middle classes, employees, small businessmen, and industrialists. This Fascism was oriented toward a collaboration with the Socialists and Populars. The other Fascism was intransigent; "it expressed the

need for direct and armed defense of agrarian capitalist interests"
and was destined to "follow its characteristic anti-proletarian
bent."[20] With regard to these early distinctions within the bourgeois
bloc, Gramsci, after the March on Rome, leaned toward an increasingly subtle view of the relation between Fascism and the bourgeoisie. He admitted that in 1921 and 1922 the industrial bourgeoisie
offered a "muffled and latent opposition" and that, even after the
March on Rome, "traditional bourgeois forces"—*Corriere della
Sera, La Stampa,* the banks, the chiefs of staff, the *Confederazione
generale dell'industria*—"would not allow themselves to be 'taken
over' by Fascism."[21]

The extreme Left's explanation, though simple, is also simplistic and unsatisfactory and fully deserving of Salvatorelli's criticisms:

> This analysis errs, not so much in what it says, but more
> especially for what it omits. The relations between Fascism
> and conservatism are real; and it is perfectly correct to say
> that Fascism is an anti-proletarian reaction of the upper
> bourgeoisie. However, if we stop at this point we deprive
> Fascism of any content or autonomy of its own: it becomes a
> mere instrument in the hands of capitalism . . . If Fascism
> were simply a militant movement in the service of capital-
> ism, if it were not an autonomous movement with a life and
> objectives of its own, three facts would remain unexplained:
> (1) the recruitment of most of its followers and, more impor-
> tant, cadres from certain social strata that are neither capi-
> talistic nor linked to capitalism; (2) the undeniable presence,
> despite differences of time and place, of a characteristic feel-
> ing of unity within Fascism; (3) the specific development of
> Fascism from the beginning of March 1919 until it came to
> power, and, subsequently, during a half-year of govern-
> ment. This development was autonomous and followed its
> own internal logic.[22]

Giovanni Zibordi attempted to explain and eliminate this
contradiction. He sought to separate Fascism into three component
parts. According to this division, Fascism was simultaneously: "a
counterrevolution of the bourgeoisie against a *red* revolution that

did not come about (as an act of insurrection) but remained a threat; a revolution, or rather a convulsion, of the middle classes that were displaced, troubled, and discontented; a military revolution." There were different mainsprings behind these components, but their driving force was Fascism's turning against the proletariat "the conscious and cold hostility of the authentic bourgeoisie, and the fanatical and aberrant aversion of these middle classes which, overwhelmed by the postwar crisis, turned on the proletariat rather than against the ruling class or regime all the ferment and resentments that characterized their discomfiture."[23] This explanation demonstrates progress in the analysis of Fascism (clarification of the roles of the various sectors of the middle classes), but it is still deficient because it places dubious elements (such as the military) in this grouping, or elements that are not of the same caliber as the chief component (the counterrevolutionary bourgeoisie is left too generic and unclarified). Zibordi's analysis is particularly interesting because it illustrates that on the Left of the political spectrum a new analysis was gaining momentum that was closer to the real nature and peculiarities of Fascism. The best example of this point of view is Salvatorelli's *Nazionalfascismo*.

The first hint of this new analysis and interpretation of Fascism was contained in "Piccoli borghesi al bivio," an article by Adriano Tilgher published in *Tempo*, December 7, 1919. It said:

> It is a fierce irony of history that the middle classes of Europe should be consumed by the same war that found in them its chief supporters. While the great barons of industry, business, and finance exacted huge profits from the war that so well served their interests, despite the fact that they had not sought it, and while the proletariat, reduced to temporary political impotence, thought only of snatching what it could from the teeth of the sharklike profiteers, the petty bourgeoisie viewed the war as a struggle for the realization of its political idealities . . . In the war the petty bourgeoisie sought neither the solution of its social problems, nor the establishment of a system of economic rewards, nor easy profits, but only the triumph of its political, nationalistic, and democratic ideals. Today, the petty bourgeoisie is dying as the result of that war that it sought to pursue to final vic-

tory. . . In the shipwreck of these ideals the petty bourgeoisie is suffering an agonizing death. The Italian petty bourgeoisie today harbors resentments against everybody:
against the government that has allowed it to languish in
starvation and that was unable at Versailles to put across
either its expansionistic or democratic programs; against the
nouveaux riches who sucked their life-blood and became fat
at their expense; against the proletariat who did not want
the war but nevertheless emerged from it richer, stronger,
and politically triumphant. The petty bourgeoisie has never
harbored such resentment against the proletariat as it does
today when it is more proletarian than the proletariat: this
state of mind explains the anti-socialist furor of the *arditi*
and of the *fasci di combattimento*, most of whose members
come from the middle classes.[24]

In 1920, 1921, and 1922, as Fascism expanded and developed
a tactical plan of action, this theme was taken up time and again.
Giovanni Ansaldo's essay "Ceti medi e operai," published in *Rivoluzione liberale* on October 19, 1922, is a well-known example.

The Italian middle classes, unprepared to endure the effort
and tension imposed by the present stage of capitalist development, pick a fight with the working class. They do not
succeed, however, in becoming resolutely anti-industrial—
that is to say, profoundly reactionary—precisely because
they are not a modern bourgeois class . . . Urban Fascism,
the Fascism of the industrial regions, is the expression of this
persistent and fatal distress.[25]

"Il fascismo e la crisi italiana," written two years later by
Mario Missiroli, is equally well known. It does not attempt to deny
that Fascism was the response of part of the bourgeoisie to the
socialist policies of the Red biennium. Missiroli, however, stressed
those remoter and, for him, more decisive origins of Fascism that
gave it the autonomy and raison d'être denied by those who sought
to make of it merely an instrument of bourgeois reaction. He was
very explicit: "I am firmly convinced that the Fascist movement contains within itself the necessary and sufficient motives for an auton-

omous existence and that it would have arisen and expanded in any
case, quite independently of the existence of Maximalism and even
of Socialism."[26]

According to Missiroli, the war had produced a "sharply
revolutionary" state of mind, but it had not created the conditions
for a socialist revolution. The basic conflict was not so much between the proletariat and the bourgeoisie as between the various
levels of the bourgeoisie. The years immediately prior to the war
had seen, as a result of Giolittian policies, a radical renewal of the
middle classes. "The old ruling circles were about to be replaced in
the political arena by new groups that arose from the working class
and from a new, broad, and quite petty bourgeoisie that followed
the leadership of the Socialist party but possessed neither the spirit
nor the intelligence of socialism." This renewal was accentuated
during the war years: wartime economic policy favored these new
strata of the petty bourgeoisie, which, "strengthened by their attainment of economic power, tended to replace the old guard in the
exercise of political power." This took place, moreover, while the
old petty and middle bourgeoisie saw its own economic and social
situation deteriorate. Missiroli viewed Fascism from this vantage
point—not as a purely idealistic and romantic phenomenon, nor as
a mere "white guard" in the service of the plutocracy and giant
industry, but as a more complex phenomenon whose development
("the idealist and romantic element is followed by a psychological
and moral element, which in turn is followed by a reactionary revolt") took place *pari passu* with the struggle for political power
between the new and old middle classes. It was significantly influenced by ranks swollen by individuals who had axes to grind against
the new classes and the organized proletariat (though this does not
justify our equating Fascism simply with that group).

Missiroli reached these conclusions after studying the situation in Emilia-Romagna, where the development of these new forces
of the middle bourgeoisie had recently taken place. This accounts
for the cogency of his remarks, as well as the difficulty we have in
applying his interpretative scheme to the whole of Fascism. It explains how even Missiroli resorted to a dual interpretation of Fascism. According to him, Fascism had been used by "reactionary
classes," with Giolitti's advice, to silence the Socialists; however,

these same "reactionary classes" tended simultaneously to use, to their own advantage, "their" middle classes against Fascism. As the success of this two-pronged maneuver was not yet certain, Missiroli concluded by asserting that the "reactionary classes" probably would suffer bitter disillusionment: "Fascism will be the mature conscience of the new democracy, and, as such, it will have to reconcile itself to socialism, or it will be worse than nothing; a tardy and impossible reactionary attempt . . . It must learn to interpret the soul and voice of the new middle classes, speaking to them in terms of loyalty and idealism; otherwise it will be doomed to disappear as a tragic episode."[27]

Missiroli's analysis contributed in a major way to the deflection of attention from the generic, and widely agreed upon, reactionary nature of Fascism toward its true and characteristic element: the middle class. Hereafter this was the direction taken by the more astute and attentive observers, such as Cappa and Salvatorelli, to mention two among the most conspicuous examples.

Although for the purposes of our discussion, Luigi Salvatorelli is the most important of these authors, the writings of Alberto Cappa are of interest for two reasons that should not be underestimated. Cappa was the first author who attempted to place Fascism within the historical development of the post-Risorgimento era. He did this by linking the postwar crisis of the middle class to their previous social and political dissatisfaction:

> Fascism is the expression of the crisis of the old Italian middle class that had been economically dispossessed by Giolitti's policies—policies which attempted to create within the proletarian movement those very elites who during the postwar period took action to exercise their respective political responsibilities, a step which was imperative if they were to consolidate their hard-won economic gains.
> The crisis of the middle classes, we have said, is a postwar political problem. It consists in the imbalance between the economic power that the working class acquired during the Giolitti dictatorship and the scant political weight it carries in the formulation of national policies. The problem was to integrate in the State the new conservative forces, the new

middle classes, incorporating as much as possible of the remnants of the old middle classes.

This, on the political level, is the position of the two antagonistic classes. It developed as the result of the loss of economic power of the petty and middle bourgeoisie, and of the gradual development and consolidation of the interests of the socialist classes. The political resolution of the conflict will, however, have to be brought about—and this is the immediate result of the Fascist movement—by their acceptance of the "ideological values" of the military victory of November 4, 1918.

In a direct line with the history of the Italian Risorgimento, Fascism continues the traditional revolt of the middle classes. The latter, although they had much innovative and daring spirit, never succeeded in producing a united and autonomous effort to bring about the Italian unity which they were the only ones to seek; they were forced to accept the means offered by the Piedmontese monarchy; subsequently, when a strong knot of interest groups had gathered around the Monarchy, they were forced to accept the means as an end, adapting themselves to the moderate program of the Piedmontese Monarchy brought into being by the adroit policies of Count Cavour.

After 1862, when the House of Savoy appeared to be the only national reality in the peninsula and conducted its admirable and successful policy of assimilation of antagonist forces, those splinter groups of the middle classes finally had to turn to the Piedmontese State for fulfillment of their slightest needs. Nevertheless, the myth of the middle classes continued to be the myth of Garibaldi, and their basic nature continued to be subversive and hostile to the State!

They attempted an uprising with the help of Crispi but were immediately overcome by the Giolitti dictatorship, which provided an outlet for their imperialism in the Lybian war. Then the dissatisfied middle classes attempted to mask the facts of national politics by focusing attention on the war. They failed, because they could not make use of the war for their purposes, and in order to win it they had to rely on the help of all classes in the nation, especially their principal foes, the proletarian classes.

Even the Fascist revolt, a new expression of the torment and exasperation of these middle classes who are unable to function in national life, has failed in its anti-Socialist objective. Fascism is unable to resolve the problem of their integration into the State and to show them to best advantage. It strengthens the Monarchy, when in fact the Monarchy's policies are its true foes.[28]

Besides the importance of the middle classes, Cappa stressed that a large part of the Fascist base consisted of very young people who had not fought in the war. If Fascism's "initial and dominant" feature was "the revolt of the petty and middle bourgeoisie against the new middle class made up of the working class and its socialist organizations and reinforced by Giolitti's policy of privilege and paternalism," it was not necessary to underestimate the role of the younger generation, which through its active participation in the civil war demonstrated its hostility toward "the parents" and sought to assert itself against their "conservatism."

Salvatorelli's Nazionalfascismo

The most important and mature contribution to the understanding of Fascism was Luigi Salvatorelli's *Nazionalfascismo.* More than a half-century after its publication this work still provides the most valid general interpretation of the origins of Fascism.[29] For Salvatorelli, the characteristic and decisive element of Fascism was the petty bourgeoisie; all other explanations were unacceptable. He was not the first to expand on this theory, but others who had investigated the question of the petty bourgeoisie had done so in conjunction with other elements—which was where they erred. Salvatorelli defines the petty bourgeoisie as "that part of society which, neither belonging to capitalism nor constituting an element in the productive process, remains distinct from the proletariat, not so much for economic reasons as out of 'bourgeois' social habit and because of its own awareness of not belonging to the proletarian class." According to him, "What should be considered . . . is that not only is the petty bourgeoisie the dominant numerical factor in Fascism, it is also the characteristic and ruling element."

Fascism was the expression of this particular element of society. Without mincing words, Salvatorelli asserts: "Fascism reflects the 'class struggle' of the petty bourgeoisie, wedged as a third force between capitalism and the proletariat."

Having said this, we have also explained the phenomenon of the contradictory duplicity, the "two faces" and the "two souls" that has so troubled the critics of Fascism. Fascism is really a single phenomenon. But precisely because it simultaneously confronts two social forces that are themselves opposites—even though they may be complementary—Fascism acquires different connotations, depending on whether it is viewed from a capitalist or an anti-proletarian stand. To many people, even friends of Fascism, it will seem absurd to speak of Fascist anti-capitalism. But it is a fact . . . If, however, the Fascist struggle has hitherto taken place predominantly—or even exclusively in the social and economic field—against the proletariat, this is the result of a variety of causes: the petty bourgeois psychology, which, at the time of the postwar efflorescence of the workers, became more hostile toward the proletariat than toward the capitalists; the presumed imminence in postwar Italy of the proletarian revolution, which was viewed by many as the gravest danger; the unremitting power of materialism that forced people to seek help from capitalist circles against the proletariat and take advantage of the tolerance and connivance of a State that was far more inclined to favor capitalism than the proletariat; and finally, the patriotism of the petty bourgeoisie, whose impulsive coarseness and myopic rhetoric naturally turned it against the proletariat because the latter seemed to deny the fatherland, while the upper middle class had always been shrewd enough not only to support the nation but to identify itself with it.[30]

The Italian petty bourgeoisie was not "technically minded"; it was not intimately linked to the structure of capitalist society. It was "humanistic," made up of State employees, bureaucrats, and professional men, imbued with rhetoric and confined to the margins of real social development.[31] It was democratic and somewhat socialist, "as long as it believed these forces were struggling for its own ideal"; it became anti-democratic and anti-socialist when it became aware that democracy and socialism did not support this ideal, and, on the contrary, was producing new bourgeois elites from within the ranks of the proletariat. At that point the petty bourgeoisie became nationalist (the Nation was viewed as the negation of class and class struggle), and hence Fascist. At the time Salvatorelli was writing (less than six months after Mussolini came to power), Fascism could not yet be considered a "revolution," merely a "revolt made possible by the complicity of the upper middle class." The idea of revolution existed, to be sure, at least psychologically, but Salvatorelli did not think this possibility could be translated into fact:

> We have already remarked that the notion of an autonomous and radical revolution was a part of Fascism; we have shown how the Fascist petty bourgeoisie has a revolutionary class psychology. But it is a psychology devoid of a true substratum, precisely because the "humanistic" petty bourgeoisie is not a real social class with its own functions and forces; instead, it is a group that exists on the fringes of the productive process essential to capitalist civilization. The nationalism that makes up its ideology, rather than being a physiological product of capitalism, or constituting—as most people think—the political projection of capitalist economy, is a retarded ideological phase of this process. It is the lack of synchronism between economic reality and the ideology of the so-called educated classes (the petty bourgeoisie) that lies at the root of the war and the postwar era in Europe. We cannot conceive of a decisive victory for national fascism without the ruin of capitalist civilization; and we cannot believe that this would be the case. At the same time, we cannot eliminate the possibility that national fascism may carry out its revolutionary attempt after winning its superficial and temporary victory over the proletariat.[32]

Despite the criticism (specific and general, direct and indirect) Salvatorelli's interpretation has generated, it remains the most convincing view of Fascism advanced to date. Within the limits of our discussion, it is even confirmed by the writings of several Fascist authors of the period.

Fascists on Fascism

The Fascist literature on Fascism until 1924 was neither prolific nor particularly significant. We need consider only three works, in chronological sequence, by Dino Grandi, Pietro Gorgolini, and Agostino Lanzillo. As one would expect, in these works the problem of the social basis of Fascism is not examined in a scholarly fashion. This can be attributed either to the fact that the Fascist myth of the Nation and the propagandistic interest in presenting Fascism as the expression of all "national" and "healthy" forces precluded their authors from dwelling on the subject, or to the need to offer a historical perspective on the Fascist phenomenon and at the same time to outline how Fascism was to develop after its conquest of power. It is symptomatic that the essays of both Gorgolini and Lanzillo refer to the middle classes as the backbone of true Fascism.[33] Grandi's essay referred to the same subject less explicitly when, in speaking of the future tasks of Fascism, he called it a "new national democracy," which had to cast away "old free-trade and collectivist concepts" in order "to make the masses adhere to the National State" and bring about the "national syndicalism" of the "producers."[34]

In conclusion, I should stress a third point on which it is possible to find agreement—which, although it is not complete, is at least very broad and, therefore, highly significant. Except for Fascist authors (and there were exceptions among them), and except for those who regarded Fascism as a phase of capitalism's crisis and thus inherent to the system, the vast majority of its contemporaries considered Fascism protean chaos, an aggregate bound together by negative attitudes and devoid of a positive program, whose true nature had yet to come to the fore. Moreover, precisely because of its protean and negative position, they were convinced that Fascism could not long endure. They believed that, once it had exhausted its reactionariness, it would transform itself or even disappear.

In this way many people deluded themselves that Fascism could be normalized and constitutionalized and thus coopted into the liberal system. This explains how even the firmest anti-Fascists considered Fascism a kind of broom that, quite apart from its defects, would eventually have the merit of ridding the political scene of the old ruling class of the Giolittian era. After the Fascist interlude a new ruling class would arise that would truly serve the needs of Italian society. "Fascism will be emptied like a wine-skin"; Fascism "is headed for twilight"; "the only thing that can be said serenely about Fascism is that in its present form it cannot endure." Such was the prevailing tenor of public opinion. It is corroborated by many contemporary essays and articles. And this public opinion must be taken into account if we are to understand the events of those years and, in particular, the attitudes of various political groups toward Fascism.

7

Interpretations during the Fascist Regime

The Matteotti assassination and the turning point of January 3, 1925, signaled a decisive moment in Italian political life. Illusions, doubts, and expectations vanished. In political terms, the two events created a watershed: Fascism stood on one side; anti-Fascism on the other. Although there was some division among the traditional anti-Fascists, they were united in their single-minded and unanimous rejection of Fascism.

The consequences of this new political situation were soon felt among the philosophers and others concerned with the interpretation of Fascism. This situation obtained, even though the pressures of the struggle caused the anti-Fascist camp to apply its energies against the policies of Fascism, rather than in an examination of the events that led to its rise. If there were such an examination, Fascism's origins were usually overshadowed by the more immediate problem of its transformation into a dictatorial regime. Thus, most scholars abandoned the path so fruitfully explored by Tilgher, Cappa, and, especially, Salvatorelli.

Three categories can be distinguished in the historical and political literature published between 1925 and 1943 that dealt with developments prior to January 3. First are the writings published in Italy in 1925 and 1926, prior to the suppression of freedom of the press, as well as the foreign publications conceived prior to the dictatorship. Second, mention must be made of the writings emanating from exiled anti-Fascist groups. And, third, I shall refer to the Fascist writings of the time.[1]

Publications, 1925 and 1926, before the end of freedom of the press

Without minimizing other works of interpretative interest,[2] I shall concentrate on the most significant book of the first group: *La rivoluzione meridionale* (Revolution in the South), by Guido Dorso. Completed at the end of 1924 and published by Gobetti about a year later, this book, as its title implies, promised not so much a study of the Fascist phenomenon as an examination of political evolution following unification, with particular reference to the South. Nevertheless, Dorso devotes considerable attention to the postwar period and to Fascism, whose developments, especially subsequent to the March on Rome, he studies in perspicacious detail.

Dorso emphasized why analyses of Fascism tended to reflect the capitalist reaction explanation. He noted that Fascism had come to power by means of compromise and that, "although it was basically a revolutionary movement, it was directed by an elite that had already compromised with all the preceding conservative social forces." In this situation, "all of the avenues that might have been available to the revolution" were precluded. Fascism "had to be content with instituting only those reforms that had been conceived by the bureaucracy to save itself in previous times of crisis and that had then been filed away when the danger passed." Thus, "Fascist policy, represented by De Stefani's fiscal programs that supported the wealthy classes at the expense of the poorer classes, fostered the conviction among many people that Fascism was purely and simply a reaction of the private employers' sector and that all other aspects of its development could be neglected."

Such a simplistic conviction resulted in certain consequences against which Dorso felt he must react. He was the first writer to underscore the importance of the transformation of the original Fascism into the Fascism of the Regime. Simultaneously, he was the first to indicate very precisely the close link between the Fascist crisis of 1923-24 and the subsequent imposition of the Fascist Regime. Dorso detected in the latter scant remnants of the Fascist revolt of the middle classes against the proletariat and capitalism. He pointed to the radical changes that took place during this period in the social composition of the Fascist Party. He wrote: "Such simplistics masked the true nature of the problem, which was that the crisis of Fascism originated at the very moment of Fascism's rise to power in Rome."[3]

"Theoretized as class struggle on the part of the petty bourgeoisie," Fascism reached a crisis at the same time these classes suffered their first disillusionments. The best proof of this was to be found in the conflict that arose between the government and Fascist intransigence. Dorso clearly understood the significance of this fact, just as before January 3 he predicted the precise means by which Mussolini was to triumph—even though he did not draw all the appropriate conclusions therefrom. With regard to the origins of the crisis, Dorso expressed himself as follows:

> While the so-called constitutional groups, who after the March on Rome had hastened to join the ranks of the new party, agitated to reincorporate the submissive petty bourgeoisie into the stagnant antiquated scheme of the prewar unified State, the original Fascist revolutionary forces, who were afraid to be construed as conservative elements and who, moreover, did not know how to carry out their tasks, returned ever more strongly into the ranks of *squadrismo*, revealing thereby the instrinsic weakness of the so-called strong State.[4]

In his analysis of Mussolini's policies from the March on Rome to the Matteotti crime and during the first months of the Aventine government, Dorso obviously could not have known the means Mussolini would use in 1925 and 1926 to react to this political situation. Yet he accurately predicted the steps, even though he tended to suggest a conclusion that never actually transpired. Unable to "dispel the old liberal fiction that the government stood above parties," and because he could not "fully articulate the Jacobin concept of the State as party," Mussolini resorted from the outset to a pendulous policy, oscillating between the "flankers" of Fascism (the traditional ruling class) and the Fascist intransigents—a policy that was nothing more nor less than a new version of the old

system of *trasformismo*. However, after the Matteotti assassination
the parameters of this pendulous policy were considerably restricted. This resulted from the fact that the "flankers," who were
"suspicious of the revolutionary origins of the man and the movement, and who had already derived from that early phase of government the conviction that they should detach themselves from
Fascism for obvious reasons of conservatism," were preparing to
abandon Fascism. "For this reason, he will increasingly exhaust
himself with retreats in the direction of trasformismo, until he finally falls victim to the revenge of the flankers." This extremely
lucid and coherent analysis had two limitations. It did not sufficiently take into account Mussolini's ability to delay events by remaining receptive to all contingencies and to use the time thus
gained to obtain his own ends: the transformation of the Fascist
Party into a bloated, bureaucratic organization, devoid of social
characterization and unable, therefore, to articulate in the slightest
way the revolt of the middle classes. Also, Dorso's analysis underestimated the consequences of one particular feature of the Aventine
secession. One of the limitations of the Aventine, he felt, was that it
claimed and asserted "the abstraction of freedom, without defining
its limits, its possibilities, and its privileged classes." For Dorso, this
limitation constituted one of the reasons for the final success of the
"flankers." In actual fact it was the real reason for Mussolini's victory. Faced with uncertainty as to the true political and social nature of the Aventine bloc, on the one side, and the possibility, on
the other, of a conservative agreement with Mussolini, who was
especially eager not to lose power, the traditional ruling class finally
opted in favor of such a conservative agreement with him.

　　　Francesco Saverio Nitti's book *Bolscevismo, Fascismo e
Democrazia* also deserves attention.[5] Published in exile, it was conceived in Italy during the years prior to the Regime. Although
many of its assertions do not differ substantially from more publicized interpretations, certain points should be stressed. The first
item of interest in Nitti's examination of the European crisis produced by the war is the link between Russian Bolshevism and Italian Fascism. As he saw it, the war had brought the idea of freedom
into crisis and had replaced it with the concept of force. The Soviet
regime represented "an important historical event of world propor-

tions." Fascism, on the other hand, was merely a minor occurrence that was not supported by an ideal ("not even a false one"), because its only basis was the use of force and the practice of violence. Nevertheless, the two phenomena had elements in common. "In this phase of European life, Bolshevism and Fascism represent the two integral rebuttals of the liberal system and democracy: Fascism is a phenomenon of white reaction; Bolshevism is a Communist attempt." Both had their origins "in men trained in revolutionary socialism." Nitti contended that "two tendencies and two spirits" existed simultaneously within Fascism. The first was more specifically Fascist: "Mussolini and his more intimate collaborators, having been revolutionaries all their lives, not only retained that mentality, but probably the hope of turning once again to the people." The second was Nationalist in origin: "the Nationalists, because they are all more or less reactionary, can only be disposed toward a reactionary situation." This contradiction led Nitti to believe that Fascism would remain an isolated phenomenon, "which will not only have no imitators but will also be unable to endure."

> Either it will continue along its present violent path and inevitably provoke a reaction whose extent cannot be foreseen; or, as is less probable, it will gradually divest itself of its present nature and return to the constitutional framework. At any rate, Fascism is more the result of individual attitudes than of a program; it is more the recollection of antiquated methods than a forerunner of future systems. It is a conquest, not a government; it is the exercise of a legal power; it is a product that is devoid of charisma and light, that will inevitably burn itself out.[6]

The relation between Fascism and Bolshevism in terms of their mutual negation of the methods of freedom is also discussed in the writings of Luigi Sturzo. In *L'Italie et le Fascisme*, published in 1927, the founder of the Popular Party elaborates on this concept, asserting that Fascism, "a genuine child of the war," was "born at the time of the Bolshevik movement and was animated by similar sentiments." However, our main interest in this book lies in the passages that discuss the first steps of Fascism, its rise to power,

and, especially, those pages where Sturzo delineates the causes of
the weakness of Fascist Totalitarianism. According to him, during
its first two years of life Fascism had not yet found its true orientation and "appears as Socialism disguised under a cloak of victory
and of national interests, while Socialism was, on the other hand, a
disguised Bolshevism." This is the root of Fascism's political inconsistency. Its success can be attributed to Fascism's change of direction and the subsequent new attitude of the political class which,
although it was in full decadence, not only did not resist Fascism
but, on the contrary, favored its development as long as it did not
interfere with its own power.

> Fascism owes its success to the attitude of the wealthy and
> conservative classes which, thanks to this new force, have
> maintained their hold on the powers of the State, overcom-
> ing the Socialists on the one hand and the Popolari on the
> other. This revolutionary attitude on the part of the conser-
> vatives merely continues the tactics they have constantly
> employed in order to preserve their hold on the policy of the
> country. Thus they were Liberal Conservatives during the
> predominance of the Left, and are Fascist Conservatives in
> the "New Era." The persistence, under varying political
> forms, of a conservative domination in revolutionary guise,
> does not mean that power has ever been held by a real Con-
> servative Party, responsible for its actions and with a pro-
> gram to be defended against the other parties. Its predomi-
> nance has been reached through the medium of the men,
> parties, and ideologies which, at a given moment, have met
> with success and risen to the top. This was possible only
> through a species of dictatorship, masked or apparent.

Despite the fact that the Mussolini government had a totalitarian nature, the Fascist Regime born under these circumstances
was undermined by a fundamental contradiction that over the long
run would have made coexistence of conservatism and Fascism impossible. In this regard Sturzo said:

> There is such intrinsic contradiction between the two
> terms that their co-existence is not possible, unless one of the

two loses all substance, leaving a body without life, an appearance, not a reality. Today the conflict between the two contradictory terms has been avoided, because one of the two, cannot, will not, or finds it inconvenient to react and assert itself, or else it has come no longer to have any vitality, that is, it has become a political nonentity . . . In these conditions, unnatural and contrary to economic laws (which have their rhythms and their own requirements), it may happen that, for a certain time, the dualism of interests can be eliminated or, better, neutralized, and that one side, the weaker, may have no means of asserting itself in the political field by which the economic field has become so unduly overshadowed. However, since dualism is in the nature of things and cannot be suppressed—or for long coerced—it will inevitably rise again and re-assert its rights with all the more vehemence the longer the coercion and the graver its consequences.[7]

Works of exiled anti-Fascists

The second category of writings concerning the origins of Fascism is composed of works that derive from the anti-Fascist emigration. They can be divided into four subgroups, all positions generally more polemical than historical, that evolved during the period of the Anti-Fascist Concentration in Paris (1927-1934). The subgroups include opinions that arose from traditional democratic anti-Fascism predating the Matteotti crime and the Aventine secession; positions developed by certain anti-Fascists on the fringes of the Concentration that were in conflict with the latter and may be considered heterodox; the Communist positions; and the genuinely historical literature that emerged from the emigration.

The first subgroup is the most fertile and subtle. In a sense it constitutes the bridge between the most widely publicized interpretations in Italy prior to 1925 and those most popular after World War II. On the whole, however, it is the least original of the four, so I shall examine only its foremost exponents.[8]

The most famous essay dealing with the judgment that democratic anti-Fascism rendered of the origins of Fascism probably is Filippo Turati's "Fascismo, Socialismo e Democrazia." It was published in part in May 1928, in a commemorative issue sponsored by a North American anti-Fascist group.[9] The Socialist leader considered that Fascism was nascent in all capitalist countries and that, although it had developed macroscopically in Italy, "it is nevertheless not an exclusively Italian phenomenon." As Turati stated that same year at the Socialist International Congress in Brussels, "the Italian phenomenon is but a manifestation of a general situation." Even taking into account all its peculiarities, which it would be an error to generalize about, along with the characteristics incumbent on it by virtue of history and national psychology, Fascism was the result of the plutocratic degeneration of capitalism, and as such it could be of concern to all countries where this degenerative process was in progress.[10] The primary cause of Fascism was the war: "Fascism is war being extended *within* and *against* every single nation." "Fascism would have been neither possible nor conceivable without the precedent of the Great War; this was true for a variety of political, economic, and psychological reasons." It was "the collision of the plutocratic interests, on the one hand, and, on the other, the creation during the war and the postwar period of new classes of dispossessed people who—with the help of governments that were accomplices or at least noncombative and because of the absence of a resistance on the part of weak and indecisive democracies—allowed Fascism to develop and triumph." If it was untrue that Fascism had saved Italy from Bolshevism (when Fascism arrived on the scene "the Bolshevik spark was in the process of being completely extinguished"), it was true to say that, "as the result of philo-Bolshevik intemperance . . . the childish and fanciful fear of the moneyed classes of losing their privileges" was a very real and significant fear. "Once fear was conquered and apprehension of imminent catastrophe was dissipated, these were replaced by the desire and frenzy for a posthumous reprisal . . . that would be preventive." "The Bolshevik wave, despite its inherent inconsistencies, provided the opportunity for the newly rising Fascism to intervene, but it also provided a magnificent *pretext* to present itself as a savior. This tendency was then and still is widely exploited. It is safe to say that without it the plutocratic-Fascist link would not have been possible."

Democratic anti-Fascism was never to diverge from this interpretation, one that harked back to Fabbri's theories and, in general, to the notion of bourgeois reaction.[11] At the most, it can be said that it was enriched by certain specific elements, such as the observation contained in Pietro Nenni's *Sei anni di guerra civile* that if Fascism "had merely been a movement of social and political reaction, it would have been immediately liquidated."

> Fascism would never have found among the middle classes the supports it needed to retain command, if it had not presented itself as a nationalistic movement devoted to righting the real and imaginary wrongs inflicted on the country during and after the war. The only spontaneous recruits to Fascism were exasperated patriots. And it is on this terrain that Fascism is still gaining some ground.
>
> Italy is suffering from an inferiority complex. It was late in arriving at the European concert; it fought for national unity at a time when other countries were undergoing colonial expansion; it was relegated to picking up the crumbs left over from the imperialist banquet; it was brave but poor at a time when the war was a question of money and raw materials; it was mistreated by the Allies in 1919. Italy is continuously at the mercy of those who know how to foment its rancor against fulfilled imperialisms.
>
> This rancor was manifested in two ways: the working masses expressed it in terms of enthusiasm for the Russian revolution, which they viewed as a permanent revolt against conservative forces and the status quo; the bourgeoisie expressed it by means of their adherence to nationalism.
>
> Fascism successfully gambled on the mood of the bourgeoisie and made nationalism the focus of its policies, placing dictatorship in the shadow of exasperated and bellicose patriotism.[12]

"La Libertà" by Claudio Treves contains specific elements added to this interpretation.[13] In this essay Treves attempted to illustrate the characteristic aspects of various European Fascisms by relating them to their respective national peculiarities. He thus derived an embryonic general interpretation of the phenomenon that transcended the immediate and macroscopic aspects of Fascism.

The heterodox and democratic anti-Fascists who were opposed to the Concentration articulated their thoughts along a very different path. Members of this second subgroup are especially well represented by Giuseppe Donati and, on a different level, by Mario Bergamo and Francesco Luigi Ferrari.[14] For them the relevant historical (hence, political) problem hinged not so much on a determination of how Fascism had arisen and of which forces inspired and nurtured it, but rather on the less immediate but more substantive reasons why its birth took place. In lively debate with the other anti-Fascists, Donati denied that Fascism could be considered "a 'calamity,' an 'adventure,' an 'act of piracy,' a 'whatnot' that had capriciously arrived on the Italian scene and might well produce serious problems, but that in the final analysis would never take hold or be justified."[15] Fascism had merely swept away, "with more brutality than courage," the "political shams that were devoid of philosophical ideals and will power." Fascism was not "a work mishap, it was a chronic disease of history and of the Italian personality," and its rise to power had "a close and fatal cause-and-effect relation with its political and parliamentary pre-Fascist predecessors."

> The parliament condemned and sentenced itself by dint of the monstrous and incessant proof it gave during four years of its inherent inability to maintain legally its control of the State. Indeed, parliamentarism proved to be an instrument pure and simple of disorder and paralysis rather than a force of life and discipline . . . The moral responsibility for the failure of the Italian parliamentary system is shared by all parties, because in all of them the leaders and the ruling elite proved to be inferior or impotent in the face of the situation.[16]

Donati and the other heterodox anti-Fascists looked to a much earlier period than the Great War for the historical roots of the failure of parliamentarism. They ascribed this failure to the traditional characteristics of the Italian people as well as to the manner in which unification had been achieved. In this respect the heterodox anti-Fascists were more or less consciously linked to the philosophies of Gobetti, Dorso, and, especially, Giustino Fortunato. Fortunato was often remembered by post-Liberation journalists and historians as the proponent of the theory that looked upon Fascism as a revelation of age-old ills. He advanced this thesis in 1921, in an essay on the Italian situation subsequent to the "subversive" war, and he reexamined the subject in an essay written in 1926.[17] In fact, however, Fortunato's positions had not then been widely disseminated, partly because they were derived from the arguments of the historical Right. This research into the "age-old ills" was defined ethically and politically by Mario Bergamo as a need for a "historical opposition" that would not be limited to anti-Fascist struggle but would also investigate the roots of the "disease." By virtue of these objectives the heterodox writers constituted a link with that school of interpretation whose most important post-Liberation advocates were Giulio Colamarino and Fabio Cusin. In the period under consideration this philosophy was the basis for Giuseppe Antonio Borgese's *Goliath: The March of Fascism*, where the author views the "Italian disease" against a historical background that had its roots in the remotest past.[18]

Significant as was the work of Donati, Ferrari, and Bergamo, the heterodox writer par excellence was Carlo Rosselli. At this time his works attempted to absorb the ethical and historical writings of Gobetti and Salvemini, the earliest political evaluations of Fascism, and the first self-examinations of the Fascist experience that had been undertaken during the last phase of the period of legality by the best of the Italian Socialists. Such self-scrutiny was particularly evident in the columns written by Nenni and Rosselli in *Quarto Stato*. For Rosselli, Fascism was "the most passive result of Italian history, a gigantic step back into the past, an abject phenomenon of adaptation and resignation," and its success was the consequence of "an almost universal desertion" that took place "as the result of a long series of consenting compromises." It had no revolutionary characteristics. To understand its birth, initial development, and temporary victory, it was necessary to seek out all its roots in the remote and immediate past. Its most intimate nature had to be scrutinized and simple and obvious explanations avoided. A typical example of Rosselli's thought is contained in the following passage from *Socialismo liberale:*

The impotence of Marxist Socialism in the face of the problems posed by liberty and morality is even more obvious in the light of its evident inability to comprehend the Fascist phenomenon. It sees in Fascism only the brutal phenomenon of class reaction. It detects in it the typical modern form of capitalist reaction. Fascism is merely the bourgeoisie resorting to violence as a means of counteracting the rise of the proletariat; all the rest, according to the Marxists, is an ideological fog. With facile oversimplification, that it would have us mistake for realism, they completely ignore the moral aspect of the problem—everything that the Fascist phenomenon denounces as specifically Italian. But this is an enormous error: Fascism cannot be explained merely as simple class interest. The squadristi did not come into being simply in response to the blind anger of the subversive reactionary segments of the population. Factions, spirit of adventure, love of the romantic, petty bourgeois idealism, nationalistic rhetoric, sentimental reaction to the war, restless longing for nobody-knows-what—Fascism would not have come into being without all of these motives.

Fomented by obvious class interest, while it was also deeply imbued with characteristics that were independent of class motives, it is as though the Fascist phenomenon was born as the result of the explosion of secret ferments within the race and from the accumulated experience of generations. It is possible to trace back to the pro-Bolshevik movement of 1919 many internal and external features of Fascism. Fascism's roots extend deeply into the Italian subsoil; it expresses the profound vices, latent weaknesses, and miseries of our people, of all of our people.

We should not believe that Mussolini triumphed only through brute force. He won because he knew all too well how to play on certain keys to which the psychology of the Italians was extraordinarily sensitive. Fascism was, to a certain extent, the autobiography of a nation that relinquishes political struggle, possesses a cult of unanimity, shuns heresy, and dreams of the triumph of glibness, faith, and enthusiasm.[19]

Rosselli's interpretation of Fascism is not limited to a study of the origins of the phenomenon. His writings from exile contain many illuminating observations referring to the Fascist Regime. They often anticipate conclusions that historians have only recently adopted—and not without disputes. Typical of this tendency is Rosselli's position in 1932, when he examined and rejected the Communists' equation of Fascism with the bourgeoisie and demonstrated that he had understood one of the most characteristic and fateful aspects of the Fascist Regime: the progressive "autonomization" of the dictatorial mechanism with regard to the social forces that had brought it into existence.[20]

The Communist position, our third subgroup, should be examined with care. In their strictly Italian sector and as an early historical evaluation of the origins of Fascism, the Communists' conclusions made theirs (especially if one keeps in mind their totally negative—except for Gramsci's—point of departure) the most articulate and convincing interpretative effort developed in this period of Italian anti-Fascism. The Communists accomplished this in part by elaborating points that had been made by Salvatorelli and Dorso. Their efforts were impugned, however, by an attempt on the political and practical levels to superimpose the "Soviet component" on what I have termed "the purely Italian component." But at a time when all efforts were focused on the struggle against Fascism, the historical interpretation could not be separated from the political one, and the latter inevitably had to prevail. Moreover, at this time the Communist International increasingly tended to identify itself with the policies of the dominant Soviet group. And the Soviet component (which had some Italian precedents) eventually reduced the Italian component to a subordinate position where it lost much of its value.[21]

In 1928 Palmiro Togliatti acknowledged that the Communist interpretation of Fascism "adopted as its premise the fact that Fascism was purely and simply a capitalist reaction." Despite various attempts to resist, and after several years of an excessively schematic interpretation (which, Togliatti himself said in 1928, "was based on the assertion that Fascism was purely and simply capitalistic reaction"), the Communist Party tended to adopt a more accurate view of how Fascism arose, developed, came to power, and was evolving into a dictatorial regime. This can be de-

tected in the Theses of Lyon—especially the Fifteenth—of the Third
Congress of the Communist Party of Italy (January 1926) and in the
fragments of discussion of that issue that are available.[22] The Fifteenth Thesis stated:

> Fascism, as an armed reactionary movement that pro-
> poses to disband and disorganize the working class in order
> to immobilize it, fits into the framework of the traditional
> policies of the Italian ruling class and of the struggle of cap-
> italism against the working class.
>
> Its origins, organization, and orientation cause it to be
> favored indiscriminately by all of the old ruling groups, but
> especially by the landowners, for whom the threat from the
> rural masses is very great. On the social level, however, Fas-
> cism's base is to be found among the urban petty bourgeoisie
> and in the new agrarian bourgeoisie that arose as the result
> of the transformation of rural landownership in certain
> areas (agrarian capitalism in Emilia; the appearance of an
> intermediary category of rural workers; "land exchange" of-
> fices [*borse della terra*]; reassignments of landholdings). This
> fact, plus the fact that Fascism has also found a new ideo-
> logical and organizational unity in the military groupings
> that keep alive the traditions of the war [*arditismo*] and are
> useful in the war against the workers, have made it possible
> for Fascism to conceive and carry out a plan of conquest of
> the State against the old ruling circles.
>
> It is absurd to speak of a revolution. The new classes that
> rally around Fascism derive from their origins a homogene-
> ity and common mentality that can be characterized as "na-
> scent capitalism." This explains how their struggle against the
> political figures of the past is possible and how they are able
> to justify it by means of an ideological construction that is
> different from the traditional theories of the State and its
> relation to the citizenry. In sum, Fascism modifies the con-
> servative and reactionary program that has always dom-
> inated Italian politics merely by means of a different view of
> the process for unifying the reactionary forces. Instead of
> pursuing the tactics of agreement and compromise, it pro-
> poses to bring about organic unity of all the forces of the
> bourgeoisie in a single political entity controlled by a central
> organization that would guide the party, the government,

and the State. This proposal corresponds to the determination to resist any revolutionary attack, and it permits Fascism to gain the adherence of the more decidedly reactionary segments of the industrial bourgeoisie and of the land-owners.[23]

In this respect, a direct line links the Theses of Lyon with Togliatti's famous "A proposito del fascismo," published in 1928. The most thoughtful and mature piece of writing by a Communist during this period, the essay contains at least three fundamental arguments. The first concerns the nature of Fascism in general.

> Fascism is the most important reactionary system that has come into existence in those countries where capitalism has attained a significant degree of development. This assertion is not made on the basis of ferocious terrorist acts or on the significant number of assassinated workers and peasants, or on the cruelty of the system of torture applied on a vast scale, or on the severity of the prison sentences; it is prompted by the systematic and total suppression of any form of autonomous organization of the masses . . . How are we to explain this particularly characteristic aspect of Italian Fascism? It would be absurd and wrong to seek its causes in the especially ferocious intentions of Fascism . . . or to discover in it that type of collective sickness that the doddering ideologists of pure democracy and of cretinous pacifism have chosen to call "wartime psychosis," "disease of violence," and so on. The total suppression of democratic freedoms . . . corresponds to the particular needs of the Italian capitalist regime and its stabilization.

Until this point we cannot say that Togliatti's general interpretation differs greatly from the interpretations of other Marxists. However, the debate widens and becomes more articulate in the second argument, where he examines the origins of Fascism.

> In the beginning, the social base of Fascism must be found in certain strata of the rural and urban bourgeoisie. More precisely, in the countryside it was made up at most of the middle-level peasants, farmers, and sharecroppers, who

were exasperated by the absurd policies of the socialist organizations . . . Even in the cities Fascism was supported at
first by the petty bourgeoisie; they were partly laborers
(artisans), specialized workers, and tradesfolk, and partly
those who had been uprooted by the war (former officers,
war casualties, *arditi*, and volunteers). If we consider the
aspirations of these social groups, we will find that some of
them were impelled by their interest in the struggle against
the working class; others, however, were imbued with a certain objectivity and even the beginnings of anti-capitalist
tendencies. It has been observed elsewhere that historically
the middle social groups can, on occasion, ally themselves
with the bourgeoisie, while at other times, under special and
precise circumstances, they can join the proletariat. It is
clear that within the strata that constituted the base of Fascism, at the time of its origin, there did exist an anti-proletarian tendency; there was, however, no attempt on their
part to establish the dictatorship of big industrial and financial capitalism. What was the element that prevailed and
determined the general orientation and evolution of the
movement? As we know, the anti-proletarian group held the
advantage. The large bourgeoisie and the landowners succeeded in dragging Fascism as a whole into the battle for the
conquest of a decidedly reactionary goal. There were, however, acts of resistance, hesitations, and even compromises.
The big bourgeoisie and the landowners succeeded in influ-
encing the movement decisively only after they passed
through a series of changes; even when they attained their
goals, they could not prevent Fascism from gaining and
maintaining the characteristics of an autonomous political
movement, and it was in this guise that Fascism undertook
the conquest of power, displacing part of the former governing class . . . One of the most interesting facts that must be
kept in mind is that, after the conquest of power, Fascism
had to become reactionary within its own organization; it
was obliged to put its structure and social composition
through a fairly rapid, general, and widespread transformation . . . As a result of this process Fascism definitively manifested itself not only as a tool of repression and reaction but
also as a center of political unity for all the ruling classes:
financial capital, large industry, and the landowners. At the
present stage of its evolution, it *identifies itself with Italian*

capitalism. Thus, the Fascist party tends to lose the characteristics of an autonomous movement of intermediary social strata that it originally possessed, and it becomes welded, along with its own organization, to the economic and political structure of the ruling classes.[24]

Even greater caution with respect to facile generalizations is applied by the author in his third argument, where he warns against the tendency to seek easy analogies among the various European "Fascisms." Italian Fascism came about because Italy was characterized by a weak economic structure, because it lacked political equilibrium, and because there were many middle-class and petty bourgeois strata in its society. Under other historical, economic, and political conditions, "it would be possible for certain characteristics of the Italian phenomenon to be reproduced; the general reactionary nature of the political transformation of bourgeois society would remain, but it would be difficult to recreate the fundamental characteristics of Fascism."

This was the quintessential Italian argument and, in more than one aspect, a construction of the Italian Communist Party. Another position existed, however—that of the Communist International—that undermined the basis of the first argument. It can be summed up by an expression typical of the Communist political language of the time: the struggle against "Social-Fascism." This theory, which asserted that Social Democracy was a wing of the bourgeoisie and, in the final analysis, an ally of Fascism, had an exclusively political value.[25] In practice, though, indirectly it exercised a notable influence on the broader interpretation of Fascism. In the first place, it was easy to apply it retrospectively to events that had accompanied the appearance of Fascism, thereby distorting the political and social character of every opposition group other than the Communists and allowing the unilateral equation of anti-Fascism with Communism. The second reason for the influence of this theory was that it facilitated a single view of Fascism (both chronologically and geographically), which, although it had a political aim of encouraging struggle against it, almost completely eliminated the possibility of reaching a realistic historical evaluation of individual Fascisms, and the Italian one in particular.

The 1970 publication of the "lessons" on Fascism taught by

Togliatti during the first months of 1935 at the Lenin Institute in Moscow demonstrates that where analyses and "internal" studies of the Fascist phenomenon in general, and of Italian Fascism in particular, were concerned, the leadership of the Italian Communists was considerably more broad-minded and realistic than can be deduced from its public pronouncements. Moreover, the leadership was clearly aware of the complexity of the Fascist problem and of the superficiality and partiality of certain schematizations still prevalent at the time in campaign literature and propaganda.

Togliatti's "lessons" are of the utmost interest for two reasons: because they are for "internal" use, they are less imbued with political caution; and they deal primarily, not with the early years of Fascism, but with the years of the Regime. They analyze the Regime in its most important light as a reactionary mass phenomenon, and they examine each of its components (party, military-propaganda organizations, trade unions, *dopolavoro* leisure-time activities, agricultural policies, corporativism) in the context of its individual contribution to the structure of the Fascist dictatorship and the unification that took place around it of the broadest social strata. Togliatti also examines the birth, growth, and transformation of these elements in relation to such real events as the economic situation and its repercussion on the masses. Thus, despite their didactic and elementary nature, these lessons often provide a methodological model that can easily be applied to historical research as well as to a practical political analysis. In a typical passage Togliatti argues against those who believe that imperialism necessarily leads to dictatorships of a Fascist type. Another example of his thought is found in the pages aimed at those who viewed all actions stemming from Fascist policies as reflections of a precise and predetermined reactionary plan. He wrote:

> It is a grave error to think that Fascism took off in 1920, or even during the March on Rome, with a predetermined plan for a dictatorial regime such as it was to become in the ten years that have transpired and as we see it today. This would be a grave error. All historical facts about the development of Fascism contradict such an idea. And not only that, from this premise, one falls inevitably into the Fascist ideology . . . We must counteract this erroneous notion with

the true, equitable view of the Fascist dictatorship. The Fascist dictatorship was forced to adopt its present form by objective and real factors: by the economic situation and by the mass movements brought about by this economic situation. We do not mean by this that the element of organization should not be considered. The danger lies in selecting the latter element without recalling the objective situation, the real situation that obtained at that precise time. The bourgeoisie is always present as an element of organization.[26]

Togliatti delineates three stages of Fascism. A first stage closes with the March on Rome. He assigns it two substages: 1919-1920, when Fascism was predominantly petty-bourgeois and reflected the positions of the urban *fasci*; and 1920-1922, which witnessed the rise of agrarian Fascism, the *squadre*, which spread to the cities in mid-1921. The second stage dates from the end of 1922 to 1925, "a period that can be defined as an attempt to create a non-totalitarian Fascist regime." A final stage, from 1925 to 1930, was "the period of the birth of totalitarianism and the beginning of the great economic crisis."

The prevalent attempt, subsequent as well as prior to 1925, was to establish an overall interpretation of Fascism that explained in a single-minded manner its origins and political and social significance, as well as its historical trajectory. This attempt culminated not in a single interpretation, but in several, each of which stressed a particular aspect of the problem and each of which was derived on the basis of political and ideological positions and, frequently, from the personal observations of the formulator. Before its demise very few authors attempted to study Fascism from a historical point of view. Aside from purely Fascist literature, there was no dearth of studies conducted about individual aspects and manifestations of Fascism; however, because of the specific nature of their themes and the political intentions exhibited by their authors, these writings did not deal with the problem of Fascism's historical aspect or its origins.[27]

Indeed, in the fifteen years following October 1922 the historical perspective of Fascism was studied by only two authors. They were extremely dissimilar, but their works constituted the first concrete attempts on the part of anti-Fascists to examine the events that led to the Fascist victory. The first of these works viewed the question from the socialist perspective; the second attempted an overall reconstruction of the postwar crisis and of the attitudes of the various parties. The former was *Storia di quattro anni*, by Pietro Nenni; its circulation was very limited because at the end of 1926 most of the extant copies were confiscated. The latter, *The Fascist Dictatorship in Italy*, by Gaetano Salvemini, was published in London in 1928. It was of primary importance, especially in Anglo-Saxon countries, because it offered foreigners documentation that was hard to come by. (And, in instances such as the Matteotti crime, it provided previously unpublished material.) Also, it effectively counteracted the picture painted by the Fascists of Italian events between 1919 and 1926. However, I consider these books somewhat less important than *La naissance du fascisme*, by Angelo Tasca, published in Paris in 1938 and translated into several languages. Today this book is considered a classic, and with it the literature on Fascism, if not exactly for the first time, at least in its most complete form, reached the level of genuine history.

As I have said, Nenni examined the origins of Fascism from the socialist perspective; and Salvemini embraced all aspects of Italian life and, because of his skill as a historian, successfully pointed out the essential reasons for Fascist success. Tasca went beyond this. His thorough knowledge of the facts was buttressed by research and minute reconstruction that made use of all available documentation as well as a series of documents and testimonials obtained from anti-Fascists of greater and lesser importance. He painted a picture of events from the end of the Great War to the March on Rome that was the richest, most complete and critically thought out examination possible at the time. But this was not his only merit, nor, in my opinion, his chief merit. His importance lay in the fact that he recognized the need to trace the internal history of Fascism. In this task his great political intelligence was even more important than his historical training. As Tasca explained when his book was finally published in Italy, with the massive body of notes that it had not been possible to include in earlier foreign editions, his motivation for writing it was a sense of "political duty." His effort was intended as a concrete revelation of the anti-

Fascist struggle. To study Fascism in the context of the struggle against Fascism was a "political duty." If one hoped to write a politically effective study, one could not limit the debate to a mere ethical and political argument or to the application of one of the interpretations of Fascism fashionable in anti-Fascist circles at the time. Each of these interpretations—"definitions," Tasca called them— "contains, more or less, some element of truth, but none of them can be accepted *sic et simpliciter.*" But he did not intend his book to elaborate a new interpretation:

> A theory of Fascism can only . . . emerge from the study of all the forms of Fascism, covert or overt, repressed or triumphant, because there are various forms of Fascism, each of which implies multiple and often contradictory tendencies that can evolve and even succeed in transforming some of their fundamental characteristics. To define Fascism means to catch it precisely during this process of becoming, to grasp its "particular difference" in a given country and at a given time. Fascism is not a subject for which it is sufficient to seek out all the attributes; it is the result of an overall situation from which it cannot be dissociated. The errors of the workers' parties, for example, are as much a part of the "definition" of Fascism as the use made of Fascism by the ruling classes.[28]

Thus, we reach Tasca's historiographic and political conclusion: "for us *before we can define Fascism we must first write its history.*" And writing its history involved not only its general aspects, but all its facts and nuances, "because it is impossible to reconstruct an era, to transfer a great experience, if events are not first viewed through their component parts, through the interaction of things and men that leads to the cell, that microscopic kingdom without which even for history there can be no progress."

Fascist writings

During the years of the Regime a very extensive body of literature was specifically Fascist. But because it rarely transcended the categories of memoirs, apologies, and propaganda, it is difficult to point to significant historiographical works.[29] Beyond its being a journalistic account of the events of 1919 and 1920, *Storia della rivoluzione fascista*, by Giorgio Alberto Chiurco, has little to recommend it. It is an official and extremely biased reconstruction of Fascist events prior to the March on Rome, published on the tenth anniversary of the creation of the *fasci* and totally devoid of historical or political insight. *Storia della rivoluzione fascista* and *Storia del fascismo*, both published at the end of the thirties under the name Roberto Farinacci (though written, for the most part, by Giorgio Masi), are at least more interesting because they provide a glimpse of the personal position of their official author, leader of the intransigently Fascist opposition to Mussolini's policies. Nor should we forget *The Awakening of Italy: The Fascist Regeneration*, by Luigi Villari, which was largely responsible for the dissemination abroad between 1921 and 1924, especially in the Anglo-Saxon countries, of the Fascist view.[30]

For the specific problem of Fascism's origins we should consider *Storia del movimento fascista*, by Gioacchino Volpe.[31] Of the entire body of Fascist literature, only this work retains a measure of historiographic dignity. It does not lack interesting observations and suggestions that reveal beneath his Fascist garb the vigorous personality of a historian and man who was not blinded by the ideology and myth in which he believed. Limiting our study to the part of Volpe's work concerned with the origins of Fascism, we can detect certain questions that complete the panorama we have undertaken.

The first such question concerns the link between Fascism and earlier national developments. For Volpe, Fascism's origins should not be sought "too far afield," because "every event, *in its essential and intrinsic nature*, belongs to its own time." It is best to leave out remote precursors. But one can turn to the nineteenth century, to "the effort to imbue Italy with a full national conscience, the effort to create a unified State with warm hopes of attaining a future equal to its past." Even more deserving of attention were the twenty or thirty years that preceded the Great War and were characterized on all sides "by innovative impulses of varying degree and nature, that were fostered by the conviction that the nation was better than its government, that its rulers were worn out, that it was necessary to change leaders and methods of government."

Most important, it was imperative to look to the war, the true cata-lyst of the crisis, and to the ferments operative in it:

> We must keep in mind all the events in Italian life between 1914 and 1919. The crisis of the old parties, revolutionary interventionism, the discrediting of institutions and classes, the polemic violence of Socialists who had become interven-tionists contrary to the party line, the deeper concern in-stilled in the best soldiers for national as well as economic problems created by war, the disillusionment and nationalis-tic exasperation with Italy's former allies, as well as against the Government, which was mismanaging the victory, the renewed and more bitter Socialist offensive against the war, the self-confident hopes of an imminent and total revolution of the Russian variety—all of these must be kept in mind in order to explain Fascism.[32]

The second question addressed by Volpe is the social char-acterization of the original version of Fascism:

> This original Fascism included an element that transcended politics and its problems—an abundance of young people and, consequently, a rejuvenated nation. The Fascist revolu-tion was at least half their work, not only the work of the war veterans but of sons of veterans. Is all of this "bour-geois," "bourgeois class," "bourgeois interests"? There can be no doubt that bourgeois interests were also at play in it.
> There can be no doubt that the bourgeoisie is at the heart of this reaction; it was subdued and discordant after the war, but now it is regaining its strength and a certain sense of unity . . . But we must keep in mind that it was an agrarian bourgeoisie, rather than an industrial or businessman's bourgeoisie. The latter were at odds with Socialism in mat-ters of class and internal relations, but were in agreement with it where international or supranational questions were concerned. It was not the upper bourgeoisie, but rather the petty and middle bourgeoisie, a bourgeoisie that was at-tracted by ideas of nationalism and carried over to Fascism some of these nationalistic notions . . . It was a bourgeoisie that included many intellectuals who did not have any riches

to defend. Finally, it was a bourgeoisie that had survived the war, that efficient solvent of class egoisms; and as it now entered the fray and sided with the Fascists, it was represented especially by veterans and young people who were most amenable to fighting for an idea and to pursuing dreams of glory, rather than limiting their action to specific economic interests . . . Thus, it was indeed a bourgeoisie: but, above all, as a collection of spiritual values, it was acceptable to and accepted by the non-bourgeois.[33]

By 1921 the expanding circle of "humble people" had come increasingly close to the bourgeoisie in its aspirations, mentality, and problems. This "in some measure provided a counterweight to the equally large admixture of the bourgeoisie." Thus, "Fascism knowingly began to appear as a great revolution of the people, indeed, the first revolution of the Italian people since the bourgeois minorities brought about the Risorgimento."

This assertion, which summarizes Volpe's interpretation of Fascism, is almost directly in accord with the more official interpretation. In the pages he devoted to the resolution of the crisis that took place after the Matteotti assassination we might glimpse an indirect modification of this interpretation. According to Volpe, what did the resolution of this crisis contribute to Fascism? More than anything else, the fear of "a new and worse chaos" occasioned by the prospect that Fascism might eventually collapse into "a great mass of the people belonging to no party, a mass that sways with every wind, yet carries no small weight in shaping the course of the parties." A mass different from that which had supplied most of Fascism's earliest supporters, one that would modify the appearance and policies of Fascism. All of this is indicative of the transformations that Fascism was undergoing at the time; it adds a special value to the later assertion that, after the crisis of 1924, Fascism emerged "a bit whittled down, *but more homogenous, and with reinvigorated determination and objectives.*"

In the lucid essay "Natura storica del corporativismo italiano," published in 1932, Giulio Colamarino addresses two problems in particular: the effective social base of Fascism between 1919 and 1922, and the general characteristics of the Fascist revolution. For this writer the March on Rome succeeded "because the middle classes . . . accepted or desired the Fascist experiment, viewing it as the last and only social solution that remained after the failure of Socialism and Giolittianism." (For Colamarino, Fascism was not to be confused with liberalism; it was its "most radical negation.") Without the middle classes, Fascism would not have triumphed:

> The road to power for the Fascists was not cleared by the compliance of the bourgeoisie, or the support of the conservatives, the nationalists, and the military. Although we cannot deny that a good part of feudal and reactionary Italy . . . did everything within its power to ally its cause with that of Fascism . . . we emphatically deny that these bourgeois and reactionary elements constituted the decisive factor in the advent of Fascism . . . Without mentioning the damage done to Fascism by the adherence of these elements, it should be stressed that the support given to the revolution by the old political class and plutocratic circles was accompanied with all the provisos, reservations, and disloyalty that characterize those who act exclusively in their own interest. The reactionary intention was to curb and intercept the Fascist effort, to distract it from its objective, mutilate its ideals, point it toward compromise, and, finally, make it fail as a revolution. The shirts of many colors that suddenly, toward the end, were mixed in with the Blackshirts clearly revealed the limited faith the bourgeoisie placed in Fascism, as well as the intentions of surveillance and entrapment inherent in the old political classes who were afraid of being unsaddled by the movement that they had cultivated with the hopes of taming it.[34]

Colamarino maintained that the Fascist "revolution" was more social than political. This was especially true because it was the child of the progressive middle classes and because of the Regime's policy of "guardianship of the workers, the great proletarian masses, and the petty bourgeoisie."

The specifically historical discussion of Fascism's origins can, if necessary, be integrated with the more general, theoretical arguments with which Fascism sought to reconstruct its own historical position and elaborate its ideology. The most significant texts in this respect are the pages Mussolini devoted to the "Fascist doctrine," which were included by Giovanni Gentile in the *Enciclo-pedia italiana* entry on Fascism; two lectures by Alfredo Rocco, "La dottrina politica del fascismo" (1925) and "Genesi storica del fascismo" (1927); and the work by Giovanni Gentile, "Origini e dottrina del fascismo" (1927).[35] They do not specifically concern our present discussion, which is focused on historical judgments and interpretations of Fascism. It would not suffice to examine only these four works. Were we truly to study Fascist reality in a non-schematic manner, we would have to consider many other writings that are less well known, though not less important to an under-standing of Italian Fascism in all its complexity, all its components, and all its most significant moments.

8

The Post-Liberation Debate

During the years when Italy was under the Fascist Regime a lively debate concerning the nature of Fascism developed. It led to a series of interpretations of Fascism that accurately mirrored the political and ideological points of view of the various camps. At the same time, as Tasca's writings demonstrate, it led to a recognition of the need to examine thoroughly and rise above such interpretations through research and historiographic systematization. Nevertheless, contrary to what might have been expected, with the fall of Fascism, after the Liberation and for some fifteen years following the situation did not change substantially. The path pioneered by Tasca had very few followers. His work was not even translated until 1950, and then it occasioned more political than historiographic interest. Debate continued to explore the need for a general characterization and interpretation to explain the Fascist phenomenon and situate it within the framework of Italy's national history.

The dearth of writings on Fascism, the 1950s
There were many reasons for this scholarly inertia. Objectively speaking, Tasca's road was still difficult to follow. New scholarly and practical interests blocked the path; the political and cultural forces in the limelight attracted more attention than Fascism did. These gave rise to an abundance of research and studies, especially with regard to the Socialist labor movement (particularly

its nonreformist and pre-Communist aspects) and the Catholic movement. There was considerable difficulty in gaining access to the sources (the dispersal of libraries and archives, legal restrictions against consulting state documents dating back to the Fascist era, and so on). In addition, there were, understandably, stumbling blocks of a subjective nature: Fascism was a wound as yet too fresh to foster a desire to study it from a historical point of view; it was deemed preferable to shroud it in the veil of oblivion or, at best, to recount the story of its definitive death and condemnation sanctioned by events.[1] The retelling of the history of an era, an event, or a man is an attempt to understand it, and understanding brings the risk of minimizing any condemnation of something still so much a part of the people's flesh and spirit. Benedetto Croce's writings were a case in point.

In a famous passage of *Teoria e storia della storiografia*, the Neapolitan philosopher states:

> History cannot discriminate between good events and bad, progressive or regressive eras. It begins only when the psychological conditions that created these antitheses have been overcome and when we substitute for them the spiritual act that seeks to define the purpose served by the event or era that had earlier been condemned, that is, when we determine what it produced. And because in their own fashion all events and all eras are productive, none of them is subject to condemnation in the eyes of history; all are laudable and venerable. An event that is condemned, an event that is denounced, is not yet a historical proposition; it is barely the premise for a historical problem that must yet be formulated. Negative history is non-history if its negative ways supplant positive thinking, if its practical and moral bounds are not observed along with the poetical and empirical limits that allow us to speak (speak, not merely think), as we do all of the time, about evil men and decadent and regressive eras.[2]

In accordance with this position, after the Liberation Croce found it impossible to write the history of Fascism because of a keen sense of revulsion. "It is repugnant and tiring for me to speak of Fascism," he observed on October 13, 1943, in his diary. In February 1946, responding to an invitation to write the history of Fascism, he observed: "I have not written it, nor shall I write it, because I hate Fascism so much that I forbid myself even to attempt to think about its history."[3] But four years later, in discussing the subject with students at the Italian Institute for Historical Studies, he observed:

> Even if I had decided or could ever decide to undertake such a work, you can be sure that I would never depict an entirely black scene, filled with shame and error. And since history is the history of man's positive achievements and not a catalogue of negative acts and inconclusive pessimism, I would discuss evil only where it was necessary to the unfolding of the tale, and I would emphasize the good that to a greater or lesser extent came into the world at that time, along with the good intentions and attempts, and I would likewise do justice to those who adhered to the new regime, motivated not by evil intentions but by generous and noble sentiments, even though they were not buttressed by appropriate self-scrutiny, as occurs with immature and youthful souls. In the eventual transition to the historical, it seems that even negative elements are, to a certain extent, converted into positive elements that can be considered as ingredients and stimulus to good that invigorates and ennobles the will.[4]

Croce's statements hold the key to an understanding of why during the 1950s there was a dearth of historiographic effort concerning Italian Fascism. It also explains why, during the 1960s, scholars turned their efforts in this direction, as a new generation of researchers came to the fore. Although these researchers had not experienced Fascism directly, they were able to confront it more freely, without revisionistic preconceptions or psychological inhibitions and with a sound ethical and political awareness of what Fascism had represented for Italy. They sought to understand it within a historical context and to reintegrate it into the corpus of Italian history.

The dependence on general interpretations

In this psychological climate authors increasingly preferred to concentrate on general interpretations and characterizations. Once the historical approach had been renounced this became the focus of attention, because only by resorting to generalizations that were more or less moralistic or more or less mechanical could one explain the emergence of such an important phenomenon that was still so alive and had so many implications. In addition, this path seemed to be the most productive at a time when political and ideological tension characterized the postwar period, and Fascism was blamed for the errors, selfishness, and conniving of one's respective adversaries.

If we set aside personal and extreme positions that engendered no following—such as the writings of Giulio Colamarino and Fabio Cusin—and if we set aside for the same reason the writings of the latter-day epigones of Fascism itself, the prevailing interpretations during the 1940s and 1950s were essentially the classic interpretations discussed in Chapter 2.[5] During this second postwar period historians, and especially journalists, were inclined to join the interpretation of Fascism as a revelation with the interpretation that viewed Fascism as a class reaction. They expanded on both theories in a series of motifs and suggestions that had been elaborated by anti-Fascist writers in the heat of battle (during the earliest period of Fascism and during the emigration). They replaced the liberal stamp that Fortunato, founder of the revelation interpretation, had given his work with a strongly radical, even Marxist, flavor.[6]

The evaluation of this interpretative phase is another matter of concern. A negative judgment would be unjust and abstract. All three interpretations and schematizations that we have discussed contain an element of truth. If nothing else, they have the merit of stressing certain of the components of Fascism; and, as a whole, they demonstrate the complexity of the Fascist phenomenon. This is also true of the interpretations that flourished abroad, which were studied earlier in this book. The latter are so foreign to Italy's intellectual life that they have had very few reverberations there.

A negative judgment would also be unfair because certain of their systematic applications have demonstrated the partiality, insufficiency, and deception of these interpretations. Such is the case with scholars who confused the national movement of the 1800s with the nationalisms prevalent in this century and projected the shadow of 1922 on the events of 1861; similarly, in Germany they related events of 1933 to 1871 occurrences. Thus, Mussolini became a descendant of Mazzini, and Hitler was viewed as an heir to Bismarck.[7]

A similar error was committed by those who attempted to explain the vicissitudes of thirty or more years of European history as a blast of collective insanity or as Hitler's demonic folly, and by those who viewed the Fascist success of 1922 as a mere plot of the landowners and industrialists. Such interpretations bespeak their own inadequacy. Sooner or later they lead to paradoxical contradictions that cause amusing turnabouts in perspective, making us speculate about the validity of such rigid schematization. For example, if we accept certain characterizations and interpretations, how can we explain that as late as 1925 Croce supported what was shortly to become the essentially Marxist theory—that Fascism was "a movement that aimed at the defense of the social order and was mainly fostered by industrialists and landowners." Yet such important leaders of Italian Communism as Gramsci and Togliatti had asserted, a year and a half after the March on Rome, that "the industrial classes" were suspicious of the new regime and refused to be "concerned" with Fascism, whose success they had insured "in 1921-22 in order to prevent the collapse of the state."

The need for historical understanding

Such obvious conflicts and contradictions can be understood and explained today only in a much wider perspective. It must focus on the specific historical moment and avoid superimposing periods and problems for the sake of schematizations that might have had some value at the time of the anti-Fascist struggle but are devoid of it now that the Fascist experience has come full circle; its condemnation must be motivated by historical understanding. Such a perspective, as Tasca maintained in 1938, cannot be found in old or new definitions of Fascism; it must be sought through concrete historical study. Indeed, recent historiography has again turned to Tasca. But even before this return, these same conflicts and contradictions placed in motion the critical mechanism within history writing that overcame the tendency to schematize. Croce was the first to argue, on more than one occasion, against the interpretation that viewed Fascism as a class reaction. At the time he met with little success. The philosopher denied that Fascism had been essentially a class movement directed against another class. He recalled that Fascism "found its adherents and supporters in all classes and among all economic and intellectual levels, among industrialists and landowners, among the clergy and the old aristocrats, among the proletariat and the petty bourgeoisie, among workers and peasants, but it also met with strong opponents in all of these same classes." He reiterated his own ethical and political interpretation: "in the face of the reality of Fascism, it is ingenuous to believe that one can find its roots in the superficial and mechanical concepts of economic classes and their opposites; it is necessary to go much deeper, into the brains of men, and there discover the disease."[8] And he countered the revelation theory with a famous passage:

> Despite the praise that it has kindly been granted, a refrain of criticism has been leveled at me as the result of the account I gave of Italian history between 1871 and 1915, because it contains a flaw in that it "does not explain" how liberal Italy, which was cautiously but continually progressing in every aspect of its life, was supplanted by that mad Italy that turned itself and its destiny over to a man and a band of men who led it to ruin; therefore, that former Italy must have contained within itself the seed, that I overlooked, of the Italy that was born thereafter. And I must respond (although I would rather not) that this is an observation that has no critical value and is purely and simply a naiveté (not to say foolishness). If a man who is healthy and strong contracts a terminal illness, it is certainly true that he carried within him the possibility of disease, even though he had previously been judged to be as healthy and strong as a man can be, although he did not carry within him the immunization against possible diseases and epidemics that may occur. In the same manner, the most honest man in the world carries within him the possibility of dishonesty and evil; and for this reason he is always wary of himself. He is modest,

v9cp ‖even humble, and prays to God to help him, and he flees ‖from pride and overconfidence, intuiting them as sins that attract punishment. This is a generic moral truth that should never be forgotten and that should always be presupposed; it is not the precise and particular historical event that history has the specific obligation to understand and narrate; it can be changed or contaminated by that moral truth that can contribute a pathology of possible diseases and a trembling contemplation of the fact that *omnia periculis sunt plena.*[9]

This passage was examined and developed in 1952 by Federico Chabod, who was discussing Croce's position with regard to the interpretation of Fascism. Chabod's series of observations, which essentially closed the general debate on Fascism, can be considered definitive. (It is not by chance that they were linked to Tasca's writings.) In discussing the parenthesis theory, Chabod wrote:

It can no longer be claimed that Fascism was a mere "adventure" that came about spontaneously in Italian history, as though from external sources. It appears to me to be beyond argument that in Fascism there appeared in the broad light of day motifs and attitudes of Italian life that had been latent for some time. The nationalist spirit was not simply an imitation of foreign events, even though it prospered and derived incentive from similar foreign attitudes . . . Except that—and here Croce is entirely correct—these germs did not *necessarily* lead to Fascism . . . It is true that during the origins of Fascism—that is to say, during the crisis of the Italian ruling class between 1919 and 1922—certain dispositions and attitudes obtained that had also been present in the period between 1870 and 1914; but where they had formerly existed on a secondary level, they now came to have decisive weight. However, this transformation into effective and decisive political reality of elements that theretofore had been purely *potential* or of insignificant weight, took place at that time, at that precise moment, because of men and errors of that moment and not because of the actions of men in 1860 or 1880. They were faults and errors that can be traced especially to the liberal government of 1919, heir to the Risorgimento; but—we must finally take note—these

faults and errors can also be traced back no less to those
political, Socialist, and Catholic groups that were not linked
in any way to the experience of the Risorgimento and the
postunitary period, and who, in a certain sense, represented
and wanted to represent the anti-Risorgimento . . . It was
then that the "precedents" of Nationalist attitudes, etc. could
become strong and even decisive elements: nevertheless,
right up to the end, the outcome was not predetermined by
fate . . . In the history of Italy from 1859 on, there was nothing that "had" to lead to this result; to study the history of
Italy between 1860 and 1915 and project onto it, with the
benefit of hindsight, the shadow of 1922 and 1925 and evaluate it only as a function of this shadow, is totally erroneous
and is not conducive to an accurate representation of history.[10]

After Chabod adopted this position, debate might well have
been considered closed, at least insofar as the revelation and parenthesis theories were concerned. As for the Marxist-Communist
thesis, rather than insisting aprioristically on it, it would have been
advisable to study events, conduct ad hoc, in-depth research without preconceptions, bearing in mind the ways the approach was
being translated into reality on both the historical and the political
level. Such a study would have had the additional merit of illustrating the uncertainties, discussion, and vicissitudes that led to formulation of the interpretation. In short, it would have been advisable
to pass from the phase of interpretation-characterization, which
had occupied postwar debate on Fascism, to a phase of concrete
historiographic reconstruction.

   This should have been even more obvious in that the few
serious historical works on Fascism by Gaetano Salvemini and,
especially, *Nascita e avvento del fascismo* by Angelo Tasca indicated not only that this was an avenue that could be explored but
also that it was the only means for reaching a satisfactory response
to a series of increasingly pressing questions. A pioneering attempt
in this direction was made by Luigi Salvatorelli and Giovanni Mira
in *Storia del fascismo* (1952), which was the first and remains the
only overall study of Fascism conducted in a scientific manner and
within a solid ethico-political framework.[11] However, from a docu-

mentary point of view it left much to be desired because it did not extend its research to the State archives, Fascist documents, and Mussolini's papers. [12] This sort of research was essential to an understanding of Fascist events and to a comprehension of the internal, substantive, and motivating aspects of the Italian situation between the wars.

Unfortunately, the road that had so auspicious a start found no other followers. Indeed, for several years the study of the period between the wars was viewed not as a study of Fascism, but rather as the study—at times inquisitorial and seeking to assign true or presumed singular and collective responsibility—of the crisis of the Liberal State, of the non-Fascist political parties and movements, or of the anti-Fascist opposition. Many works in this vein were published. Some are very important, especially those by Nino Valeri and Gabriele De Rosa; they have helped to clarify a series of problems related to the history of the period between 1914 and 1926.

Although the study of the history of the concept of Fascism remained virtually unexplored, many forays of a general nature were made at this time and have helped prepare the proper climate for the younger generation of scholars. [13] These investigations of the historical and moral basis of Fascism were carried out by scholars, mainly of a Catholic orientation, whose writings bespoke the cultural need for a new approach to the reality of Fascism, one providing a deeper and more persuasive interpretation than had hitherto been offered by the various popular schools of historiography.

9

More Recent Cultural and Historiographic Orientations

In the 1960s the question of the interpretation of Fascism reached an important turning point in Italy. It influenced all aspects of Italian culture, although thus far its effects on historiography are most obvious. The arduous debate characteristic of earlier decades was supplanted by questions, especially as expressed by the younger generation, that stemmed from discussions that originated in the 1950s. Instead of reflecting specific historiographical choices, the new problems are defined in terms of states of mind and cultural needs as yet unclear. Schematic interpretations, rigid determinism of an ideological and political nature, certain theses of a demonological type, all are proving increasingly unsatisfactory and unconvincing. At the same time, new inquiries, stimuli, hypotheses, and research ideas have come from abroad. Although works such as those by Fromm, Parsons, Lipset, Nolte, and Arendt are not entirely satisfying and find few counterparts in the Italian scholarship, they have served a useful purpose: they have attracted attention to certain aspects of Fascism and its history that previously had been undervalued or ignored. They have been instrumental in drawing attention previously focused almost exclusively on the origins of Fascism to the years of the dictatorial Regime and the particular mechanism of the Totalitarian State. They have provoked a comprehensive comparison of the realities of the various Fascist movements, parties, and regimes. And they have focused attention on individual positions that previously had been neglected.[1]

Contrary to what might have been expected, the social sciences, sociology in particular, have contributed little.[2] Except for informative accounts summarizing the writings of foreign scholars, research has been limited to an outline of the problem of the generations under Fascism and in relation to Fascism.[3] The ties between the middle classes and Fascism, a topic reexamined once more in the period immediately after the Liberation, was not followed up.[4] The only contribution of interest thus far has been *L'industrializzazione tra nazionalismo e rivoluzione*, by L. Garruccio. The philosophers, on the other hand, have provided stimulus that, though not abundant, is nevertheless significant. Besides the works of Del Noce, *Quale umanesimo? Ipotesi su Croce, Ugo Spirito, Mussolini* (1966), by R. Mazzetti, should be studied. Although many aspects of this book are controversial, it illustrates some of the central problems of the relations between Fascism and culture. It proposes general hypotheses and interpretations that cannot help but be considered and discussed.

The most important contribution, however, derives from the historiographical field—especially from a group of scholars with varying backgrounds and orientations who have recently undertaken the study of the Fascist era. Their results occasionally have given rise to vociferous and bitter debate; nevertheless, they have influenced the work of other scholars who are more closely bound to traditional forms of interpretation and judgment. Because of the nature of this book, and because I consider myself part of this group, I shall not linger on the achievements of these scholars.[5]

In my opinion, a unitary motif can be found in the work of this group. It is represented by the rejection—whether implicit or explicit is unimportant—of any single one of the traditional interpretations. In practice, this rejection is expressed by the acceptance of Tasca's assertion that in order to define Fascism, one must, above all, write an account of its history. It follows that, in order to write its history, it is necessary to research even the most minute of clues and individual manifestations, including those that might seem irrelevant. This group of scholars has based its research on

very extensive and intensive archival investigations, which are now
facilitated by an especially enlightened and liberal legislation.
Thus, we are confronted with a double effort: first, to avoid any
avulsion of Fascism from the context of Italian reality and to study
Fascism in its full relation to Italian life; and, second, to go beyond
an external and superficially unitary view of Fascism and distinguish the complex realities and illustrate the components and their
dialectical relation.

This tendency is apparent in all the works in question. Suffice it to recall the writings of Delio Cantimori, published in 1962,
when studies of this type were just beginning to appear. Cantimori
should be considered representative of another generation and discipline, but he was able, as few others were, to sense the deeper
meaning of the evolution of historiography and the intimate requirements of the young:

> it is not possible historically, that is, critically, to speak of
> "Fascism" as though Fascism had been a kind of whale that
> swallowed everything indiscriminately, or that satanically
> carried everyone to their destruction, like Moby Dick. It is
> necessary to discern the variety of currents, movements,
> tendencies, individuals, fantasies, inconsistencies, and so
> forth, that allowed Mussolini and his followers to seize
> power, maintain it, and retain it; just as it is also necessary
> to discern the variety and difference of ideas, political con-
> cepts, interests, and personalities, and so forth that consti-
> tuted "anti-Fascism"—both general characteristics of the
> period and the chronological facts . . . If we do not begin to
> look at things in this manner, and if we hold fast to general
> schemes, we run the risk of losing all sense of proportion
> and perspective, both of recent events as well as of those in
> the past, and we run the risk of succumbing to the most
> heinous of moralisms: historical and political moralism. Fas-
> cism viewed as a bloc, anti-Fascism viewed as a bloc, with-
> out differentiating either one or the other, will not allow us
> to recall the political history of those years prior to 1926, the
> fondness of the Liberals (whether as a party or as individ-
> uals) for Mussolini, without being accused of blaming them
> for "Fascism"; we will not be able to define the differences
> that existed among a Grandi, an Arpinati, a Bottai, and a

Mussolini or a Farinacci. Nor will we be able to refuse to consider that period aprioristically or negatively without being accused of being nostalgic. In the opposite instance, the game certain people play of continuing to exhibit photographs of such and such political figure dressed as an "avanguardista" or as a youthful Fascist is out of place; all of this may be useful for daily polemics, but only to a certain extent and up to a certain point. On the whole, this approach does not help us to understand the history of Fascism, of anti-Fascism, or of the recent political events in Italy.[6]

At this point a question arises: does this new historiography of Fascism lead to a type of "historiographic revisionism," such as occurred in several countries after World War I and has been attempted upon occasion by foreign scholars? Is what Croce predicted coming to pass?[7] Will some writers, seduced by paradoxical, ingenious, and brilliant theses, attempt a *Rettung*, a rehabilitation of Fascism and its leader? I cannot believe it. As scholars are aware, the overall historical evaluation of Fascism can neither be changed nor substantially revised. In fact, the efforts of younger writers may bring about exactly what Croce considered the real need: an investigation and understanding of how Italian and European history had "brought to power such men" as Mussolini and Hitler. Because they were trained in a moral and political climate different from that of the preceding generation, and because, as Croce also pointed out, they were led not merely to discriminate between good and evil but to seek "the purpose served in the development of events by the facts or eras that were previously condemned," these younger writers are more detached and historical and their tone is less strident.

In 1959, at the Genoa meeting of the National Institute for the Study of the Liberation Movement in Italy, Gabriele De Rosa vigorously emphasized "the need to write history without sowing blame and accolades right and left, and to write it with political sensitivity and detachment from the events under consideration." "Historical debate," he warned, "cannot be the same as courtroom debate."[8] In a sense the new historiography has merely put this preaching into practice. It has sought to avoid attributing to men and political forces plans that are excessively conscious and preordained—for instance, where a certain premise dictates certain conclusions. Instead of illustrating assumptions, it has attempted to let the facts speak for themselves. All of this corresponds to a tendency, after more than a half-century of drastic ideological confrontations, that is widespread in the most modern and serious Western historiography.

In a passage that might well be applied to Italy, the British historian Alan John Percivale Taylor exhorted scholars of the contemporary age to doubt everything and to search out, even more than before, documentary proof of everything, so as to avoid attributing to men and movements, plans and intentions that they very often did not have but that had been attributed to them as a result of political conflicts or of post facto reconstructions by historians of a later date. He invited modern scholars to "let our assertions or conclusions evolve from our narrative and not vice versa." This new trend he described as follows:

> I think a general change is taking place in the habits of historians that should make things easier, and to which, incidentally, I hope to have made a personal contribution. Until a short while ago historians attributed conscious plans and intentions to statesmen. It was supposed that great men— Louis XIV, Napoleon, Bismarck—knew exactly what they were aiming at and how they would obtain it . . . Now we have come to consider these policies as constructions imposed on events by the historians themselves . . . This may be an essentially English type of empiricism, and we must not carry it too far (as I perhaps do at times) to the point where we declare the opposite, that statesmen have no preconceived plans. Nevertheless, even when they do have plans, these rarely are translated into reality in the intended manner, so that we arrive at almost the same result. The only sure rule for historians is to doubt everything: to doubt that statesmen had plans and to doubt that they had no plans. Naturally, this is a rule for perfection. Every historian tends to lean one way or the other and with regard to Hitler almost all historians have held fast to the notion that he knew what he was doing. Here we must make an important distinction. Hitler certainly wanted to gain power in Germany and make Germany powerful in Europe. I doubt that

anyone would take objection to this notion or deny that Hitler was more dynamic and had more vigorous impulses than other statesmen. It is another thing to pretend that Hitler had clear and definite plans on how to achieve one or the other of his objectives. This assertion cannot be imposed as a dogma; it must be supported by documentary proof, and increasingly numerous documents lead one to doubt that such is the case . . . It is my opinion that even the old interpretations of Hitler's policies can no longer be sustained. At one time it was supposed that Hitler proceeded by means of logical steps, that had previously been established, from the day in which he withdrew from the 1933 Disarmament Conference to that on which he declared war against the United States in 1941. Now we have come to acknowledge that he seized the occasions that others offered him to achieve his successes or to perpetrate his errors.[9]

The new historiography seems motivated, not by a search for absurd revisionism, but by the desire to stimulate intensive reflection on the significance of a half-century of recent Italian history. Despite the fact that such reflection is intimately and necessarily concerned with the realities of our time, and with the moral and political values that rule it and that are rooted in anti-Fascism, it does not pursue polemical objectives and policies that are not within the province of the historian. It is a position, as Romeo correctly observed, that brings to mind the stance of those historians, "who several decades after 1870 began to study the Risorgimento historically and who wrote about the Kingdom of Naples, or the Grand Duchy of Tuscany as historically concluded facts that history itself had located in the past."[10] It seems, however, that along this path the interpretation of Fascism has entered an entirely new phase, one in which all previous interpretations have been negated.[11] A new interpretation will result from new analysis and deep rethinking of the events that transpired between the two wars, and all Italian contemporary history—pre-Fascist, Fascist, and post-Fascist—viewed as a unified, uninterrupted whole.?

Conclusions

I have asserted and hope to have shown that I do not personally ascribe absolute validity to any of the individual interpretations of the Fascist phenomenon so far put forth. Although I cannot deny the existence of a common denominator among some of the movements, parties, and regimes generally defined as Fascist, in order to achieve a historically effective explanation of the Fascist phenomenon in general and of the various individual forms of Fascism in particular it is necessary to keep in mind and adapt all the interpretations advanced to date. It is especially important that, rather than generalize about the significance of Fascism's characteristics, we stress the specifically national characteristics that are concretely related to historical events—economic, social, cultural, and political—in countries where Fascist movements, parties, or regimes have arisen. I am convinced, as Angelo Tasca has declared, that a definition of Fascism implies above all else writing the history of Fascism. Although this path of historical reconstruction of the various Fascisms has been the object of considerable work, especially in recent years, much remains to be done.

We can outline a provisional balance sheet of the results thus far achieved. Such an evaluation is all the more necessary in that there exists an inclination to obliterate—perhaps as a reaction to those who expanded the term Fascism excessively—the notion of Fascism as a phenomenon and to lose sight of that modicum of common denominator to which I have referred. Without awareness of this common denominator, we would lose the ability to comprehend the creation of a bloc of states opposed by another bloc that was unquestionably heterogenous and provisional but that was brought into existence by its opposition to the first bloc. The history of Europe and the world between the two World Wars would be explained in mere diplomatic terms verging on the casual: if certain errors had not been committed at Versailles, if Fascist Italy had not joined forces with Nazi Germany, if the French advocates of military intervention with Finland against the USSR had prevailed, if Hitler had not destroyed the Ribbentrop-Molotov pact, and so on.

The means to historical understanding

Thus, at the risk of making some inevitable schematizations, I shall recapitulate the elements that must be emphasized in order to attain a historical understanding of the Fascist phenomenon.

The first is geographical and chronological. Fascism was a European phenomenon that developed within the time span encompassed by two World Wars. Undoubtedly certain moral and social roots and preconditions antedated World War I, but they were closely linked to the cultural and economic situation in Europe, especially to that of certain specific European countries. (No comparison can be made with situations outside Europe, whether of the same period or later, because of radical differences in historical contexts—in the broadest sense of the term.) However, these roots and preconditions were "marginal," and nothing indicates that they would have developed without the direct and indirect trauma of World War I and its immediate and long-term consequences, the Great Depression of 1929, for example. The crisis provoked by the war was the only real cause of their eruption and extension to social groups that had previously been immune. It infused these roots with additional contents of a moral, political-moral, economic, and social nature.[1] Thus, in the postwar period the upheaval became active and general and afflicted the whole spectrum of society in all its levels and in all its respective values.

We must not draw excessively broad conclusions from this assertion. In different countries the crisis had different manifestations and dimensions, because of the individual contemporary and historical situations of these countries, and, as Chabod has explained, because of the abilities, faults, and errors of the men of that time and of the traditional ruling classes.[2] Moreover, the political parties whose roots and strengths came from different classes and social strata than those of the ruling classes hoped for different resolutions to the crisis. The Fascist or authoritarian resolution in certain countries was in no way inevitable and conformed to no necessity. It was the result of many factors, all rational and all avoidable. It was the result of misunderstandings, errors, lack of foresight, illusions, fears, fatigue, and, for only a minority, of blind resolve that often led unexpectedly to Fascism.[3]

The second element that must be taken into account if we are to have a historical understanding of the Fascist phenomenon concerns its social base. Those who, like Croce, maintained that Fascism was not the expression of a specific social class, but found supporters and adversaries among all classes, were correct. But Fromm's disciples were even more correct when they observed that, although the working class and the liberal and Catholic bourgeoisie displayed a negative or resigned attitude toward it, Fascism found its most ardent supporters among the petty bourgeoisie. Indeed, the relation between Fascism and the petty bourgeoisie, and, more generally, between Fascism and the middle classes, is one of the crucial elements of the historical problem. Though this was especially true at the time Fascism came to power, it also pertains to later years. It is not by chance that the problem has drawn much attention, in the historical and sociological literature on Fascism as well as in the propaganda of numerous political currents. The analysis of the arguments that stressed the relation between Fascism and the middle classes can be summarized as follows:

(1) After World War I, in several European countries, whether vanquished or victorious, the middle classes underwent a serious crisis, in cases such as Italy and Germany, an extremely serious one. Some of the causes of the crisis predated the war; they were related to the transformation of social structures and the incipient emergence of a "mass" society in progress in these countries. The causes also derived directly from the war, from the accelerated transformation of society and social mobility, especially upward

mobility, provoked by the war. They were also the result of the grafting onto the above of still other causes that derived from the socioeconomic crisis of the immediate postwar period, and later from the Depression.

(2) On the economic and social level this crisis took shape in somewhat different ways, depending on whether the middle classes in question were the traditional ones (farmers, merchants, professionals, small businessmen), whose members possessed a certain degree of personal autonomy and constituted a fairly homogenous and integrated social entity, or whether they were those that had risen in the scale more recently (white-collar employees, accountants, and salaried intellectuals), who lacked personal autonomy and were only slightly integrated. All the middle classes were confronting a society in the process of rapid transformation, best represented by the growing strength of the proletariat and the upper bourgeoisie. The middle classes had to acknowledge this transformation in the midst of adverse economic circumstances (inflation, high cost of living, reduction of fixed incomes, rent controls, and so on), without, in the majority of instances, adequate instruments for collective bargaining and in a situation of steady loss of social and economic status.

(3) On the psychological and political level, this crisis manifested itself as social frustration that was often translated into profound unrest, a confused desire for revenge, and a blind struggle (that often assumed subversive and revolutionary overtones) with a society in which the middle classes felt themselves to be the chief, if not the only, victims— all the more galling since they had assumed that the war would bring them "democratic" and moral hegemony. At its inception, this frustration could have been used and directed by the Socialist movement to establish an effective alliance with at least a part of the middle classes. However, the errors of the workers' parties and the fear of Bolshevism impelled a great many members of the middle classes toward Fascism, which they viewed as yet another revolutionary movement aiming to assert its social and political power against the proletariat and the upper bourgeoisie.

(4) Thus, for some authors, Fascism was the attempt to give political life to a third force, opposed to both Communism and the parliamentary democracy of the capitalist countries, that found its

prime movers among the middle classes, which considered themselves an autonomous social force. Nor does the fact that Fascism aimed its blows chiefly at the proletariat invalidate this interpretation. In the short run, the antiproletarian offensive was explained by the fact that the middle classes felt more threatened socially and politically by the proletariat than by the upper bourgeoisie, and therefore had worked out a temporary *modus vivendi* with the latter, aimed against the former. Nevertheless, in the long run, a basic tendency reappeared in both Italian and German Fascism: the expansion of public enterprise and transferral of economic leadership from the capitalists and private enterprise to State functionaries, while avoiding any revolutionary change in the basic system of private enterprise.

Although it may be conceded that the foregoing is a comprehensive interpretation of Fascism, its analysis of the relation between the middle classes and Fascism is too unilateral, and therefore unacceptable. Like all other interpretations that seek to explain Fascism, it underestimates important aspects of Fascist reality and ignores still others.

Three of these neglected aspects are especially important. First, the secondary mobilization of the middle classes cannot be separated from the simultaneous acceleration of the primary mobilization of the proletariat. In the crisis situation on which countries such as Italy and Germany verged, this second type of mobilization met with greater difficulties than before in finding its own legitimate or tolerated channels—a point Gino Germani has made. And, as Richard Löwenthal noted, the increase in the nonproductive sectors of society vis-à-vis the total population affected the proletariat in general, and the working class in particular, since that group felt its repercussions most heavily. Among the results that interest us particularly was the formation within the proletariat and the working class of a series of conflicting interests that weakened their unified action. This caused even greater social stress among the classes and a radicalization of the political struggle. At the same time, it produced in the proletariat and its class organizations (upon occasion created artificially and coercively) centrifugal tendencies that propelled certain sectors of the proletariat—consisting mainly of the unemployed—into an ambiguous psychological and political situation. (Just as it is possible to refer to the "dispossessed" among the bourgeoisie, it is possible to speak of the "dispossessed" among the proletariat.) In this ambiguous situation they wavered between dichotomous extremes, and many turned to Fascism. This was especially true in Germany at the beginning of the 1930s, as Werner Conze described: "Unlike the Socialist Party, the Communist Party was not a party of the unemployed. Thus, it is understandable that during those years the exchange of members between the KPD and the SA of the NSDAP became ever more frequent until, in 1932, it affected 80 percent of the membership."[4]

A second aspect of Fascism that is ignored is that in all the vicissitudes of Fascism from the beginning to the end, in the upswing as well as during the crises, the role of youth was particularly important. This is only partially explained by the common social origin of the various categories of youths who participated in these events. I shall not linger on this aspect, so admirably investigated by Germani.[5]

Third, if Fascism was essentially a phenomenon of the middle classes, so was its elite, although with a characteristic that cannot be underestimated. Especially during the period of Fascism's "origins," most Fascist leaders came from two specific backgrounds that were often commingled: either they had been party militants or were involved in movements of the extreme Left where they held responsible positions, or they were war veterans.[6] This background characterized their attitude in new situations where it was necessary to be open-minded, unscrupulous, aggressive, capable of leadership, brave, sensitive to the changes of heart of the masses, and aware of the psychology and revolutionary techniques of the enemy. It was an elite that was able to elaborate a revolutionary and nationalistic "ideology" that corresponded to the psychology, resentments, inclinations, and aspirations of the masses on whom it had to rely if it wished to attain power.

Various elements have been wholly neglected by scholars who view the relation between Fascism and the middle classes as the comprehensive interpretation of Fascism. The most important of these elements, indeed the decisive one, was the progressive move—once Fascism became a regime—toward an autonomous Totalitarian mechanism, a step which meant breaking away from

the forces that had contributed to the rise of Fascism and its instal-
lation as a regime. This shift toward an autonomous Totalitarian
mechanism affected precisely that petty and middle bourgeoisie
that had provided the main strength of the action squads during the
time of the 1921-22 armed confrontation. Once Fascism had attained power, these elements of the bourgeoisie hoped to control
the workings of the Fascist parties by democratic means. They
viewed the parties as conveyor belts for carrying out their own economic and social demands and, thus, as instruments of their own
autonomous social role. However, even more than the other social
forces that had contributed to the growth of Fascism, this segment
of the bourgeoisie found itself cast aside.

Another important aspect that has been neglected—although
it was attributed its proper importance by those who viewed Fascism as a variant of Totalitarianism—is the "technological" instru-
mentation adopted by Fascism, especially National Socialism, to
bring about this autonomous role of the Totalitarian state and,
more generally, to exert its own Totalitarian control over all aspects of life in the countries it dominated.

Noteworthy differences between Italian and German Fascism existed. They can be attributed to at least three causes: the distinct nature of the two peoples; the fact that in National Socialism
the *Volk* ideology played a role and had a more radical basis and
tradition than did any other component of the other Fascist ideologies; and the manner of achieving Totalitarian control of national
life.

To understand the true Fascisms historically, particularly
the Italian and German forms, and to distinguish them from other
movements, parties, or regimes that were only superficially Fascist
or were not Fascist at all, as well as to detect that minimal common
denominator, one must keep in mind the relation between the middle classes and Fascism.[7] If not, it is difficult to appreciate the novelty and differences inherent in Fascism with respect to the conservative and authoritarian movements that preceded, accompanied,
or followed it. It also precludes the possibility of understanding the
origins and characteristics of Fascism and the consensus it achieved
in Italy and Germany. Such consensus cannot be explained as the

result merely of a police state, regime of terror, or monopoly of the mass propaganda.

If we do not consider the rapport between the middle classes and Fascism, we cannot appreciate the two elements that are perhaps most characteristic of Fascism. Classic conservative and authoritarian regimes have always offered values and a social model that have been tested in the past and are considered able to prevent the disruptions and mistakes of certain recent revolutionary interludes. The strength of Fascism, on the other hand, has been to give the masses the impression that they are always mobilized, that they have a direct relationship with the leader (because he can interpret their aspirations and translate them into fact). They are led to believe not only that they can participate in and contribute to the restoration of a social order whose limits and historical inadequacy they have experienced, but that they can be prime movers in a revolution that will gradually lead to a new and better social order.

It was this feeling that accounted for the consensus enjoyed by Fascism, a consensus that can only be understood in the light of the moral and cultural values that fostered it and the hypothetical social order that sustained it. Such values were typical of the middle classes, and of the limited sectors of the remainder of society which the cultural hegemony of the middle classes was able to influence. It was a consensus that was broad, though not as broad as possible. It was a consensus that could easily dissolve in the face of a prolonged stalemate in social progress. Where social progress was nonexistent, the consensus could be maintained only through irrational substitutes aimed outside the national collectivity. Such was the case in Germany of the myth about the racial superiority of the Aryans, and in Italy of the myth about the rights of the "proletarian" and "youthful" nation against the "plutocratic" and "old" nations. It was not by chance that both were typically petty bourgeois myths.

Nor are these the only knots in the history of Fascism that an examination of the relation between Fascism and the middle classes can untie. Consider, for example, Fascist ideology and its models, and, more generally, the presence in Fascism of old, conservative elements inherited from the past coupled with new, renovating elements characteristic of modern mass societies. Both are typical of a mentality, a culture, and interests that are individually the expression of the middle classes. [8]

Nor can we underestimate the contribution of the middle classes to the political and social crisis experienced by some countries between the two wars. This diminishes the ideological nature of the errors committed by the workers' parties at the time of the rise to power of Fascism. How much did underestimation of the middle classes contribute to these errors? How much responsibility for the errors should be attributed to the refusal to grant any social autonomy to Fascism? How much to the insistence on considering the Fascists mere adventurers and dispossessed persons in the pay of agrarian and industrial capitalism? Today we consider the problem in historical terms. In the past, however, when it was considered in dramatically political terms and in terms of struggle, would not a less schematic analysis of the problem of the middle classes have avoided certain errors and, especially, their repetition in other countries?

Fascism in Italy

If we pass from the general to the specific and examine the case of Italy, the petty and middle bourgeois characterization of Fascism finds much to validate it. Corroboration is found at all levels—in the writings of the most astute contemporary observers, in police documents, in documents of the Fascist Party, and in the increasingly numerous recent studies of Fascism. On the basis of these data, notices, testimonies, and judgments, it is possible to assert that once the Totalitarian regime was established and until adherence to the PNF became increasingly a mass action and a practical necessity, the social base of the Fascist Party was constituted largely by the middle classes, predominantly the urban and rural petty bourgeoisie.

These factors, impressive on their own, gain even greater significance when examined alongside contemporary news accounts and Fascist propaganda. The latter's ambivalence and oscillation between conservatism (regarding the proletariat) and subversiveness (with respect to the upper bourgeoisie), between free-trade and protectionism, between authoritarianism and social democracy, between realism and romanticism, reflect the mentality, aspirations, interests, culture, contradictions, and even the phraseology of the Italian middle classes and their internal stratifications. They clearly indicate the effective hegemony of the middle class over the upper bourgeoisie and the proletariat.

Mussolini and the Fascist leadership (moderate Fascists, Nationalists, fellow travelers, *commis d'État*) that had come to the fore with the implementation of the compromises of October 1922 and 1925 assiduously attempted to eliminate this hegemony. During the March on Rome, however, it was instrumental in deciding the ultimate fate of Fascism. The hegemony enabled Fascism to become a mass party and prevented it from losing political autonomy (as Giolitti and a significant part of the old Liberal ruling class had hoped would happen). It allowed the new leaders to penetrate ever deeper into the bureaucratic and military apparatus and dissolve its connective tissue, in many cases severing the disciplinary ties between the center and the periphery. On another level, the hegemony permitted the new leaders to lure a large number of members away from the more typically petty bourgeois parties, the older traditional parties, and the Popular Party, toward which, immediately after the war, a significant part of the more integrated and traditional middle classes had turned.

Thus, on the morrow of Mussolini's rise to power so astute an observer of the Italian social and political scene as Luigi Salvatorelli could assert in no uncertain terms that the middle classes were the characteristic and decisive element for understanding Fascism. This future historian of Fascist Italy viewed Fascism in 1922 and 1923 as, and it bears repeating, "the *class struggle* of the petty bourgeoisie that was wedged between capitalism and the proletariat, as the third combatant between two others."[9]

There could be no disputing the fact that the Fascist petty bourgeoisie had a revolutionary class psychology and aspired to its own "autonomous and radical" revolution. However, this psychology had no real substratum because the petty bourgeoisie "is not a real social class imbued with its own functions and forces; it is rather an agglomeration that exists on the fringes of the productive process that is essential to capitalist civilization." For Salvatorelli, this explains the nature of the Fascist "revolt"—not "revolution"—

and its inane demagoguery. It is also the premise for his two fundamental judgments of Fascism: the revolt of the petty bourgeoisie
was made possible by the complicity of the upper bourgeoisie,
which was set on making Fascism the instrument of its own immediate class interests; and, given its heterogeneity, the only common
ideological element of the petty bourgeoisie was nationalism. This
line of argument gave rise, finally, to Salvatorelli's judgment regarding the "antihistoricity" of Fascism: Fascism as the "anti-Risorgimento."

Today, considering the changes that have taken place in advanced capitalist societies, it is difficult to deny—as Salvatorelli did
in 1923—that the middle classes constitute a well-defined social reality that has its own functions. By and large, however, Salvatorelli's analysis and judgment, insofar as they refer to Italian society
after World War I, must be accepted. When viewed along with the
slightly later work of Guido Dorso, they provide a better historical
focus for Fascism at the time of the March on Rome and during the
years of the Regime than does anything else.

As I pointed out in my biography, the policy of Mussolini
and the Fascist leadership during the Regime confirmed and perfected the compromise of October 1922 that brought Mussolini to
power. This was achieved with the help of the pre-Fascist ruling
political and economic class and with social forces such as the upper bourgeoisie and what remained of the aristocracy. A direct result, and one of the most important effects of this strengthened
compromise, was the need for Mussolini and his Regime to effect a
transformation and revision of the PNF. This alienated a significant
number of those Fascists, chiefly former squadristi, who were most
intransigent and bound to a destructive political and social perspective of a petty bourgeois type. The purge that took place between
1926 and 1928 radically changed the social physiognomy of the
PNF, which lost its autonomy and was reduced politically to being
an instrument of Mussolini's policies.

The transformation of the PNF is extremely significant, and
two important facts must be stressed: the original Fascist base that
most accurately reflected the crisis and the desire for change on the
part of the middle classes was so much more radical than the Regime that it was judged incompatible with it; and it was not able to

prevent its own political liquidation. The first statement is so self-evident that it needs no further examination. An explanation of the second can be deduced from Salvatorelli's statement to the effect that the middle classes, especially the petty bourgeoisie, were not able on their own to express a viable alternative; their revolutionary aspirations were no more than whimsies. Another, somewhat longer, explanation should be added. As the sociologists have noted, when Fascism rose to power, Italian society and a large part of European society were experiencing a period of intense social and psychological mobilization; it was a period of lively confrontation—highly revolutionary yet at the same time strongly authoritarian—of hitherto legitimate structures. Even the middle classes aspired to their own revolution; in Italy, they thought they could attain it by means of Fascism. This mobilization was followed, in sociological terms, by a traditional process of reintegration and demobilization. The first years of Fascist government in Italy dissipated many hopes for Fascism and brought to the fore the fear of new upheavals and of a leap into the dark. In sum, a new atmosphere existed that discouraged those who might wish to brave unpopularity and the repressive machinery of the Fascist State.

This voluntary and coerced demobilization of the middle classes, with the consequent emergence during the second half of the 1920s of the Fascist Regime as a substantial political and social compromise between the pre-Fascist ruling class and a moderate Fascist elite that had only recently risen in social status but was already quite integrated, should not lead us to believe that the Italian Fascist Regime of the thirties had completely lost the petty and middle bourgeois character that had been the salient feature of Fascism in the twenties, and responsible for its rise to power. Even within the limits of the significant political and social compromise to which Mussolini's Fascist leadership had to acquiesce, and even in the face of the widening margins of Totalitarian autonomy that separated the Regime from the social forces that had created it, there can be no doubt that the real social base of the Italian Fascist Regime remained the middle classes. Two facts confirm this contention. During World War II, when the Regime showed increasing evidence of cracking, individuals from the old Fascism were rehabilitated and brought to the fore (the case of Carlo Scorza is typical), and an attempt was made to relaunch Fascism in terms of a "return to the origins" that for so many years had been considered heretical. Besides its petty bourgeois efforts to vindicate national "honor" and its respect for the "betrayed" alliance, the Italian Social Republic of 1943-1945 advocated a political and social return to the positions occupied during the earliest Fascist period. This could not have been otherwise if we take into account its origins (and those of its principal leaders) and the objective attitude of the remaining two great components of Italian society of the time.

Despite the advantages it gained from Fascism, the upper bourgeoisie never completely accepted the movement. This is explained by psychological and intellectual reasons as well as elements of style and taste and fear. The upper bourgeoisie feared: Fascist interference and control of economic activity; the Fascist elite's tendency to become an autonomous ruling class and to alter the balance of compromise for its own benefit; and Mussolini's increasingly aggressive foreign policy, which overlooked both the real interests of Italy and of the upper bourgeoisie. Part of the upper bourgeoisie was especially interested in the export market; it was more realistic than Mussolini was about the risk of conflict inherent in an alliance with Germany. As for the proletariat, even at the time of the Regime's greatest success, its adherence to Fascism was quantitatively small, tenuous, and characterized by wide areas of discontent and latent opposition. This situation was not buttressed by support from other areas which were also being eroded. Thus, the stronghold of Fascism remained, for better or worse, the middle classes—nor is it by chance that even today the middle classes still express vestiges of neo-Fascism and of nostalgia. The adherence of the middle classes to Fascism persisted, although it was gradually weakened by the Spanish Civil War, the racial campaign, the Axis, and participation in World War II. Although it cannot be said that they constituted the part of Italian society psychologically and culturally most suited to nationalist demagoguery, the middle classes derived, or thought they derived, from the Fascist Regime the major "moral" and economic advantages as well as advantages of social advancement and participation in civil society.

All of this must be recognized in order to understand the Fascist phenomenon in general and, more particularly, Italian Fascism. We must avoid being taken in by Fascism's "proletarian rhetoric" or by the intermittent attacks on the "bourgeois spirit" that it aimed against the upper bourgeoisie and the cultural hegemony it still retained (and to some extent was regaining during the final years of the Regime).

The social bases of Fascism

Having finished this digression on Italian Fascism, let us consider the social bases of Fascism as a phenomenon. Obviously Fascism cannot be considered the product of capitalist and antiproletarian reaction. Yet this is the thesis of those who viewed Fascism as the inevitable result of senescent capitalism. I shall not deny that Fascism must be viewed as a manifestation of class struggle: it was not only a "bilateral" class struggle of the petty bourgeoisie, but it also emanated from the capitalist bourgeoisie. The real problem is to avoid reducing everything to these terms in order to explain Fascism.

At least three reasons dictate against such a simplistic explanation. The first is that the characteristic element that permitted the strengthening of Fascism was the middle classes; we would have to provide a convincing explanation for the fact that, despite the subversivism, revolutionarism, and anticapitalism of the middle classes, the capitalist bourgeoisie succeeded in gaining hegemony over them from the beginning.

Second, as even a Trotskyite such as Guérin recognizes, the capitalist bourgeoisie did not have a univocal attitude toward Fascism. According to Guérin, those who resorted to the Fascist solution to avert the revolutionary threat and regain the position lost during the crisis were "the magnates of heavy industry (iron and steel, mining) and . . . bankers with a stake in heavy industry." "Light industry or finished goods industry" was "noncommittal and sometimes even hostile" toward Fascism; in no way wished to see it triumph; would not have been averse to finding a *modus vivendi* with its own dependents; and, unable to bar the road to Fascism, was only at the end induced "by class solidarity to put aside all diversity of interests" and become "resigned" to Fascist success.

And on that day when fascism, to their amazement, had become a considerable political force in its own right, a pop-

ular movement which could no longer be checked without
the use of armed force, light industry and its liberal politicians put class loyalty ahead of the conflict of interests.
They were loath to shed the blood of "patriots." They resigned themselves to the triumph of fascism. The entire capitalist class united to put fascism into power.[10]

Third, nothing proves that the basic aim of capitalism was
to foster Fascism's rise to power. For capitalism, Fascism was an
ambiguous force, potentially if not substantially alien to its very
nature. Even if Fascism was dominated, there were great risks—as
events demonstrated in Germany especially, but also in Italy—and
it pursued objectives that would increasingly diverge from the natural goals of capitalism. The opinions of authentically Marxist
writers such as Paul A. Baran and Paul Marlor Sweezy are significant in this regard:

> The history of recent decades is particularly rich in ex-
> amples of the substitution of authoritarian for democratic
> government . . . In general, however, moneyed oligarchies
> prefer democratic to authoritarian government. The stabil-
> ity of the system is enhanced by periodic popular ratifica-
> tions of oligarchic rule—this is what parliamentary and
> presidential elections normally amount to—and certain very
> real dangers to oligarchy itself of personal or military dicta-
> torship are avoided. Hence in developed capitalist countries,
> especially those with a long history of democratic govern-
> ment, oligarchies are reluctant to resort to authoritarian
> methods of dealing with opposition movements or solving
> difficult problems, and instead devise more indirect and
> subtle means for accomplishing their ends . . . By these meth-
> ods . . . democracy is made to serve the interests of the oli-
> garchy far more effectively and durably than authoritarian
> rule.[11]

The relation between the upper bourgeoisie and Fascism
should be viewed, not in a mechanistic and unilateral, but in an
articulated manner that relates the attitude of the capitalist forces,
especially the financiers and industrialists, to the broader attitude
of the contemporary ruling classes. From this perspective it be-

comes clear that Fascism was understood and used by individual
and local groups of capitalists as a "white guard" to crush the resistance of proletarian class organizations and to avoid turmoil related to the "freedom of work" and so on, but had no support from
the "central" organizations.[12]

In a later phase, when Fascism was well on the way to becoming an autonomous mass movement, the fact that support of it
became more consistent did not in any way signify that the upper
bourgeoisie contemplated relinquishing its power. Part of the upper
bourgeoisie merely wanted to use Fascism to smash the labor movement, whereas the majority wanted a return to normalcy from a
situation of chronic and intolerable political crisis.[13] But, by granting Fascism a place in coalition governments during this later period, the financial and industrial upper bourgeoisie, who had not
understood the true nature and novelty of Fascism, committed the
same errors of judgment that the political and liberal democratic
class had made in both Italy and Germany. They believed that by
granting Fascism a place in the government they could resolve the
political crisis and simultaneously "normalize" and "constitutional-
ize" Fascism—in short, establish hegemony over it and absorb it
into the system. But this did not mean that the great majority became Fascist. Bauer illustrated this psychological and political process when he wrote with regard to Germany:

> Could it be that the capitalist class and the Junkers had be-
> come National Socialists? Not at all. Basically, they had
> contempt for "the housepainter" who aspired to power and
> for the totally plebeian movement—supported by the petty
> bourgeoisie, peasants, and all manner of dispossessed indi-
> viduals, and imbued by a utopian petty bourgeois anticapi-
> talism—that they sustained. But, just as in Italy Giolitti
> thought he could use Fascism to intimidate, push back, and
> tame the rebellious working class, so in Germany the capi-
> talists and the Junkers believed they could use the National
> Socialist movement to overcome the influence of social
> democracy and the trade-unions; to break the resistance of
> the working class to reduced salaries, the annulment of legis-
> lation governing protection of labor and social insurance, to
> the policies of deflation of capital dictatorship and large
> landownership. But in this respect also Fascism soon slipped

away from the control of the capitalist classes. In Germany, too, the time came when the Junkers and the capitalists had no other alternative but to overthrow Fascism and thus displace the power relationship in favor of the working class, or to hand over the State power to Fascism. Faced with this situation, the Junkers, who made up Hindenburg's circle, decided to grant Hitler power over the State. As in Italy, the representatives of the historical bourgeois parties became a part of the first Fascist government, here too they thought they could dominate and assimilate Fascism in the government. But, even more rapidly than in Italy, German Fascism, once in power, used it to expel the bourgeois parties from the government, to dissolve bourgeois parties and organizations, to impose their own "totalitarian" dictatorship.[14]

The consequences of these errors of judgment were soon felt. Under Fascism the upper bourgeoisie certainly did not lose its position of rank; certain sectors even derived far-from-negligible benefits. But even the upper bourgeoisie had to come to terms, in Germany especially, with the steady drift toward autonomous Totalitarian power. The so-called capitalist magnates often witnessed the destruction of some of the interests they had most jealously defended. Gradually their political power was eroded, and they often found themselves in opposition to the new Fascist elite, concerning specific sectoral problems as well as basic policies that Fascism sought to apply to the national economy. The upper bourgeoisie was unable to dictate its own policies because of insufficient imagination and excessive caution, and because in effect it had lost political power.[15] In the final analysis, its members risked being swept away by the fall of Fascism; where they were able to avoid this eventuality, they had to pay a stiff price for their errors.

The changing state and the revolutionary nature of Fascism
So much for Fascism's social base. At least two other elements must be kept in mind for a historical understanding of the overall phenomenon of Fascism. The first concerns certain economic, bureaucratic, institutional, and social aspects of Fascist states. These aspects have been discussed a great deal in recent

years, and we have much clearer notions about some of them.[16]
What should be emphasized, however, is that, where basic motivations are concerned, a sharp distinction often is not made between
what is typically and intrinsically Fascist content and what should
be related to the objective demands of the times—to the development of a mass society that could no longer be ruled with the instruments, techniques, and mentality of an earlier age. To understand
the historic reality of Fascist regimes, we cannot overlook their
Totalitarian form. But this Totalitarian form must not be confused
with growth and changes in the functions of the State which, as
Löwenthal has stressed, are typical of modern pluralistic capitalist
societies. One sign of this is the growing tendency of the State to
centralize and influence production and to subsidize and plan certain activities. Let us bear in mind the increasingly widespread
social insurance and social security systems and the importance
assumed by collective contracts and their "standardization." If this
distinction is not made, we not only fail to plumb the depth of Fascist reality, but we run the risk of attributing to Fascism a trend
present in all countries that have attained a certain degree of development. This would reinforce recent investigators of Fascism
whose vision is blurred by ideological and political prejudices
toward the existing political and social system, and who actually
claim to perceive in them a "subrosa reevaluation of the neoauthoritarian, reformist State."

The second thing that must be taken into account in any historical judgment of the Fascist phenomenon is the unquestionable
revolutionary nature of Fascism. Many scholars, Löwenthal among
them, have recognized it. In a historical analysis, acknowledgment
of this obvious fact is hampered by a fairly widespread ideological
and political prejudice that has assigned a magical, binding, and
unique meaning to the word "revolution." Jules Monnerot has written: "The word 'revolution' is always construed in a positive light;
when this shall no longer be the case, we shall have entered a new
epoch."[17]

The refusal to consider Fascism a revolutionary phenomenon stems from this idea. It is a refusal that cannot be accepted in
historical scholarship, because it precludes an understanding of the
narrow and indissoluble tie between Fascism and mass society and

the role Fascism played in what Del Noce calls "the age of secularization."[18] Under such circumstances, Fascism's uniqueness in comparison with classical authoritarian regimes would not be appreci-
ated; neither would its novelty in regard to occasional revolts that
lacked an effective institutional outlet. Nor would we be able to
understand the important difference between Fascism and other
contemporary revolutions, such as Communism's illusory political
and social revolution, neocapitalism's falsely democratic technical
revolution, and that "necessary" revolution of values which, according to Jacques Ellul, can be the only *true* revolution.[19]

Notes

Chapter 1. Fascism as a Problem of Interpretation

1. Pelham Horton Box, *Three Master Builders and Another: Studies in Modern Revolutionary and Liberal Statesmanship* (Philadelphia, Lippincott, 1925); Herbert Wallace Schneider, *Making the Fascist State* (New York, Oxford University Press, 1928); Schneider, in collaboration with Shepard Bancroft Clough, wrote *Making Fascists* (Chicago, University of Chicago Press, 1929). Other studies include that of Carmen Haider, *Capital and Labor under Fascism* (New York, Columbia University Press, 1930).

2. George Macaulay Trevelyan, *The Historical Causes of the Present State of Affairs in Italy* (London and New York, Oxford, 1923); Paul Hazard, *Italie Vivante* (Paris, Perrin, 1923), and *Les livres, les enfants et les hommes* (Paris, Flammarion, 1932). For Hazard's position with regard to Fascism, see Giuseppe Recuperati, "Paul Hazard," *Belfagor* (September 1968), pp. 579 ff.

3. Herbert Lionel Matthews, *The Fruits of Fascism* (New York, Harcourt, Brace, 1943), p. 5, observed: "Once upon a time, a great many of us, even in our democratic countries, were saying that what we needed was another Mussolini. Those were the days when tourists and observers who had gone to Italy used to point out that the trains ran on time, that strikes ceased, and that the Italians were no longer burning down buildings or breaking each other's heads in street fighting. If you are inclined to laugh at these ingenuous people now, it may be well to think of those more recent years of 'appeasement' when the Axis had persuaded so many millions in so many countries that the future of the world was theirs, that poor old democracy and liberalism were dying, that here was a new, young and vigorous way of life."

   Matthews' work, which was deservedly praised by Croce, has been generally forgotten by students of Italian Fascism. It is well worth consideration, not only because it is astute and balanced, but also because at the time it was written and published every discussion of Fascism was often grossly schematic and characterized by unrelenting demonology.

Interesting insight into the acceptance Italian Fascism met abroad is found among certain American writings of the New Deal. For a summary that also covers the first half of the thirties, see Arthur Meier Schlesinger, Jr., *The Age of Roosevelt*, 3 vols. (Boston, Houghton Mifflin, 1957-1960).

4. George Douglas Howard Cole, *A History of Socialist Thought: IV, Communism and Social Democracy, 1914-1931,* part II, (London, Macmillan; New York, St. Martin's, 1958), p. 851.

5. Henry Stuart Hughes, *Contemporary Europe: A History* (Englewood Cliffs, N.J., Prentice-Hall, 1961), p. 238, points out that in international circles, until the outbreak of World War II, Italian Fascism, and Mussolini in particular, were viewed more favorably than National Socialism and offered "the more characteristic model for a fascist control of society."

6. John Strachey, *The Menace of Fascism* (London, Gollancz, 1933).

7. The publication of Hermann Rauschning's *Die Revolution des Nihilismus: Kulisse und Wirklichkeit im dritten Reich* (5th ed., Zurich and New York, Europa, 1938) signaled an important phase in this debate. Rauschning, an ex-Nazi who had broken with Hitler, drew attention to the coexistence in National Socialism of conservative and revolutionary elements and the significance of this amalgam. He considered National Socialism the consequence of the disintegration, begun some time before, of the ruling class and its spheres of influence and of the general dissolution of all traditional classes, including the peasants. He particularly viewed it as the result of a new primitive elite expressed by the masses, who were looking for elementary political forms, for a "plebiscitary democracy of the masses."

8. For Italian Fascism, see Louis Rosenstock-Franck, *L'économie corporative fasciste en doctrine et en fait: Ses origines historiques et son évolution* (Paris, Librairie Universitaire, 1934); Herman Finer, *Mussolini's Italy* (New York, Holt; London, Gollancz, 1935; new ed. Hamden, Conn., Anchor Books, 1964); William George Welk, *Fascist Economic Policy: An Analysis of Italy's Economic Experiment* (Cambridge, Mass., Harvard University Press, 1938); Carl Theodore Schmidt, *The Corporative State in Action: Italy under Fascism* (New York and Toronto, Oxford University Press, 1936).

9. For perhaps the most refined and thoughtful attempt to reduce the classic interpretations to the moral-disease theory, see Leo Valiani, "Il problema politico della nazione italiana," in Achille Battaglia, ed., *Dieci anni dopo (1945-1955)* (Bari, Laterza, 1955), pp. 4 ff.

10. The essays of M. Bardèche bear witness to this incapacity; see *Qu'est-ce que le Fascisme?*, whose appendix contains a debate on the subject conducted in France in 1962 and the author's reply. See also Giulio Cesare Andrea Evola, *Il fascismo: saggio di una analisi critica dal punto di vista della destra* (Rome, Volpe, 1964).

11. In the literature of the 1950s and 1960s on ideologies and their crises, the problem of Fascism was often mentioned and in most interesting observations. Of special importance are the comments of Raymond Aron, *L'opium des intellectuels* (Paris, Calmann-Lévy, 1955), where the author denies that Fascism and National Socialism were "a scarcely original variation of the reaction or an effect of the State superstructure of monopoly capitalism." He stresses several common aspects of "Totalitarianism of the Right" (Fascism) and "Totalitarianism of the Left" (Communism), asserting that "neither Fascism nor National Socialism was entirely or essentially, counterrevolutionary" in that they did not strive for, especially in the latter instance, a return to the past, but "broke with the past as radically as did Communism."
     More recently small groups of the extraparliamentary Leftist opposition have conducted an exasperated review of the ideology of Fascism. According to these new interpretations, there is no substantial difference between Fascism and its " 'liberal' parallel or the systems that succeeded them (for example, the New Deal in the United States, or the Federal Republic of Germany at the beginning of the Cold War)"; *La ribellione degli studenti* (Milan, 1968); quoted sentence by W. Lefèvre, p. 179. For an evaluation of Italian Fascism see Renzo del Carria, *Proletari senza rivoluzione: Storia delle classi subalterne italiane dal 1860 al 1950* (Milan, Oriente, 1966), II, 145 ff. According to the author, Fascism should be viewed as "the joining of aggressive 'nascent capitalism' of the middle class with the terrorist reaction of monopolies in crisis."

12. Helio Jaguaribe, "Brésil, stabilité sociale par le colonialfascisme?" *Les Temps Modernes* (October 1967), pp. 602 ff., has actually elaborated a model of "colonial Fascism," that is, of Fascism in semi-colonial countries such as Brazil. For

an understanding of so-called Fascist Latin American political regimes, studies such as those of Gino Germani (to be
mentioned later), or those collected by Virgilio Rafael Bel-
trán in *El papel político y social de las Fuerzas Armadas en
América Latina* (Caracas, 1970), are of much greater value.

13. The article "Goldwaterism" in the *Monthly Review* (September
    1964) is significant. Not only does it decry the indiscriminate
    use of the Fascist label "for all reactionary police states" and
    attempt to group the principal characteristics of Fascism that
    can be deduced from the German and Italian experiences,
    but it also notes overall differences between certain con-
    temporary regimes or movements that can be considered
    Fascist, and others to which the term is misapplied. The
    authors' explanations of why the term cannot be used with
    reference to the Gaullist regime are extremely astute; their
    attempts to consider Goldwaterism as a proto-Fascist move-
    ment are much less convincing.

14. Theo Pirker, ed., *Komintern und Faschismus 1920-1940* (Stutt-
    gart, Deutsche Verlags Anstalt, 1965); Wolfgang Aben-
    droth, ed., *Faschismus and Kapitalismus* (Frankfurt, Euro-
    päische Verlags-Anstalt; Vienna, Europa, 1967); Ernst
    Nolte, *Theorien über den Faschismus* (Cologne and Berlin,
    Kiepenheuer u. Witsch, 1967); and Milorad Ermečic, *Os-
    nove gradanske diktature u Europi izmedu dva svjetska
    zata* (Sarajevo, Zavod za izdavanje udzbenika, 1965); Franz
    Leopold Neumann, *Demokratischer and autoritärer Staat*
    (Frankfurt, Europäische Verlags-Anstalt; Vienna, Europa,
    1967).

15. The records of the two meetings were published respectively in
    S. J. Woolf, ed., *The Nature of Fascism: Proceedings of a
    conference held by the Reading University Graduate School
    of Contemporary European Studies* (London, Weidenfeld
    and Nicolson, 1968; New York, Random House, 1969); and
    in *Fasišmus a Evropa. Fascism and Europe*, 2 vols. (Prague,
    1969-1970).

16. Boris Removich Lopuhkov, *Fašizm i rabočee dvizenie v Italii
    (1919-1929)* (Moscow, Harka, 1968), is significant.

17. Ernst Nolte, *Der Faschismus in seiner Epoche: Die Action Fran-
    çaise, Der Italienische Faschismus, Der Nationalsozialismus*
    (Munich, Piper, 1963); trans. Leila Vennewitz, *Three Faces
    of Fascism: Action Française, Italian Fascism, National
    Socialism* (New York, Holt, Rinehart and Winston, 1966).

18. The most mature and important book is George Lachmann Mosse, *The Crisis of German Ideology: Intellectual Origins of the Third Reich* (New York, Grosset and Dunlap, 1964), which outlines the more significant features of National Socialism and the basic differences between it and other Fascist manifestations, Italian Fascism especially.

19. A warning about the pitfalls of this thesis can be found in a neglected article by "P. Davila" (pseud. Claudio Treves?), "Charakteristik des italienischen Faschismus und des balkanische Faschismus," *La Fédération balkanique* (Vienna; April 1, 1929). Here the characteristics of Italian Fascism and the Fascisms of the Balkans are examined. For Davila, they differed to the degree that they represented two different stages of economic and political development. True Fascism (Italian Fascism) was marked by the struggle of the capitalist bourgeoisie against an evolved and organized proletarian movement; to prevent its gaining a foothold, the capitalist bourgeoisie destroyed the liberal and democratic institutions it had created, which the proletariat wanted to use for its own purposes. On the other hand, Fascism in Eastern Europe and the Balkans recreated situations that had already occurred in the rest of Europe. Although they, too, had recourse to the violent methods of Italian Fascism, the youthful bourgeoisie and residual feudal military groups in these countries tried to prevent a still backward proletariat from gaining strength within the liberal democratic state— without, however, destroying the institutions of the state but, rather, using them against the proletariat.

    We must be more cautious with the period around World War II, for at this time the needs of the moment often and significantly modified the original characteristics of the various Fascisms. Certain Quisling regimes were actually expressions of the Nazi occupation and contingent situations rather than true Fascist regimes.

20. There has been mention of a Japanese Fascism—see Masao Maruyama, *Thought and Behaviour in Modern Japanese Politics*, trans. Ivan Morris (London and New York, Oxford University Press, 1963)—and even more insistently of an Argentine Fascism, Peronism—see Robert Jackson Alexander, *The Perón Era* (New York, Columbia University Press, 1951). In my opinion it is impossible to consider these Fascist, even though certain aspects of political phenomena in both countries recall European Fascisms. The historical contexts and social aspects of these presumed Fascist movements, however, are completely different. Insofar as Argen-

tina is concerned, the differences are made very clear in the studies of Gino Germani (although he inserts Peronism in the Fascist model), "Algunas repercusiones sociales de los cambios económicos en la Argentina (1940-1950)," *Cursos y Conferencias del Colegio libre de Estudios Superiores* (Buenos Aires), 40:238-240 (January-March 1952), and *Integración politica de las masas y el totalitarismo* (Buenos Aires, 1956).

21. The close bonds between Fascism and mass society were first noted explicitly by José Ortega y Gasset in the essay "Sobre el fascismo," and then in *La rebellión de las masas* (Madrid, Revista de Occidente, 1930).

22. The element that should be most thoroughly studied and applied for relevance is nationalism. For bibliographical information on the subject see Ottavio Bariè, "Les nationalismes totalitaires," in Max Beloff, ed., *L'Europe du XIXe et du XXe siècle, III, (1914-aujourd'hui)* (Milan, Marzorati, 1959-1964), I, 155 ff.

23. See, for Fascism, Renzo De Felice, *Storia degli ebrei italiani sotto il fascismo* (Turin, Einaudi, 1961).

24. For the mass psychological and political significance of this myth see David Krech and Richard S. Crutchfield, *Théorie et problèmes de psychologie sociale* (Paris, 1952), II, 568 ff.

25. See the definition of Henri Michel, "Introduction sur le 'Fascisme,' " *Revue d'histoire de la deuxième guerre mondiale* (Paris; April 1967), p. 1. According to this, the Fascist regime was conservative but not reactionary (in that it did not seek a return to "the golden age of the past"), and it was revolutionary in its techniques of power. For analogies and differences between the classic Right and Fascism, see René Remond, *La Droite en France de la Première Restauration à la V république* (3rd ed., Paris, Montaigne, 1968); trans. into Italian as *La Destra in Francia dalla restaurazione alla V Repubblica (1915-1968)* (Milan, 1970), pp. 224 ff.

26. Compare George Lachmann Mosse, "La genesi del fascismo," *Dialoghi del XXX* (April 1967), pp. 20 ff.

27. Hughes, *Contemporary Europe*, pp. 332 ff.

28. For an overall picture see Renzo De Felice, "Faschismus" in the

Herder encyclopedia, *Sowjetsystem und Demokratische Gesellschaft.* See also the entry under "Fascismo" by Renzo De Felice in the Italian edition of the Feltrinelli-Fischer encyclopedia (*Storia*), which largely follows previous editions of this book.

Chapter 2. The Classic Interpretations

1. Benedetto Croce, *Scritti e discorsi politici, 1943-1947* (Bari, Laterza, 1963), I, 7 ff.; II, 46 ff., 357 ff.

2. Friedrich Meinecke, *The German Catastrophe: Reflections and Recollections,* trans. Sidney B. Fay (Cambridge, Mass., Harvard University Press, 1950), pp. 1-2.

3. On some potential Totalitarian aspects of modern democratic thought (and on their possible evolution into full Totalitarianism, of the Left or of the Right) and on their first concrete manifestations during the French Revolution, see the important study by Jacob Leib Talmon, *The Origins of Totalitarian Democracy* (London, Fecker and Warburg, 1952).

4. Meinecke, *The German Catastrophe,* p. 37.

5. Ibid., pp. 44-45.

6. Ibid., p. 51.

7. Gerhard Ritter, *Die Dämonie der Macht* (Munich, Leibniz, 1948; Stuttgart, H. F. C. Hannsmann, 1947), p. 167. Other works by Ritter include *Europa und die deutsche Frage: Betrachtungen über die geschichtliche des deutschen Staatsdenkens* (Munich, Münchner, 1948); "The Historical Foundation of the Rise of National Socialism," in Gerhard Ritter, ed., *The Third Reich* (London, 1955); "Le origini storiche del Nazionalsocialismo," in *Nuove questioni di storia contemporanea* (Milan, Marzorati, 1968).

8. See discussion in Chapter 8.

9. Golo Mann, *Deutsche Geschichte des 19. und 20. Jahrhunderts* (Frankfurt, S. Fischer, 1958); trans. Marian Jackson, *The History of Germany since 1789* (New York, Praeger, 1968), pp. 416-417.

10. On the attitude of the German army toward National Social-

ism until 1933, see Thilo Vogelsang, *Reichswehr, Staat und NSDAP* (Stuttgart, Deutsche Verlags Anstalt, 1962). For an evaluation tending to stress the role and responsibility of the armed forces and industrial spheres in the establishment of National Socialism, see George Wolfgang Felix Hallgarten, *Hitler, Reichswehr und Industrie: Zur Geschichte der Jahre 1918-1933* (Frankfurt, Europäische Verlags Anstalt, 1955). For a criticism of Hallgarten's views see H. A. Turner, Jr., and Ernst Nolte in the *American Historical Review* (October-December 1969).

11. Mann, *History of Germany*, p. 447.

12. Hans Kohn, *The Twentieth Century: The Challenge to the West and Its Response* (New York, Macmillan, 1957; 1st ed., 1949), p. 50.

13. Ibid., pp. 56-57.

14. Ibid., p. 75.

15. Nino Valeri, "La marcia su Roma," in *Fascismo e antifascismo, I (1918-1936)* (Milan, Feltrinelli, 1962), pp. 104-105.

16. By Edmond Vermeil see also *L'Allemagne contemporaine: Sociale, politique et culturelle, 1890-1950* (Paris, Aubier, 1952-1953); trans. L. J. Ludovici, *The German Scene, Social, Political and Cultural, 1890 to the Present Day* (London, Harrap, 1956).

17. Gerhard Ritter, *Staatskunst und Kriegshandwerk: Das Problem des "Militarismus" in Deutschland* (Munich, Oldenbourg, 1954-1960); trans. Heinz Norden, *The Sword and the Scepter: The Problem of Militarism in Germany*, 4 vols. (Coral Gables, Fla., University of Miami Press, 1969-1973).

18. A description of the debate is found in Bariè, "Les nationalismes totalitaires"; see Chapter 1, note 22.

19. Denis Mack Smith, *Italy: A Modern History* (Ann Arbor, University of Michigan Press, 1959), p. 140. See Walter Maturi, *Interpretazioni del Risorgimento: lezioni di storia della storiografia* (Turin, Einaudi, 1962), pp. 686 ff.

20. In the sphere of Crocean thought numerous essays have stressed the particular "germs" of the Fascist phenomenon. Four arti-

cles by Carlo Antoni, significant because of their treatment
of Nazism as a cultural phenomenon, appeared in *La nuova
Europa* (Rome; Dec. 17, 1944, Jan. 14, 28, Feb. 25, 1945).

21. The criticism raised against the revelation interpretation in *La
    Rivista trimestrale* (Turin), nos. 19-20 (September-Decem-
    ber 1966), pp. 404 ff., is significant in the second sense, espe-
    cially because of the obvious influence of Chabod's argu-
    ments. "At the time of the most important crisis under
    Giolitti . . . all possibility of effective bourgeois hegemony
    had been used up. Consequently, it had exhausted the hege-
    mony of the homogeneous political forces, which had taken
    the lead in the formation of a unitary state. Thus, the sub-
    sequent vacuum of power, which was impossible to fill by
    democratic and positive means, made the country prey to
    the Fascist adventure.
        "This extreme and catastrophic operation, brought about
    by the inability of the bourgeoisie to sustain hegemonic di-
    rection and by the resultant shattering of free-trade liberal-
    ism and its political and State figures, could only have been
    avoided by a *transfer of hegemony* corresponding to the
    very development of national reality, that is, the coming to
    power (and hence to constructive responsibility for the gov-
    erning of the nation) of those new social forces—the Catho-
    lics and the proletariat—that had of necessity organized in
    parties able to effect an internal critique of the ways in
    which the State had developed during the Risorgimento:
    these were the Socialists and the Catholic Democrats. We
    refer to an *internal* critique because the Catholics, with
    Sturzo, had definitely come to accept the State, but placed
    themselves in the opposition; and because the Socialists,
    although they were the natural expression of policies anti-
    thetical to the bourgeoisie, were born and became *organized*
    forms of the proletarian class because they recognized the
    historical and dialectical positiveness of capitalism.
        "As we have noted, these two political forces were unable
    to make the transition in time from the role of critics to that
    of hegemonic partnership. In that crucial time immediately
    following the war they allowed themselves to be conditioned
    throughout by their respective ideological exclusivism, so
    that they confronted the Giolitti forces with prejudice and,
    therefore, in vain. Moreover, they confronted and competed
    against each other. This explains, we think, why both were
    defeated by Giolitti, and later by Giolitti and Fascism. The
    responsibility for the advent of Fascism must therefore be
    borne not only by the Giolittian forces because of their ob-

jective limitations—nor just by the Monarchy and the Vatican—but also, and especially, by Turati, Sturzo, and Bordiga."

22. Gerhard Ritter, *The German Resistance*, trans. R. T. Clark (London, Allen and Unwin, 1958; New York, Praeger, 1959), pp. 37-39. The first two paragraphs quoted are from the Clark translation; the remainder, not included in his abridged version of Ritter's book, can be found in the original German publication.

23. Maurice Herbert Dobb, *Political Economy and Capitalism: Some Essays in Economic Tradition* (London, Routledge, 1937), pp. 262-264.

24. Paul A. Baran and Paul Marlor Sweezy, *Monopoly Capital: An Essay on the American Economic and Social Order* (New York, Monthly Review Press, 1966), pp. 156-157.

25. See also Maurice H. Dobb, *Problemi di storia del capitalismo* (Rome, 1958), p. 413.

26. Arthur Rosenberg [Historicus, pseud.], *Der Faschismus als Massenbewegung* (Karlsbad, 1934); reprinted in Abendroth, ed., *Faschismus und Kapitalismus*, pp. 75 ff.

27. August Thalheimer, "Über den Faschismus," *Gegen den Strom* (Berlin), nos. 2-4 (11, 18, and 25 Jan. 1930); reprinted in Renzo De Felice, ed., *Il Fascismo: Le interpretazioni dei contemporanei e degli storici* (Bari, Laterza, 1970), pp. 272 ff.

28. Thalheimer was referring primarily to Karl Marx, *The Eighteenth Brumaire of Louis Bonaparte*, trans. Daniel De Leon (New York, International Publishing Co., 1898), and Karl Marx, *The Civil War in France: An Address to the General Council of the International Workingmen's Association* (London, Truelove, 1871), and to *Gewalt und Ökonomie bei der Herstellung der neuen Deutsches Reiches* by Engels.

29. Otto Bauer, *Der Faschismus* (Bratislava, 1936); reprinted in De Felice, ed., *Il Fascismo: Le interpretazioni dei contemporanei*, pp. 355 ff.

30. Ibid., pp. 371 ff.

31. George Douglas Howard Cole, *A History of Socialist Thought: V, Socialism and Fascism (1931-1939)* (London, Macmillan, 1960), pp. 3, 5.

32. George Douglas Howard Cole, *A History of Socialist Thought: IV, Communism and Social Democracy (1914-1931)* (London, Macmillan, 1960), II, 454.

33. Cole, *History of Socialist Thought: V,* pp. 5-6.

34. Leo Huberman and Paul Marlor Sweezy, *La controrivoluzione globale* (Turin, 1968), pp. 68-69.

35. Some Marxist-Communist views about the rise of Fascism in certain countries are found in "Les origines du fascisme," *Recherches internationales à la lumière du marxisme* (Paris, May and June 1958).

36. See, for example, the Hungarian journal *Történelmi Szemle,* 1962, nos. 3 and 4, and, especially, Boris R. Lopukhov's book on Italian Fascism in the years between 1919 and 1929.

37. Enzo Collotti, "Fascismo internazionale: un aggiornamento bibliografico," *Il Movimento di Liberazione in Italia* (July-September 1968), p. 114, observed that "dogmatic and fatalistic schematizations by the Communist International not only made discussion about Fascism sterile and carried it beyond its objective roots, but they had significant consequences in the concrete political field in determining the tactics of the Communist parties (especially the German Communist party) before the coming to power of National Socialism in Germany, in the sense that on the basis of these schematizations not only was it impossible to determine the qualitative differences between National Socialism and the bourgeois regimes that had preceded it, but it was not even possible to organize anti-Fascist opposition within a realistic framework." Compare Heinz Brahm, "Die Bolschewistische Deutung des deutschen 'Faschismus' in den Jahren 1923 bis 1928," *Jahrbücher für Geschichte Osteuropas* (Munich, 1964), no. 3.

   For first-hand information on the Social Fascism theory see Siegfried Bahne, " 'Sozialfaschismus' in Deutschland: Zur Geschichte eines politischen Begriffs," *International Review of Social History,* no. 2 (Assen, Netherlands, 1965);

and Paolo Spriano, "L'esperienza di Tasca a Mosca e il 'socialfascismo, '" *Studi storici* (Rome, 1969), no. 1.

38. B. R. Lopukhov, "Il problema del fascismo italiano negli scritti di autori sovietici," *Studi storici* (April-June 1965), p. 255.

39. For the principal official positions of the Third International, see Jane Degras, *The Communist International (1919-1943): Documents*, 3 vols. (London and New York, Oxford University Press, 1956-1965). For their analysis, see J. M. Cammett, "Communist Theories of Fascism (1920-1935)," *Science and Society* (Paris; 1967), no. 2; E. Lewin, "Zum Faschismus: Analyse durch die Kommunistische Internationale," *Beiträge zur Geschichte der deutschen Arbeiterbewegung* (Berlin, 1970), no. 1; Jules Monnerot, *Sociologie de la révolution: mythologies politiques du XXe siècle, marxistes-leninistes et fascistes, la nouvelle stratégie révolutionnaire* (Paris, Fayard, 1969), pp. 614 ff.; Nicos Poulantzas, *Fascisme et dictature: La Troisième Internationale face au fascisme* (Paris, Maspéro, 1970).

40. With regard to Italian Communists, see the editorial in the first issue of *Lo Stato Operaio* (Milan and Rome; March 1927); reprinted in Franco Ferri, ed., *Lo Stato operaio (1927-1939)* (Rome, Riuniti, 1964), I, 3 ff., esp. 5-6.

41. Degras, *Communist International*, II, 484. Passages translated in the Degras book are interspersed with others which the author quoted from a more complete Italian version on the International.

42. For these and other observations on Fascism, see Georgi Dimitrov, *La Terza Internazionale*, trans. Giorgio Kraisky (Rome, O.E.T., 1945), p. 4.

43. Degras, *Communist International*, II, 377.

44. For the position of Karl Radek, see "L'internazionale comunista davanti al fascismo," *Pagine Rosse* (Aug. 5, 1928), where it is asserted that "the roots of fascism are in the proletarization, as a result of the war, of the important masses of the urban lower middle class," and where Fascism is defined as a type of "socialism of the middle classes" from which the latter expect what they had hoped for but never obtained from the traditional lower-middle-class parties and from the Socialists.

45. For a more precise frame of reference for the resolution, see the unabridged intervention of Klara Zetkin before the Executive in June 1923, partially reprinted in Ernesto Ragionieri, *Italia giudicata (1861-1945)* (Bari, Laterza, 1969), pp. 533 ff. An interesting example of the opinions about a political evaluation of Italian Fascism circulating in Communist circles before the Matteotti assassination is found in the small volume by Mátyás Rákosi, *Italianskij fascism* (Leningrad, 1925).

46. Degras, *Communist International*, II, 41.

47. Dimitrov, *La Terza Internazionale*, pp. 3 ff.

48. Leon Trotsky, *Ecrits* (Paris, Marcel Rivière, 1958), II, 5-6, 61 ff., 158 ff., 123 ff., 12 ff., 49-50; *Ecrits* (Paris, Marcel Rivière, 1959), III, 111 ff., 123 ff., 397 ff., 29 ff., 270 ff. For Trotsky (III, 272-273), although the bourgeoisie needed Fascism to retain power, it did not like "plebeian" methods of Fascism.

49. An updated edition appeared in 1965. Also by Daniel Guérin see *La Peste brune a passé par là: Un témoignage sur les débuts du régime nazi* (Paris, Editions universelles, 1945). Of particular interest is Guérin's attempt to study the different attitudes that heavy and light industry took during the initial phases of Fascism. According to him, the former subsidized and supported Fascism; the latter proved to be reserved and occasionally hostile.

50. Richard Löwenthal [Paul Sering, pseud.], "Der Faschismus," *Zeitschrift für Sozialismus* (Karlsbad; September-October 1935); reprinted in De Felice, ed., *Il Fascismo*, pp. 296 ff., 319 ff. The essay was the second part of a larger work that might usefully be consulted in its entirety. Löwenthal [Sering, pseud.] published another work on Fascism ten years later, entitled *Jenseits des Kapitalismus: Ein Beitrag zur sozialistischen Neuorientierung* (Nuremberg, Nest-Verlag, 1946).

51. Löwenthal, "Der Faschismus," pp. 326, 328.

52. György Lukács, *Die Zerstörung der Vernunft* (Berlin, Aufbau-Verlag, 1954). Herbert Marcuse, "The Struggle against Liberation in the Totalitarian View of the State," in *Negations;*

Essays in Critical Theory, trans. Jeremy J. Shapiro (Boston, Beacon, 1968).

Chapter 3. Other Interpretations, 1930s-1960s

1. In this chapter we shall study three of the minor interpretations: the Catholic, Totalitarian, and Transpolitical forms of Fascism. The restricted scope of this book prevents a discussion of interpretations related to the three classic forms, and precursors or offshoots of the varieties of Fascism treated in the next chapter will be discussed along with their main branches. Other minor varieties include individual positions that, although not devoid of interest or historical import, are tangential to our present purpose.

   Mention should be made of an interpretation put forward by James Burnham in *The Managerial Revolution* (New York, John Day, 1941). According to Burnham, in the course of the general wearing down of capitalist society and the translation of its ideology into fact, a basic tendency emerges toward a society where control of the economic process—hence, of politics in the strictest sense—passes into the hands of the managerial class. The latter expresses its own ideologies, characteristic of its society and differing from those of capitalist society. Burnham defines Nazism, Stalinism, and the New Deal as managerial ideologies: "There is, in truth, not a formal identity, but a historical bond uniting Stalinism (communism), Nazism (fascism), and New Dealism. Against differing developmental backgrounds and at different stages of growth, they are all *managerial* ideologies. They all have the same historical direction: away from capitalist society and toward managerial society."

2. Jacques Maritain, *Humanisme intégral* (Paris, 1936); *True Humanism*, trans. M. R. Adamson (London, Centenary, 1938), pp. 152-153. A substantial part of this book is comprised of six lectures delivered in August 1934.

3. According to Maritain, there were various forms of Fascism, "whose specifications are very diverse," but which have common generic characteristics; *True Humanism*, pp. 272-274, 279.

4. Among the essays, see especially "Totalitarismo e filosofia della storia," *Il Mulino* (February 1957), and "Idee per l'interpretazione del fascismo," *Ordine Civile* (15 April 1960), collected in Costanzo Casucci, ed., *Il Fascismo: Antologia di scritti critici* (Bologna, Il Mulino, 1961), pp. 359 ff., 370 ff.;

see also the introduction to *Il problema dell'ateismo* (Bologna, 1964); and *Il problema politico dei cattolici* (Rome, 1967).

After World War II, French Catholic values shifted, often away from Maritain's interpretations, in the most varied and contradictory directions. An excellent example are the articles in a special issue of *Esprit* (December 1947) devoted to Fascism, especially that by J. M. Domenach.

5. Casucci, ed., *Il Fascismo*, pp. 362-363.

6. Ibid., pp. 360 ff. For Del Noce's refutation of various interpretations, see *Il Fascismo*, and *Il problema dell'ateismo*, p. cxlviii.

7. Del Noce, *Il problema dell'ateismo*, pp. cxxxviii-cxxxix.

8. Casucci, ed., *Il Fascismo*, p. 383.

9. Del Noce, *Il problema dell'ateismo*, pp. cl ff.

10. For views of these origins, see Les K. Adler and T. G. Paterson, "Red Fascism: The Merger of Nazi Germany and Soviet Russia in the American Image of Totalitarianism (1930's-1950's)," *American Historical Review* (April 1970), pp. 1046 ff.

11. On Latin American caudillismo, see Riccardo Campa, *Antologia del pensiero politico latino-americano: Dalla colonia alla seconda guerra mondiale* (Bari, Laterza, 1970). For Spanish caudillismo, see the interpretations of Arias Salgado, Franco's Minister of Education, quoted in Giuseppe Maranini, *Storia del potere in Italia (1848-1967)* (Florence, Vallecchi, 1967), p. 298.

12. See Wolfgang Sauer, "National Socialism: Totalitarianism of Fascism?" *American Historical Review* (December 1967), pp. 404 ff.

13. See also Carl J. Friedrich, *Totalitarianism* (Cambridge, Mass., 1945); Carl J. Friedrich, ed., *Totalitarianism: Proceedings of a Conference held at the American Academy of Arts and Sciences* (Cambridge, Mass., Harvard University Press, 1954); Hans Buchheim, *Totalitarian Rule: Its Nature and Characteristics*, trans. Ruth Hein (Middletown, Conn., Wesleyan University Press, 1968).

Certain studies of Totalitarian elites published in the United States since the 1930s can be considered individual developments of the interpretation of Fascism as a Totalitarian phenomenon. An excellent synthesis, from both a methodological point of view and one of individual research into Soviet, Nazi, Fascist, and Chinese elites, can be found in Harold Dwight Lasswell and Daniel Lerner, eds., *World Revolutionary Elites: Studies in Coercive Ideological Movements* (Cambridge, Mass., M.I.T. Press, 1965). Here the thesis is argued that if on the level of "open ideology" Fascist Totalitarian and Communist regimes were "declared antagonists," in actual fact the former merely applied Bolshevist "methodology."

For the principal scientific criticism of the Totalitarian interpretation of Fascism and of the general theme of Totalitarianism, see Alexander J. Groth, "The 'Isms' in Totalitarianism," *American Political Science Review* (1964), pp. 888 ff., and Robert D. Burrowes, "Totalitarianism: The Revised Standard Version," in *World Politics* (New Haven, Yale University, Institute of International Studies, 1969), pp. 272 ff.

14. Hannah Arendt, *The Origins of Totalitarianism* (2d ed., Cleveland and New York, World, 1961; 1st ed., 1951), pp. 372 ff.

15. On the personality of the leader and his role, see L. Dion, "Il concetto di 'leadership' politica," in Riccardo Campa, ed., *L'autoritarismo e la società contemporanea* (Rome, Edizioni della Nuova Antologia, 1969), pp. 85 ff.

16. Arendt, *Origins of Totalitarianism*, pp. 314-315. According to the author, this phenomenon was typical after World War I, especially in East Central European countries. In Russia it occurred especially in the thirties, when Communism was transformed into Stalinism. France and Italy felt it to a lesser degree, though it occurred to an alarming degree in these countries after World War II.

17. Ibid., pp. 317, 311-312.

18. Carl J. Friedrich and Zbigniew K. Brzezinski, *Totalitarian Dictatorship and Autocracy* (2d ed., Cambridge, Mass., Harvard University Press, 1965), p. 22.

19. Ernst Nolte, *Der Faschismus in seiner Epoche: Die Action Française, Der Italienische Faschismus, Der Nationalsozialismus*

(Munich, Piper, 1963); trans. Leila Vennewitz, *Three Faces of Fascism: Action Française, Italian Fascism, National Socialism* (New York, Holt, Rinehart and Winston, 1966). After this work Ernst Nolte published *Die Faschistischen Bewegungen: Die Krise des liberalen Systems und die Entwicklung der Faschismen* (Munich, Deutschen Taschenbuch-Verlag, 1966); *Theorien über den Faschismus* (Cologne and Berlin, Kiepenheuer u. Witsch, 1967); *Das Faschismus von Mussolini zu Hitler* (Munich, Kaiser, 1968); and a new and expanded edition of his 1966 volume; and in 1969 the speech made that year at the Prague convention, "Der Faschismus als Problem in der wissenschaftlichen Literatur der jüngsten Vergangenheit," in *Fasišmus a Evropa. Fascism and Europe*, I, 17 ff. See, with regard to the attacks, Ernst Nolte, *Die Krise des liberalen Systems und die Faschistischen Bewegungen* (Munich, Piper, 1968); trans. into Italian as *La crisi dei regimi liberali e i movimenti fascist.* George Lachmann Mosse's summary appeared in 1966 in the *Journal of the History of Ideas*, pp. 621 ff.

20. According to Nolte, the Fascist phenomenon can be characterized in accordance with certain fixed elements: the original territory, represented by the liberal system; its extension from Pilsudski-style authoritarianism to Hitlerian Totalitarianism; the combination of a nationalistic motif with a socialistic motif (although the latter tended gradually to recede into the background); anti-Semitism; the coexistence of a particular tendency and a universal tendency; the social substratum of middle classes with an orientation "seemingly free of classes"; and the objective. Moreover, the various Fascisms, despite their many differences, had in common "the hierarchical principle and the desire to create a 'new world,' love of violence and the pathos of youth, an awareness of the elite and effectiveness with the masses, revolutionary fire and veneration of tradition." Finally, "Fascism is anti-Marxism, which seeks to destroy the enemy by the evolvement of a radically opposed and yet related ideology and by the use of almost identical and yet typically modified methods, always however, within the unyielding framework of National self-assertion and autonomy." Nolte, *La crisi dei regimi liberali*, pp. 17 ff.; *Three Faces of Fascism*, p. 20.

21. Nolte should be reproached for using the term "Fascist" in an excessively broad sense, applying it to movements, parties, and regimes that had no Fascist elements, or very few. Suffice it to note two examples. One, already pointed out, by

Ludovico Garruccio, *L'industrializzazione tra nazionalismo e rivoluzione: Le ideologie politiche dei paesi in via di sviluppo* (Bologna, Il Mulino, 1969), p. 57, concerns the underestimation of the fact that Fascist anti-Marxism, before being dictated by ideological motives in the strict sense or by classes (anti-Communism), was often anti-internationalism. The other concerns the excessive "ideological" weight given by Nolte to expressions and terms current in political usage that in fact have very little such content (for example, the Marxist Mussolini).

22. Nolte, *La crisi dei regimi liberali*, pp. 12 ff., 14 ff.

23. Nolte, *Three Faces of Fascism*, pp. 451-453.

24. See, especially, Rémond, *La Droite en France*. For George Lachmann Mosse see, besides the essay "La genesi del fascismo," his practically definitive studies, *The Crisis of German Ideology: Intellectual Origins of the Third Reich* (New York, Grosset and Dunlap, 1964) and *Germany and Jews: The Right, the Left, and the Search for a "Third Force" in pre Nazi Germany* (New York, Fertig, 1970).

    Mosse states that: "All fascisms attempted to capture and direct bourgeois dissatisfaction which began to take a concrete revolutionary form late in the nineteenth century. At that time, youth in particular attempted to escape from the 'materialist' society in which they had been reared and tried to find a new meaning in life, a new dynamic which would enable them to recapture their own individuality. On one level this revolt led to a battle against conventions, but on another it attempted to find a new sense of 'belonging' that might be combined with the revolt to which they were committed. Fascism was far from being purely nihilistic; indeed, the discovery of a positive ideology was what enabled some fascists to succeed while their more 'negative' ideological *confrères* failed." In this sense, Fascism was certainly one of the two great subversive movements of our time. And this was true even though its initial revolt was subsequently toned down. Mosse has some truly illuminating passages on this subject.

    Among the various Fascisms there were unquestionably points held in common; in particular, all "exhibited a flight from reality into the realm of an emotional and mystical ideology. They were all a part of the 'displaced revolution' that moved from a rejection of reality to a glorification of ideology." However, there were also significant differences, in particular between National Socialism (in Germany the ideological crisis had been deeper than in any other country and was rooted in the national structure) and other Fascisms. Mosse, in speaking of Fascism, keeps these differences clearly in sight, as he does the distinction between Fascism and reactionary regimes in the true sense of the word.

25. Both works are slightly different versions of a single essay: "Appunti per una definizione storica del fascismo," in Augusto Del Noce, *L'epoca della secolarizzazione* (Milan, Giuffrè, 1970), pp. 111 ff., and "Per una definizione storica del fascismo," in R. Pavetto, ed., *Il problema storico del fascismo* (Florence, Vallechi, 1970), pp. 11 ff.

26. Del Noce, "Per una definizione storica," p. 24.

27. Del Noce, "Appunti per una definizione," pp. 117-118.

28. Ibid., pp. 133 ff. For an evaluation of the reference to "actualism" (and hence to the relationship between Gentile and Fascism), see the three essays on Gentile by Del Noce in *Giornale critico della filosofia italiana* (Messina) in 1964, 1965, and 1969. Certain aspects of these essays, essential to an understanding of Del Noce's position, can be found in "Appunti per una definizione," pp. 124 ff.

Chapter 4. Interpretations by Social Scientists

1. Until World War II, this type of study was quite rare outside the United States. Representative works include Robert Michels, *Sozialismus und faschismus in Italien* (Munich, Meyer & Jessen, 1925); Franz Borkenau, "Zur Soziologie des faschismus," *Archiv für Sozialwissenschaften und Sozialpolitik* (February 1933); and Georges Bataille, "La structure psychologique du fascisme," *La Critique sociale* (Paris; March 1934).

2. For a discussion of this aspect, first examined by Talcott Parsons in *The Social System* (New York, Free Press, 1951), see Luciano Cavalli, *Il mutamento sociale: Sette ricerche sulla civiltà occidentale* (Bologna, Il Mulino, 1970), pp. 487 ff., which is a good summary of a revolutionary situation: "To explain the revolution one must recur to a discussion of deviant behavior. 'The presence of widely diffused and suitably distributed elements of alienation within the population' is above all necessary for the formation of a deviant group

on a revolutionary scale. However, diffuse discontent is not dangerous until it is organized. The power and danger of the 'deviant movement' lies in the fact that within a new system devoid of expectations, the characters spur each other on to behavior that is not consonant with the official interpretation of values. Moreover, the deviant movement, through fundamental ambivalence and opportunism, will attempt to obtain legitimacy in terms of the institutionalized values by redefining them and thus coining a new ideology. Indeed, Parsons thinks that the success of a deviant movement depends on the presence within society of certain elements that do not jibe perfectly with the accepted system of values. For this reason, 'possession of an ideology that incorporates symbols of great and diffuse appeal to the population with respect to which the present state is vulnerable, is a condition that is essential before the deviant movement can claim supremacy over the entire society.' A fourth element, however, is necessary to the success of revolution: the crisis of the system of power . . . As an example, Parsons discusses the National Socialist revolution in Germany . . . According to Parsons, the widespread alienation was caused by the rapid industrialization of a country characterized by a particularly rigid structure; the organization was effected by a party and a man (the *Führer*) that embodied all the principal reasons for discontent and reflected all the dissatisfied tendencies of the moment; 'National Socialism's' clever ideological formula, which joined two previously widespread but antithetical ideological elements, insured the neutrality of the Left and the general assistance of the Right. Finally, the government was unstable: 'There was no balance between the class structure and the government because the upper-class groups were excluded from the government while they retained their position in society.' A series of further facts (economic depression, uncertainty of the international situation, and so on) finally tipped the balance in Hitler's favor."

3. For a psychoanalytic interpretation of Fascism, see various passages (written in 1936) of Carl Gustav Jung, *Essays on Contemporary Events*, trans. Elizabeth Welsh, Barbara Hannah, and Mary Briner (London, K. Paul, 1947). For a cursory general review of authors who have written about Fascism in a Freudian vein, see Michel David, *La psicoanalisi nella cultura italiana* (Turin, Boringhieri, 1966), pp. 29 ff.

4. Wilhelm Reich, *Mass Psychology of Fascism*, trans. Theodore P. Wolfe (3rd ed., New York, Orgone Institute, 1946). Reich's preface to this expanded edition, important to an understanding of the evolution of his position, is also found in *The Mass Psychology of Fascism*, trans. Vincent R. Carfagno (New York, Farrar, Straus & Giroux, 1970), pp. xiii ff. It might be useful to read it along with *The Function of the Orgasm: Sex-Economic Problems of Biological Energy*, trans. Theodore P. Wolfe (London, Panther, 1968), which also deals with Fascism.

5. T. W. Adorno et al., *The Authoritarian Personality* (New York, Harper, 1950); preface by Max Horkheimer. For more precise methodological and critical information and for the pertinent bibliography, see John H. Madge, *Origins of Scientific Sociology* (New York, Free Press, 1962). See also "The Lessons of Fascism," in Hadley Cantril, ed., *Tensions That Cause Wars* (Urbana, University of Illinois, 1950), pp. 209 ff.

6. Erich Fromm, *Escape from Freedom* (New York, Holt, 1941), pp. 108, 118, 119. The quotations that follow are from *Escape from Freedom* by Erich Fromm. Copyright 1941, © 1969 by Erich Fromm. Reprinted by permission of Holt, Rinehart and Winston, Publishers.

7. Ibid., pp. 140-141.

8. Ibid., p. 208. For some later developments of the mechanisms-of-escape theme, see David Riesman, *The Lonely Crowd* (New Haven, Yale University Press, 1950).

9. Fromm, *Escape from Freedom*, pp. 209, 212-216.

10. Ibid., p. 297.

11. Erich Fromm, *The Sane Society* (New York, Holt, 1955), p. 237.

12. After Fromm, the psychological aspect of Fascism, particularly that of National Socialism, was studied by a vast body of authors. In general, they followed the same path, although often they softened somewhat the argument of the author of *Escape from Freedom* and sought to avoid the most obvious

pitfalls. See especially D. Müller-Hegemann, *Zur Psychologie des deutschen Faschisten* (Rudolfstadt, 1966); P. Suri, "La psicologia sociale del nazionalsocialismo," in *L'autoritarismo e la società contemporanea*, pp. 115 ff.

13. For the first and other essays, see Talcott Parsons, *Società e dittatura* (Bologna, 1956).

14. Karl Mannheim, *Ideology and Utopia: An Introduction to the Sociology of Knowledge*, trans. Louis Wirth and Edward Shils (New York, Harcourt Brace Jovanovich, Inc.; London, Routledge & Kegan Paul Ltd., 1946), pp. 3-7.

15. See Antonio Santucci's introduction to the Italian edition, *Ideologia e utopia* (Bologna, 1957), p. xxi.

16. Mannheim, *Ideology and Utopia*, pp. 119-123.

17. Ibid., pp. 125, 130.

18. Ibid, pp. 128, 120.

19. Georges Gurvitch, *Les cadres sociaux de la connaissance* (Paris, Presses universitaires de France, 1966), pp. 215 ff.; *The Social Frameworks of Knowledge*, trans. Margaret A. Thompson and Kenneth A. Thompson (New York, Harper & Row, 1971).

20. For the political sociology of the Fascist parties, see Maurice Duverger, *Sociologie politique* (Paris, A. Colin, 1958), pp. 294 ff.; trans. Barbara and Robert North, *Political Parties, Their Organization and Activity in the Modern State* (New York, Wiley, 1966).

21. Harold Dwight Lasswell, "The Psychology of Hitlerism," *The Political Quarterly* (London, 1933), p. 374. David J. Saposs, "The Role of the Middle Class in Social Development: Fascism, Populism, Communism, Socialism," in *Economic Essays in Honor of Wesley Clair Mitchell* (New York, Columbia University Press, 1935), pp. 393 ff.

22. Svend Ranulf, *Moral Indignation and Middle Class Psychology: A Sociological Study* (Copenhagen, Levin & Munksgaard, 1938). Nathaniel Stone Preston, *Politics, Economics and Power: Ideology and Practice under Capitalism, Social-*

ism, Communism and Fascism (New York and London, Macmillan, 1967), p. 201. For a thorough evaluation of the sociological aspects of the middle class, particularly their ideology, one must take into account the influence of Henri de Man, especially *Le socialisme constructif*, trans. from German by L.-C. Herbert (Paris, F. Alcan, 1933), and *L'idée socialiste, suivi du Plan de travail*, trans. from German by H. Corbin and A. Kojevnikov (Paris, Bernard Grasset, 1935).

23. Seymour Martin Lipset, *Political Man: The Social Bases of Politics* (Garden City, N.Y., Doubleday, 1960), pp. 134, 133.

24. Ibid., pp. 133-134.

25. Gino Germani, "Fascism and Social Class," in S. J. Woolf, ed., *The Nature of Fascism: Proceedings of a conference held by the Reading University Graduate School of Contemporary European Studies* (London, Weidenfeld, 1968), pp. 65 ff.; for the most important part translated into Italian, see De Felice, ed., *Il Fascismo: Le interpretazioni.*

    To be fully understood, Germani's paper should be considered within the framework of the more recent debate about modernization as well as in the wider context of his own works. See his more recent works: *Política y sociedad en una época de transición: de la sociedad tradicional a la sociedad de masa* (Buenos Aires, Paidós, 1968), and *Sociología de la modernización: estudios teóricos y aplicados a América Latina* (Buenos Aires, Paidós, 1969).

26. For other analyses of mass society see Emil Lederer, *The State of the Masses: The Threat of the Classless Society* (New York, W. W. Norton, 1940); William Kornhauser, *The Politics of Mass Society* (Glencoe, Ill., Free Press, 1959); and, for certain specific aspects, Joseph Alan Kahl, ed., *Comparative Perspectives on Stratification: Mexico, Great Britain, Japan* (Boston, Little, Brown, 1968).

27. For Germani, mobilization is a process of social change composed of six phases that can take place synchronically or diachronically: (1) a situation of integration (in a specific social structure); (2) a process of rupture or disintegration (concerning some aspect of the existing structure); (3) liberation (of individuals or groups); (4) response to such a phe-

nomenon (that is, either availability or resignation, or psychological mobility); (5) objective mobility; and (6) reintegration (into a structure that is more or less different from its predecessor). For a broader discussion see *Sociología de la modernización.*

28. Jules Monnerot, *Sociologie de la révolution* (Paris, Fayard, 1969), esp. pp. 489 ff., 515, 592.

29. See, for example, Albert T. Lauterbach, *Libertà e pianificazione* (Bologna, 1952), pp. 43 ff. Walt Whitman Rostow, *The Stages of Economic Growth, A Non-Communist Manifesto* (Cambridge, University Press, 1960).

30. A. F. Kenneth Organski, *The Stages of Political Development* (New York, Alfred A. Knopf, Inc., 1965), pp. 7 ff., 123.

31. Ibid., pp. 136, 124 ff.

32. Ibid., pp. 155-156.

33. A. F. K. Organski, "Fascism and Modernization," in Woolf, ed., *Nature of Fascism*, pp. 19 ff., esp. 23-31.

34. Barrington Moore, Jr., *Social Origins of Dictatorship and Democracy: Lord and Peasant in the Making of the Modern World* (Boston, Beacon, 1966), pp. 447 ff.

35. Some of the theses of Garruccio's book were earlier propounded under his pseudonym of Ludovico Castelnuovo (Ludovico Garruccio is also a pseudonym): "Fascismo ideologia di transizione," *Il Mulino* (July-August 1964), pp. 309 ff. See also his "Le tre età del fascismo," *Il Mulino* (January-February 1973), pp. 53 ff. On delayed industrialization, see especially Mary Kilbourne Matossian, "Ideologies of Delayed Industrialization: Some Tension and Ambiguities," in J. H. Kautsky, ed., *Political Change in Underdeveloped Countries: Nationalism and Communism* (New York and London, Wiley, 1962), pp. 252 ff. According to Miss Matossian, besides Italian Fascism (and National Socialism), Marxism-Leninism, Kemalism, Gandhism, Nasserism, and so on are, to some extent, ideologies resulting from late industrialization.

36. Garruccio, *L'industrializzazione tra nazionalismo e rivoluzione*, p. 58.

Chapter 5. Stages in the History of Fascism and the Problem of Its Origins

1. Outside Italy some scholars have viewed World War I as the culmination of a situation that already existed and that the war had brought to a head. For the Soviet historian G. Sandomirskij, author of *Fazism* (Moscow-Petrograd, 1923), the first manifestations of Fascism occurred before 1914; the war merely brought to fruition seeds that already existed as of 1906-7—and not only in Italy, for he considered France the birthplace of Fascism. B. R. Lopukhov, in *Il problema del fascismo italiano*, p. 240, summarizes his point of view as follows: "Sandomirskij deduced this assertion from the analyses of the French so-called 'social novels'; dating from the beginning of the century where the attacks against governments that were weak and devoid of character were allied to the cult of the strong 'Nietzschean' personality, to the propaganda of the civil war waged by the bourgeoisie against the workers, to the ideas of Caesarism. According to Sandomirskij, these novels were the forerunners of Mussolini's ideas and of Fascism. In other words, Fascism reflected the disillusionment of one part of the bourgeoisie with the democratic form of state power and its desire to gain a victory against the revolutionary movement of the proletariat by means of oppression, and without trusting to the help of the government. The war had temporarily deflected the attention of the bourgeoisie from the internal enemy. But immediately after the war the Fascist seeds burgeoned. This was the case in Italy: Sandomirskij writes that Italian Fascism is a result of the World War. Its roots are to be found in the peculiarly unhealthy frame of mind produced in Italy by the war and its terrible economic consequences." Some significant passages from Sandomirskij are quoted in De Felice, ed., *Il Fascismo: Le interpretazioni*, pp. 81 ff.

2. The article was reprinted in Luigi Salvatorelli, *Nazionalfascismo* (Turin, P. Gobetti, 1923), pp. 38 ff. After World War II, Salvatorelli several times repeated his thesis, expanding on the responsibility of Victor Emmanuel III. See "Casa Savoia nella storia d'Italia," *Quaderni liberi* (Rome), V (May 10, 1944), and "Tre colpi di stato," *Il Ponte* (Florence; April 1950), pp. 344 ff.

3. Luigi Salvatorelli, *Pensiero e azione del Risorgimento* (Turin, Einaudi, 1944); trans. Mario Domandi, *The Risorgimento:*

Thought and Action (New York, Harper & Row, 1970).

4. Angelo Tasca, *The Rise of Italian Fascism, 1918-1922*, trans. Peter and Dorothy Wait (New York, Howard Fertig, 1966), pp. 338-341. (The first edition, in French, was published in Paris in 1938.) Federico Chabod, *A History of Italian Fascism*, trans. Muriel Grindrod (London, Weidenfeld and Nicolson, 1963); originally published as *L'Italia contemporanea (1918-1948)* (Turin, Einaudi, 1961). This is a collection of a series of lectures delivered in Paris in 1950.

5. Pietro Nenni, *Storia di quattro anni, 1919-1922* (Rome, Einaudi, 1946). Gaetano Salvemini, *The Fascist Dictatorship in Italy* (London, Jonathan Cape, 1928).

   With regard to Italy's intervention in World War I, we should remember the judgment rendered in 1939-1941 by Gaetano Salvemini in his essay on Italian diplomacy during World War I, published in *The World.* This historical judgment is particularly important because in 1923 Salvemini, faced with the Fascist victory, had already in political and moral terms made amends for his pro-interventionism in 1914-15. See Gaetano Salvemini, *Scritti sul fascismo*, ed. Nino Valeri and Alberto Merola (Milan, 1966), II, 96 ff.

6. See the writings of Alceste De Ambris in the summer of 1922; for example, "Dopo il trionfo fascista: Le due facce di una sola medaglia," *Rivista popolare di Politica, Lettere e Scienze sociali* (Rome; July 16-August 21, 1922). According to De Ambris, Fascism, like Bolshevism, was a typical postwar phenomenon. "In a certain respect it can be asserted that Fascism is nothing but the reverse side of the Bolshevik coin. The imprint is different, but the metal remains the same. In both cases we are dealing with movements—initially deriving their roots from fundamentally just sources—that rapidly degenerated into hateful and unpleasant forms."

7. Livio Paladin, "Fascismo (diritto costituzionale)," *Enciclopedia del Diritto*, vol. XVI (Milan, 1966).

8. Gabriele De Rosa, "Considerazioni storiografiche sulla crisi dello Stato prefascista e sull'antifascismo," *Il Movimento di Liberazione in Italia* (Milan; October-December 1959), pp. 19 ff.

9. The extremely grave crisis for Fascism precipitated by the Matteotti assassination was overcome by Mussolini during

1925-26. He was able to succeed for three reasons: the political inadequacy of the Aventine opposition; the support of intransigent Fascism; and, above all, the direct or indirect support of the typically conservative sectors and the Church who were afraid of seeing the country again open to revolutionary solutions or even to another period of internal disorders. As soon as he was able to, Mussolini got rid of the intransigents (who wanted a true Fascistization of the State and of Italian society and a renewed emphasis on the Party and the Militia as the effective instruments and agents of power) and concentrated all power in the State—without succeeding, however, in making it truly Fascist. Without a Fascist ruling class equal to the situation and without a revolutionary party, the "conditioning" of the conservative forces became decisive. The State identified itself formally with Fascism, and Fascism with its leader; however, Mussolini remained in practice a prisoner of a State that was substantially the old conservative State. Despite the corporative imprint dictated from above and certain attempts made to expand public initiative and state control, that State not only was unable to modify the social structure but it aligned itself with the traditional social dynamics that continued (albeit with some friction) to evolve along the same old lines. Mussolini's role was that of a mediator within a system that tended to return to the same old conflicts without Fascism's being able to resolve them; it merely succeeded in turning them to the advantage of the more conservative forces and thus made them worse. His was the role of a mediator for whom no course was open but that typical of nationalism: imperialist expansion, hence war, which in turn became a justification for social immobility and a necessary premise for the future well-being that was to be achieved not by solving internal social conflicts but at the expense of other nations.

During the 1930s the Fascist regime was reduced to a balance of conservative interests, upheld by a policy of social-welfare assistance, and, where that was insufficient, by a police regime and a popular consensus nourished by the habitual myth of the leader and by the faith (largely fostered by lingering patriotic traditions of the Risorgimento) in his ability to bring grandeur to the nation. This was an extremely precarious balance that was destined to crumble with the first crisis of this grandeur and to unleash all the centrifugal forces that hitherto had been appeased or suppressed. And this is precisely what happened on July 25, 1943, when, faced with military defeat, the regime crumbled, and Fascism along with it. All that survived (the Italian Social Republic) was the old intransigent Fascism, which dreamed of being able to bound back into power by refurbishing the social programs of 1919 and taking revenge against its old enemies.

Chapter 6. *Interpretations prior to the Matteotti Assassination*

1. The Biblioteca di Studi Sociali series was edited by Rodolfo Mondolfo for the Cappelli publishing house of Bologna and by the Turin firm of Pietro Gobetti. Seven of the eight essays in this series—those written by Guido Bergamo, Giuseppe De Falco, Cesare Degli Occhi, Luigi Fabbri, Dino Grandi, Mario Missiroli, Adolfo Zerboglio, and Giovanni Zibordi, with their preface by Rodolfo Mondolfo—were reprinted in Renzo De Felice, ed., *Il fascismo e i partiti politici italiani: testimonianze del 1921-1923* (Fascism and the Italian Political Parties: Testimonials of 1921-1923; Bologna, Cappelli, 1966); the exception was that of Adolfo Zerboglio, "Il Fascismo: Dati, impressioni, appunti," 1922. The same collection contains an essay, in the nature of an initial evaluation, on "Il fascismo in Italia" by Rodolfo Mondolfo, published in 1928 in German; essays by Djula Šaš (pseud. Giulio Aquila), also published in German in 1923; and a series of eight articles published in *Il Resto del Carlino* (Bologna, February-May 1922), written by noted figures in Italian cultural life.

2. Readers who wish to gain an idea of Salvatorelli's judgment of his contemporaries are referred to Luigi Salvatorelli, *Nazionalfascismo* (Turin, 1923). In addition to the essays published in the collection edited by Mondolfo, Salvatorelli examined those published in the only issue on Fascism of *La Rivoluzione liberale* (Milan), May 28, 1922: by Mario Vinciguerra, *Il Fascismo visto da un solitario* (Turin, Gobetti, 1923); by Alberto Cappa and Adriano Tilgher (whom I shall speak of further on); and by a "Deputato al Parlamento," *Il Fascismo* (Milan, 1922).

3. Giovanni Zibordi, *Critica socialista del fascismo* (Bologna, 1922), p. 8. See also numerous writings by Zibordi on Fascism in *Critica Sociale* (Milan) between 1922 and 1924. *L'Ordine Nuovo* (Aug. 9, 1921); reprinted in Antonio Gramsci, *Socialismo e Fascismo: L'Ordine Nuovo, 1921-1922* (Turin, Einaudi, 1966), p. 545.

4. Ivanoe Bonomi, *Dal Socialismo al Fascismo* (Rome, Formiggini, 1924); trans. John Murray, *From Socialism to Fascism: A Study of Contemporary Italy* (London, Martin Hopkinson, 1924), pp. 107-108. On the transformation of Fascism in 1920-21 and its conversion to the Right, see also the writings of Alceste De Ambris, including the article cited in Chapter 5, note 8, and, especially, "L'évolution du Fascisme," *Mercure de France* (Paris; Feb. 15-March 15, 1923)—also published in De Felice, *Il Fascismo: Le interpretazioni*, pp. 197 ff.—as well as those of Arturo Labriola, especially *Le due politiche: Fascismo e riformismo* (Naples, Morand, 1923), pp. 171 ff.

5. Giuseppe De Falco, *Il fascismo milizia di classe: commenti alla cronaca* (Bologna, Cappelli, 1921). The most explicit non-Fascist testimony of the positive evaluation of Fascism is found in the speech made in the Chamber of Deputies on January 31, 1921, by Gino Sarrocchi, a Liberal. See Gino Sarrocchi, *Sulla politica interna: Socialismo e fascismo* (Rome, 1921). For Sarrocchi, Fascism was "a healthy reaction . . . of an entire people who, having withstood the most intolerable abuses, having suffered a long time at the hands of violence, finally saw mobilized in its defense the best part of its youth and followed this generous vanguard." Accordingly, its "merits are infinite and superior to those of the government, which, although it disposes of material means that are directly within its reach and that cannot be easily improvised, did not and could not rearouse the public conscience in the same way that Fascism did."

Among those who expounded an intermediate position see Alcide De Gasperi, "Il fascismo nella campagna ellettorale," *Il nuovo Trentino* (April 7, 1921), where criticism of Fascism was almost entirely reduced to condemnation of the "punitive expeditions" and the "collective reprisals," and where the author suspended judgment on the rest of the phenomenon but allowed to leak out a certain willingness to distinguish between "aggressive" and "defensive" violence. Among other things, De Gasperi wrote: "In the beginning, Fascism was an impetus of reaction to Communist internationalism that denied freedom and the nation; today it is a spiritual and political movement; tomorrow it will be a party with a maximum program and a program that can be immediately realized. We suspend judgment of it as a party until it appears with a clearly defined physiognomy; to judge it as a movement, it would be necessary to formulate too many distinctions for an overall appraisal to be useful.

"From Bologna to Ferrara, where it was welcomed as a liberating force and was viewed with benevolence even by our friends—let us not forget the attitude of *Avvenire d'Italia* and the interview with Count Grossoli; from Florence and Tuscany, where it attracted even the "white" labor organizations, despite the suffering the latter underwent at the hand of Red tyranny; from Milan to Trieste, from the Cafe Aragno to the burning of the Croatian villages, the Fascist movement has displayed so many facets and attempted to attain so many different objectives as to make a synthetic judgment extremely difficult. The only judgment that seems possible is that of the means Fascism employed in many places —means that sometimes drew a word of caution from Mussolini himself. Let us be the first to say that we do not join the ranks of those who condemn all Fascist actions under the generic condemnation of any kind of violence. There are situations in which violence, although it might take on the appearance of aggression, is really defensive, and hence legitimate. Renzo, in forcing the prelate to bless his marriage to Lucia, was apparently the aggressor; but in fact it was Don Abbondio who became the instrument of the most tyrannical violence."

6. Luigi Fabbri, *La contro-rivoluzione preventiva* (Bologna, Cappelli, 1922). The fact that only a few political observers, such as Fabbri, inquired why the Fascist reaction was unleashed only after the socialist movement was on the decline cannot be explained in terms of a tacit adherence to Fascism or some other superficial label. The fact that many people did not ask this question can be explained in two ways. First, although the occupation of the factories had failed, the impression and fear it left lasted a long time. And, second, although the socialist movement was obliged to pass from the offensive to the defensive, it continued to be verbally aggressive and to hold its own in organizational and electoral terms and it was finally crushed only by the Fascist squadristi. The Fascists claimed that thereby they had averted the danger of a Bolshevik revolution, whereas that danger, if it ever really existed, had certainly disappeared by the time the squadristi appeared on the scene.

7. Pietro Gobetti, *Dal bolscevismo al fascismo: Note di cultura politica* (Turin, Gobetti, 1923), pp. 33 ff.

8. Salvatorelli, *Nazionalfascismo*, pp. 11 ff.

9. Fabbri, *La contro-rivoluzione preventiva*, pp. 11 ff.

10. Guido Bergamo, *Il fascismo visto da un repubblicano* (Bologna, Cappelli, 1921), p. 22. For the position of the Republicans, see also PAN (pseud. F. Perri), *Il Fascismo* (Rome, 1922); he considered Fascism, "a chaotic conservative movement which gathers around a negative postulate all the forces of the bourgeoisie regardless of their category" (p. 10). See also *Repubblicani e Fascisti: Pagine Documentali* (Rome, 1924).

11. De Falco, *Il fascismo milizia di classe*, p. 13.

12. Reprinted, along with other writings on Fascism by Bordiga between 1921 and 1924, in *Communisme et fascisme* (Marseilles, 1970), pp. 81 ff., 111 ff.

13. See "I primi dieci anni di vita del Partito Comunista Italiano," in Giuseppe Berti, ed., *Annali 1966* (Milan, G. G. Feltrinelli Institute, 1966), pp. 186 ff.

14. Reprinted in Palmiro Togliatti, *Opere* (Rome, Riuniti, 1967), I, 423 ff.

15. The essay, signed with the pseudonym "Giulio Aquila," is included in De Felice, ed., *Il fascismo e i partiti politici italiani*, pp. 421 ff. According to Šaš, "Fascism, seen historically, is the advance of industrial capital." Although the individual economic and political situation in Italy had given it specific characteristics, it was not just an Italian specialty but was rather a phenomenon "of maximum immediacy on the international level." It had established its roots in the economic and political situation dictated by the war, particularly in that the war had made impossible a capitalist reconstruction of the economy, "with the 'normal' exploitation of the proletariat": "the 'democratic' instruments of power, the legal democratic state apparatus are no longer sufficient, even with the active support of the social democrats, to chase away the proletariat that has been relatively reinforced in a situation of increased exploitation; for these reasons the bourgeoisie pushes aside the 'democratic' instruments of power, the democratic and legal state." In Italy the Fascist victory was not only military but also especially political. "This political victory consisted in the fact that Fascism succeeded in attracting to itself vast strata of the petty bourgeoisie and the peasant class, and beyond that even a portion of the working class, especially in the plains, and used them politically and militarily against the working class that was conscious of its own true class interests. Although Fascism, *from a historical point of view*, represents an attack of

capital against the working class . . . externally it does not appear to be, or rather did not appear to be before it came to power, a reactionary movement turned against the interests of the workers by a small group of capitalist plutocrats. Instead, it appeared to be a progressive movement, even a 'revolutionary' movement."

16. See Alfonso Leonetti, *Note su Gramsci* (Urbino, Argalià, 1970), pp. 45 ff.; see also Massimo L. Salvadori, *Gramsci e il problema storico della democrazia* (Turin, Einaudi, 1970), p. 83, who states: "according to the analysis made by Gramsci, Fascism is the result of the failure of the Giolitti plan that was based on the integration of the working class, on the political subordination of the farmers to the industrial bourgeoisie, and on the compression of the peasant masses. Fascism represents the advent to leadership of the State by the agrarian bourgeoisie, who aim at the suppression of parliamentary democracy and the substitution of a regime of violence that eliminates the possibility of an alliance between the workers and the peasants."

17. Antonio Gramsci, *L'Ordine Nuovo, 1911-1920* (Turin, Einaudi, 1955), pp. 349 ff., 365 ff.

18. Antonio Gramsci, *Socialismo e fascismo: L'Ordine Nuovo 1921-1922* (Turin, Einaudi, 1966), p. 266.

19. Ibid., pp. 12, 167-168.

20. Ibid., p. 299.

21. Palmiro Togliatti, *La formazione del gruppo dirigente del Partito comunista italiano nel 1923-1924* (Rome, Riuniti, 1962), pp. 199, 223 ff.

22. Salvatorelli, *Nazionalfascismo*, pp. 8 ff.

23. Zibordi, *Critica socialista del fascismo*, pp. 15 ff., p. 23. See also in Salvatorelli, *Nazionalfascismo*, pp. 10 ff., the criticisms leveled at Zibordi's analysis—both the general criticism (lack of a unifying synthesis among the three elements analyzed) and, more important, the criticism relative to the military component and its relation to the revolution of the middle class. Although he does not refer to a "military revolution," Gaetano Salvemini refers to a "military conspiracy" in *Scritti sul fascismo*, I, 65 ff., 555 ff.

24. Reprinted in Adriano Tilgher, *La Crisi mondiale e saggi critici di marxismo e socialismo* (Bologna, Zanichelli, 1921), pp. 175 ff.

25. Reprinted in Nino Valeri, ed., *Antologia della "Rivoluzione Liberale"* (Turin, F. de Silva, 1948), pp. 345 ff.

26. Among the most interesting reviews of Missiroli's article, see those by Benito Mussolini in *Rivista illustrata del Popolo d'Italia* (Milan; Dec. 8, 1921) and by Guido Mazzali in *Avanti!* (Dec. 8, 1921). Along the same lines as Missiroli, but with more accent on the general sociological and political elements, see Vilfredo Pareto, "Il fascismo," *La Ronda* (Rome; January 1922).

27. The essay was written in the first days of August 1921. For developments in Missiroli's position over the course of the next few months (marked by the crisis Fascism underwent as the result of the Pacification Pact and the solution to that crisis provided by the party congress in 1921 in Rome's Augusteo), see Missiroli's article "Il partito degli eretici," *Secolo* (Nov. 12, 1922); reprinted in Mario Missiroli, *Una battaglia perduta* (Milan, Corbaccio, 1924), pp. 213 ff. The anonymous articles (that must have been inspired by, if not actually written by, Missiroli) on the Augusteo congress in *Secolo* (Nov. 3, 4, and 12, 1921) are also interesting.

28. Alberto Cappa, *Due rivoluzione mancate: Dati, sviluppo e scioglimento della crisi politica italiana* (Foligno, Campitelli, 1923), esp. pp. 156 ff. (quotation on pp. 168 ff.), and Alberto Cappa [pseud. Grildrig], *Le generazioni del fascismo* (Turin, Gobetti, 1924). Besides Missiroli's influence, the more general influence of Gobetti is found in Cappa's writings. Before and after the rise to power of Mussolini we do not find a true analysis of Fascism in Gobetti's writings, but they contain perspicacious elements proving that their author had perceived many of the problems Fascism would encounter once it came to power. Rather than analyze it for its own merits, Gobetti sought to insert the Fascist phenomenon within the wider context of his study of the Risorgimento and post-Risorgimento; see especially, *Risorgimento senza eroi: Studi sul pensiero piemontese nel risorgimento* (Turin, Baretti, 1926), and *La rivoluzione liberale* (Bologna, 1924), whose last chapter is devoted to Fascism. For an analysis of the relation between these cultural positions and Gobetti's anti-Fascist activity, see Nino Valeri, "Sulle Ori-

gini del fascismo," in *Questioni di storia contemporanea* (1st ed., Milan, Marzorati, 1953), III, 733 ff.

29. For some rebuttals to Salvatorelli's essay and his answer to them, see Luigi Salvatorelli, "Risposta ai critici di Nazional-fascismo,' " *La Rivoluzione Liberale* (13 Nov. 1923); reprinted in Valeri, ed., *Antologia della "Rivoluzione Liberale,"* pp. 423 ff.

30. Salvatorelli, *Nazionalfascismo*, pp. 13 ff, pp. 16 ff.

31. Giovanni Ansaldo, "La piccola borghesia," *Il lavoro* (June 3, 1923); reprinted in Valeri, ed., *Antologia della "Rivoluzione Liberale,"* pp. 417 ff., puts forth a convincing criticism of this characterization of the Italian petty bourgeoisie. For him, the "technical" petty bourgeoisie of the North, and Milan in particular, was much more Fascist than the "humanistic" bourgeoisie (to be found especially in the South), on which Salvatorelli had focused his attention.

32. Salvatorelli, *Nazionalfascismo*, pp. 24-25.

33. Pietro Gorgolini, *Il fascismo nella vita italiana*, preface by Benito Mussolini (Turin, Silvestrelli-Cappelletto, 1922). See particularly p. 133 of the Italian third edition for a discussion of the "social maturation" of Fascism. It is pointed out that "the original interventionist nucleus . . . and the veterans were expanded by two fairly large groups consisting of the intellectual proletariat and the petty bourgeoisie that were aroused because of the abnormal state of affairs that was ruining the Nation." Agostino Lanzillo, *Le rivoluzioni del dopoguerra: Critiche e diagnosi* (Città di Castello, Il Solco, 1922), esp. p. 225; pp. 219 ff. are especially devoted to Fascism.

34. Dino Grandi, *Le origine e la missione del fascismo* (Bologna, Cappelli, 1922). The essay reproduced in large part the speech given before the Fascist Congress of the Augusteo in Rome in November 1921. For random judgments of the speech that are interesting see Guido De Ruggiero, "Intorno al fascismo," *Il Resto del Carlino* (Bologna; Feb. 14, 1922), reprinted in *Il fascismo e i partiti politici italiani*, p. 504; and Pietro Gobetti, *La rivoluzione liberale: Saggio sulla lotta politica in Italia*, ed. Gasparo De Caro (Turin, Einaudi, 1964), p. 182. Also by Gobetti, see *Dal bolscevismo al fascismo: Note di cultura politica* (Turin, Gobetti, 1923), p. 34,

and the observations on the derivation from Missiroli of the theory of the development of postwar democratic ideals.

Chapter 7. *Interpretations during the Fascist Regime*

1. A special place must be accorded Giuseppe Prezzolini's book *Fascism*, trans. Kathleen Macmillan (New York, Dutton, 1927), which represents the point of view of an intellectual who was not allied with Fascism, but in many respects was not hostile to it.

2. See in particular Carlo Avarna Di Gualtieri, *Il fascismo* (Turin, Gobetti, 1925), and Ermanno Bartellini, *La rivoluzione in atto 1919-1924* (Turin, Gobetti, 1925). See also Ettore Ciccotti, "La parabola del fascismo," in *Il Fascismo e le sue fasi: Anarchia, dittatura, deviazioni* (Milan, Unitas, 1925), pp. 401 ff.; Carlo Alberto Alemagna [pseud. General Filareti], "Genesi e parabola del fascismo," in *In margine del fascismo* (Milan, Unitas, 1925), pp. 335 ff.; Rodolfo Mondolfo, *Il fascismo in Italia* (Turin, Gobetti, 1925).

3. Guido Dorso, *La rivoluzione meridionale* (Rome, Einaudi, 1945), p. 93; originally published in Rome in 1925 by Gobetti. Quotations refer to the later edition, which is enriched by a new preface and an extensive appendix. Certain observations of this sort had already been made by Djula Šaš in *Der Faschismus in Italien;* reprinted in Mondolfo, *Il fascismo e i partiti politici italiani*, pp. 468 ff.

4. Dorso, *La rivoluzione meridionale*, pp. 94-95.

5. A first edition of the work, entitled *La libertà*, was published in 1926 in Turin; a reworked and expanded version was published the same year in Paris as *Bolchevisme, fascisme et démocratie* (Progrès Civique). The definitive edition, *Bolscevismo, Fascismo e Democrazia*, was published with few changes in 1927 by Il Solco. It is included in the second volume of Francesco Saverio Nitti, *Scritti politici*, ed. G. De Rosa (Bari, Laterza, 1961). An English translation by Margaret M. Green, *Bolshevism, Fascism and Democracy*, was published in London by G. Allen & Unwin in 1927.

6. Nitti, *Scritti politici*, II, 334.

7. Luigi Sturzo, *Italy and Fascism*, trans. Barbara Barclay Carter (New York, Fertig, 1967), pp. 100 ff., 286 ff., quotations on

230 ff.; originally published as Luigi Sturzo, *L'Italie et le Fascisme*, trans. Marcel Prélot (Paris, Alcan, 1927).

8. Among the minor authors, see especially Mario Mariani, *I Quaderni antifascisti: Le origini del fascismo* (Paris, Ceccioni, 1927); Domenico Saudino, *Sotto il segno del Littorio*, I, *La genesi del fascismo* (Chicago, Libreria sociale, 1933); Ignazio Silone, *Der Faschismus, seine Entstehung und seine Entwicklung* (Zurich, Europa-Verlag, 1934); Luigi Fabbri, *Camisas negras: Estudio crítico histórico del origen y evolución del fascismo, sus hechos y sus ideas* (Buenos Aires, Nervio, 1934); and Egidio Réale, *L'Italie* (Paris, Delagrave, 1934). Interesting observations on the Fascist crisis after the March on Rome are contained in Emilio Lussu, *Marcia su Roma e dintorni: fascismo visto da vicino* (Paris, Critica, 1933). Indirectly related to the problem of the origins of Fascism because it is a study of the middle classes is Libero Battistelli, *I fuori classe* (Rio de Janeiro, 1931).

9. Reprinted in Alessandro Schiavi, *Esilio e morte di Filippo Turati (1926-1932)* (Rome, Opere Nuove, 1956), pp. 122 ff. Most of the essay was used to sum up Turati's judgment of Fascism; see Carlo Rosselli, "Filippo Turati e il socialismo italiano," *Quaderni di Giustizia e Libertà* (June 1932), esp. pp. 40 ff.

10. See Filippo Turati, *Le problème du Fascisme au Congrès International Socialiste* (Brussels, 1928). Turati thus radically removed himself from the analysis and definition of Fascism that, on the eve of the suppression of opposition parties, had been elaborated (in October 1926) by the leadership of the Italian Socialist Party of the Workers (PSLI) in a "Declaration" that, in my opinion, remained in its preliminary draft. This "Declaration" did not stress the plutocratic degeneration of capitalism, but mentioned a "Mediterranean" phenomenon: it linked Fascism with the weak and backward economic and political structure in Italy. "The victory of Fascism followed a path that we can call *Mediterranean*, where the liberal State was a recent conception and did not have healthy autonomous roots. It had a few traditions and was both a repercussion of foreign revolutions and the reward given by the princes to the people for their support in the national wars. This political tendency coincided with a poorer, weaker, more backward economic line where modern capitalism did not appear to be healthy and where conservative agriculture prevailed over progressive industrial-

ism. In such a situation the repercussions of the war were debilitating, and the rush of the privileged classes to save themselves was violent. They did this by violently excluding the proletariat from the political scene in order to subject it, defenseless and unarmed, to the major burdens that resulted from the war." The test of the "Declaration" is published in *Il Cannocchiale* (December 1969), pp. 89 ff.

11. For a typical example of the application of this interpretative scheme see Silvio Trentin, *L'aventure italienne: legendes et réalités* (Paris, Presses universitaires, 1928). On Trentin, see Norberto Bobbio, *Italia civile: Ritratti e testimonianze* (Manduria, Lacaita, 1964), pp. 271 ff.

12. Pietro Nenni, *Six ans de guerre civile en Italie* (Paris, Valois, 1930); trans. Giuliana Emiliani, *Sei anni di guerra civile* (Milan, Rizzoli, 1945), pp. 226-227.

13. Claudio Treves, *Il fascismo nella letteratura antifascista dell'-esilio* (Rome, Opere Nuove, 1953), esp. pp. 76 ff.

14. See Mario Bergamo, *Saturnia o l'elogio della discordia* (Paris, 1932); Francesco Luigi Ferrari, *Le régime fasciste italien* (Paris, Spes, 1928). Ferrari's work was essentially historical and juridical; Bergamo's was political and polemical toward the Concentration. With regard to Fascism's individual aspects, the criticism of heterodox writers such as Donati and Bergamo was sometimes in agreement with that of dissident Fascists who had also emigrated abroad after the Matteotti assassination. See Massimo Rocca, *Le fascisme et l'antifascisme en Italie* (Paris, Alcan, 1930).

15. For this hitherto unpublished note, dated after July 1930, see Giuseppe Donati, *Scritti politici*, ed. Giuseppe Rossini (Rome, Cinque Lune, 1956), II, 430. For a definition of Fascism see the hitherto unpublished note, "La lotta di classe nel dopoguerra," II, 487 ff.

16. Ibid., II, 422 ("L'alibi Mussolini," *Il Pungolo*, Feb. 15, 1930); pp. 404 ff. ("La crisi dei partiti e l'avvento del Fascismo," *Il Pungolo*, Aug. 1-15, 1929). In volume II, see also pp. 341 ff., 381 ff.

17. Giustino Fortunato, *Dopo la guerra sovvertitrice* (Bari, La-terza, 1921), esp. pp. 25 ff., 36 ff. "The new Italy developed and was shaped by fortunate events that were turned to the

advantage of a small minority of intellectuals. It became a
reality with the loss of so few lives that, in the recent war, the
Basilicata alone suffered twice as many victims as all of Italy
had in all the national wars between 1848 and 1870. It could
not be hoped that in a mere fifty years new institutions and
new conditions of a government policy more fragmented
and disheveled than any other country's would form a State
different from that which in fact came into being, out of
thirty-five million men who had no civic discipline because
they had no moral discipline, and out of a country so seldom
favored by fortune. It became one of the shakiest and most
intolerant States in the modern world. Ours was an organ-
ism that was still diseased and still under the influence of
reactionary forces that, it was hoped, might be able to heal
it. But in fact it was caught in midstream by the most violent
hurricane history has recorded; if it emerged honorably,
bearing witness that it had not risen again in vain, it could
not but simultaneously abandon itself, at the end of its
strength, to all that was most atavistic in its nature."

Giustino Fortunato, *Nel regime fascista* (1926); reprinted
in Fortunato, *Pagine e ricordi parlamentari*, vol. II (Rome,
1947).

18. Giuseppe Antonio Borgese, *Goliath: The March of Fascism*
(New York, Viking, 1937); this book was translated into
several languages, including Italian: *Golia: marcia del fascismo* (Milan, Mondadori, 1946).

19. Carlo Rosselli, *Socialismo liberale* (Rome, Florence, Milan,
1945), pp. 110-111, 117 ff.; the first edition published as
Socialisme libéral, trans. Stefan Priacel (Paris, Valois, 1930).

The anarchist Camillo Berneri was another interesting
heterodox writer. His renewed interest in the degree of Leftism exhibited by the *fasci di combattimento* between 1919
and 1920 is significant. In 1935 he wrote: "Political movements are propelled by the wind and the rationalist aprior-
ism of the programs almost always dissolves on contact with
the irrational, that is, with history in progress. The Leftism
of the Fascist program in 1919 took in many people but it
was not deliberately misleading"; Camillo Berneri, *Scritti
scelti. Pietrogrado 1917-Barcellona, 1937* (Milan, Sugar,
1964), p. 170.

20. Carlo Rosselli, "Risposta a Giorgio Amendola," *Quaderni di
Giustizia e Libertà* (Paris; January 1932), p. 38. For Rosselli's
position, see also the work of Rodolfo Morandi and the per-

tinent polemics between the two in Aldo Agosti, *Rodolfo Morandi: Il pensiero e l'azione politica* (Bari, Laterza, 1971), pp. 163 ff.

21. Besides the 1921 cases I have mentioned, it is significant that even Gramsci in the summer of 1924 spoke of the need to destroy "not only Mussolini and Farinacci's Fascism, but also the semi-Fascism of Amendola, Sturzo, Turati"; see "I primi dieci anni di vita del Partito Comunista Italiano," p. 159.

22. Reprinted in Paolo Alatri, *L'antifascismo italiano* (Rome, Riuniti, 1961), I, 415 ff. The Communist Left always rejected any interpretation that was not "capitalist reaction." For the opinion of Bordiga's followers, see Dino, "Cosa è il fascismo," (Milan; Dec. 1, 1930); for groups close to Trotsky, see Blasco, "Les problèmes révolutionnaires de l'Italie et nos divergences," *La lutte des classes* (Geneva; July 1930); reprinted in Alfredo Azzaroni, Pierre Naville, and Ignazio Silone, *Blasco: La vie de Pietro Tresso* (Paris, Editions polyglottes, 1965), pp. 111 ff.

23. The most interesting aspect of this discussion (see *Il Terzo Congresso del Partito Comunista d'Italia—Sezione dell'Internazionale Comunista*, n.d. but see 1926, pp. 15 ff.) is the position of Antonio Gramsci. Note particularly Gramsci's assertion that Fascism should be considered not only "a fighting weapon of the bourgeoisie" but also "a social movement" and that it was necessary to "examine the stratification of Fascism itself because, given the totalitarian system that Fascism tends to establish, it will be in the heart of Fascism itself that those conflicts will materialize that cannot come to light by any other means" (pp. 40-41).

24. Palmiro Togliatti, "A proposito del fascismo"; reprinted in *Società* (December 1952), pp. 591 ff., and De Felice, *Il Fascismo*, pp. 279 ff.

25. In "A proposito del fascismo," Togliatti maintained that Italian Fascism was "clearly different" from all other reactionary regimes because it refused any compromise with Social Democracy. This assertion did not prevent many Italian Communists from subsequently accusing Italian Socialists of Social-Fascism.

26. Palmiro Togliatti, *Lezioni sul fascismo* (Rome, Riuniti, 1970), pp. 20 ff.

27. See the works by Francesco Luigi Ferrari already cited. See also Ferrari's posthumous essay *L'Azione cattolica e il "regime"* (Florence, Parenti, 1957), as well as Silvio Trentin's essay. Also, by Mario Bergamo, *De l'État barbare; ou l'arbitraire comme conception juridique dans la législation fasciste* (Marseilles, E.S.I.L., 1931), and the many studies by Gaetano Salvemini, including *Mussolini diplomatico* (Paris, Editions contemporaines, 1932), and *Sotto la scure del fascismo* (Turin, De Silva, 1948).

28. The first Italian edition was Angelo Tasca, *Nascita e avvento del fascismo: l'Italia dal 1918 al 1922* (Florence, La Nuova Italia, 1950); trans. Peter and Dorothy Wait, *The Rise of Italian Fascism, 1918-1922* (New York, Fertig, 1966). The Italian edition contains the notes that, for reasons of space, were omitted from the French edition; but the extremely important documentary appendices that were to have completed the work seem to have disappeared. The passage quoted is from the preface to the first Italian edition (p. xvi); it was not included in the second edition.

29. It may be possible—just for documentary reasons—to distinguish between memoirs that appeared prior to 1931-32 and those published afterward. The works published before that time occasionally contain suggestions and observations of interest. They facilitate an understanding of the complex origins, contradictions, and conflicts inherent in Fascism, and of the solutions proposed by certain Fascists and groups of Fascists. However, with the tenth anniversary of the March on Rome, the suggestions and observations became less frequent as Fascist literature conformed strictly to Mussolinian apologetics.

30. Luigi Villari, *The Awakening of Italy: The Fascist Regeneration* (London, Methuen, 1924). Gaetano Salvemini's work contains a continuous and systematic attempt to counter Villari's thesis and dispel the mystery from the facts it presented.

31. Especially in its first part (until 1926) the *Storia del movimento fascista* reproduces, often verbatim, Volpe's contribution to the historical portion of the entry "Fascismo" in the *Enciclopedia italiana*.

32. Gioacchino Volpe, *Storia del movimento fascista* (Milan, Istituto per gli studi di politica nazionale e internazionale,

1939), p. 20; *History of the Fascist Movement* (Rome, Edizioni di Novissima, 1936).

33. Ibid., pp. 46-47. Cf. Arigo Serpieri, *La guerra e le classi rurali italiane* (Bari, Laterza, 1930), pp. 246 ff. In explicit polemics with Salvatorelli, Serpieri denies that the social base of Fascism can be identified with the "humanistic" petty bourgeoisie. For him, the "largest part of the army" came to Fascism from the countryside: the small and middle landowners' semirural bourgeoisie, the tenant farmers, peasant landowners, and so on.

34. Giulio Colamarino, "Natura storica del corporativismo italiano," *Nuovi problemi di politica, storia ed economia* (Ferrara; January-March 1932), pp. 9 ff.

35. For "Fascismo" see the text first published by the *Enciclopedia italiana*, and enriched with notes in Benito Mussolini, *La dottrina del fascismo* (Milan-Rome, 1933). Rocco's lectures are reprinted in *Scritti e discorsi di Alfredo Rocco* (Milan, Giuffrè, 1938), III, 1093 ff., 1117 ff. Gentile's 1927 essay is included in Giovanni Gentile, *Origini e dottrina del fascismo* (Rome, Libreria del Littorio, 1929), pp. 5 ff. For its antecedents, see the Gentile anthology, *Che cosa è il fascismo: Discorsi e polemiche* (Florence, Vallecchi, 1924).

Chapter 8. The Post-Liberation Debate

1. Another, less justifiable tendency was, and sometimes is, to reduce Fascism to its most grotesque and tasteless aspects; see, for example, Carlo Emilio Gadda, *Eros e Priapo (Da furore a cenere)* (Milan, Garzanti, 1967).

2. Benedetto Croce, *Teoria e storia della storiografia* (6th ed., Bari, Laterza, 1948), p. 78.

3. Benedetto Croce, *Scritti e discorsi politici (1943-1947)*, I, 195; II, 314. A similar sense of revulsion can be detected, although in a different ideological vein, in Pavese's letter of June 13, 1945; Cesare Pavese, *Lettere 1945-1950*, ed. Italo Calvino (Turin, 1966), p. 17.

4. Benedetto Croce, "L'obiezione contro la 'Storia dei propri tempi,' " *Quaderni della Critica*, 6:36 ff. (March 1950).

5. Giulio Colamarino, *Il fantasma liberale* (Milan, Bompiani,

1946); Fabio Cusin, *Antistoria d'Italia* (Turin, Einaudi, 1948). For works of epigones see Attilio Tamaro, *Venti anni di storia (1922-1943)* (Rome, Tiber, 1953), and *Due anni di storia (1943-1945)* (Rome, 1948), written with an apologetic and nationalist tone.

On the specifically Italian translation of these classic interpretations, their precedents in political literature of the Fascist era, and the principal debates that they have occasioned, see Giacomo Perticone, *La politica italiana nell'ultimo trentennio* (Rome, Leonardo, 1945-1947), II, 39 ff.; Nino Valeri, "Premessa ad una storia dell'Italia nel postrisorgimento," in Gabriele Pepe, ed., *Orientamenti per la storia dell'Italia nel Risorgimento* (Bari, Amici della cultura, 1952); Emilio Raffaele Papa, *Il prefascismo fra storiografia e mito: fascismo parentesi o fascismo rivelazione?* (Turin, 1966). These three works identified various aspects of the three classic interpretations and have provided an impetus for the debate occasioned by them. Because these three authors limited their works to an examination of the most famous expressions of the interpretations, occasionally they excluded significant positions among earlier writings and among works immediately following World War II.

According to Antonio Graziadei, *Democrazia borghese e democrazia socialista* (Rome, Morara [1946]), pp. 44-45, 98-99, Mussolini and Hitler's Totalitarian Fascism was "desired by the large landowners and big industrialists, who were frightened by the movement of the masses during the post-World War I period." "In its potential stage it was a phenomenon that could not be separated from bourgeois 'democracy,' " which under specific conditions passes "necessarily from the potential stage to the actual." Thus, Fascism should not be considered "a new and exceptional event," for "in one form or another, it had already appeared in considerably earlier times and in countries other than Italy"—such as France during the Thermidorian period and under Louis Napoleon or England at the end of the eighteenth century.

Lelio Basso, *Due totalitarismi: Fascismo e Democrazia Cristiana* (Milan, Garzanti, 1951), pp. 258 ff., on the other hand, concentrated on the origins of Fascism. There are several significant points in his analysis. The first is his study of urban and agrarian squadrismo. The former, the expression of the middle classes, wavered in its goals between anti-capitalist and antiproletarian tones. The latter, more socially uniform, was characterized by support of the landowners' interests. Second, Basso evaluates the overall importance of squadrismo. According to him, its role was generally over-

emphasized: "squadrismo had a function of primary importance as an instrument in the struggle against the workers'
movement, in the destruction of the political trade unions
and cooperative organizations, and in the attacks against
the city halls, but it was not the preeminent factor in the
conquest of the state." If the phenomenon had been left to
fall back on itself, it would have been reabsorbed and quickly
liquidated. The success of Fascism stems from the fact that
in 1920-21 financial capital decided on "the liquidation of
the old state" and used Fascism for this purpose. "But this
use of Fascism did not exclude the utilization of other traditional means of struggle or compromise; it did not imply a
direct plan for the transformation of the State structure."
This occurred only in 1920 and 1921, when Italian capitalism experienced economic difficulties. From this fact Basso
deduces two important consequences. First, "the transition
from the liberal state to the Totalitarian state was not the result of a takeover of the state by external violence, or by
squadrismo; it was the effect of a modified Italian social
structure that came about with the rise to dominance of
monopoly capital. Monopoly capital compounded the traditional imbalance of our economy by adding to it even more
serious imbalances. These stemmed from the inability to
overcome the postwar crisis by any means other than making the state apparatus totally subservient. Monopoly
capital was responsible for the decision of the ruling class to
free itself from the old structures and to replace them with
others that were more in tune with the new requirements."
Secondly, the new Totalitarian Fascist state differed from
the old reactionary police-state of Crispi, Rudinì, and Pel-
loux precisely because the latter was the expression of the
old premonopolistic capital, whereas the former was the expression of the new monopolistic capital.

The historical anthology by Armando Saitta, *Dal fascismo alla Resistenza: profilo storico e documenti* (Florence,
La Nuova Italia, 1961), is somewhat different from the writings of Perticone, Valeri, and Papa. It addresses the same
basic questions but it adopts a richer and more modern approach. Ample space is devoted to the connection of Fascism, anti-Fascism, and the Resistance. See also the writings
of Angelo Tasca, "Per una storia politica del fuoruscitismo,"
Itinerari (October-December 1954), and Sergio Cotta, "Line-
amenti di storia della Resistenza italiana nel periodo dell'oc-
cupazione," *Rassegna del Lazio* (Rome), a special issue in
1965 devoted to the *Atti* of the National Meeting on the
Resistance.

6. Among works of a historic nature, see the essays collected in Paolo Alatri, *Le origini del fascismo* (Rome, Riuniti, 1956), esp. pp. 45 ff.

7. For a critique of such historiography, see Rosario Romeo, *Il giudizio storico sul Risorgimento* (Catania, Bonanno, 1966), pp. 141 ff.

8. Croce, *Scritti e discorsi politici (1943-1947)*, II, 46 ff.

9. Benedetto Croce, "Ingenuità dei censori della storia," *Quaderni della critica*, 6:102 (November 1946).

10. Federico Chabod, "Croce storico," *Quaderni della rivista storica italiana* (Naples; October-December 1952), pp. 518 ff.

11. The revised and expanded edition is Luigi Salvatorelli and Giovanni Mira, *Storia d'Italia nel periodo fascista* (Turin, Einaudi, 1964).

12. An early important documentary contribution, insofar as Mussolini is concerned, was the beginning of publication of Benito Mussolini, *Opera Omnia*, ed. Edoardo and Diulio Susmel, 36 vols. (Florence, La Fenice, 1951-1963). The collection, composed mainly of published writings, is still incomplete because it does not include the documents collected in the Archivio Centrale dello Stato. Based on this work, see Giorgio Pini and Diulio Susmel, *Mussolini: L'uomo e l'opera*, 4 vols. (Florence, La Fenice, 1951-1953).

13. Because it is impossible here to examine all these works, I shall indicate only the most significant ones, such as the articles by L. Colucci, "Posizione storica del Fascismo," *Stoà* (May-December 1954); Claudio Pavone, "Le idee della Resistenza: Antifascisti e fascisti di fronte alla tradizione del Risorgimento," *Passato e Presente* (Milan; February 1959); Costanzo Casucci, "Fascismo e storia," *Il Mulino* (April 1960); Vittorio Stella, "Fascismo e cultura," *Il Mulino* (August 1960), as well as those collected in the second part of Costanzo Casucci, ed., *Il Fascismo: Antologia di scritti critici* (Bologna, Il Mulino, 1961). Publication of this anthology occasioned a fruitful and lively debate that has contributed in no small measure to the formulation of a new perspective of Fascism and its place in Italian history. Articles published in response to Casucci's anthology include L. Castelnuovo, "Fascismo, ideologia di transizione," and Vittorio Stella,

"Pensiero politico e storia nell'interpretazione del Fascismo,"
as well as those by Costanzo Casucci—all published in *Il
Mulino* between July and November 1964. Writings of authors of the preceding generation include those by Riccardo
Bauer, *Alla ricerca della libertà* (Florence, Parenti, 1957).

Chapter 9. More Recent Cultural and Historiographic Orientations

1. I refer in particular to Giacomo Perticone's many essays on
   modern society and mass regimes. For a completely different
   perspective see the 1944 article by Giorgio Bassani, "Nazis-
   mo e Fascismo: la rivoluzione come gioco," *Paragone: Men-
   sile di Arte Figurativa e letteratura* (Florence; April 1966).

2. See Renato Treves, "Interpretazioni sociologiche del fascismo,"
   Occidente (Havana, 1953), pp. 371 ff. For a selection of the
   rare psychoanalytic interpretations, see Michel David, *La
   psicoanalisi nella cultura italiana* (Turin, Boringhieri, 1966),
   ch. II (with notes on the Fascist era).

3. See Renato Treves, "Il fascismo e il problema delle generazioni," *Quaderni di Sociologia* (Turin; April-June 1964). Besides this approach, see some of the observations of Giordano Sivini, "Socialisti e cattolici in Italia dalla società allo
   Stato," in Giordano Sivini, ed., *Sociologia dei partiti politici* (Bologna, Il Mulino, 1971), pp. 71 ff.

4. See Giuliano Pischel, *Il problema dei ceti medi* (Milan, 1946),
   pp. 67 ff. According to Pischel, the rise of Fascism and its
   ability to remain in power was facilitated by the middle
   classes. Nevertheless, Fascism was not to be viewed as a
   phenomenon limited to the middle classes; it was the instrument of "much broader reactionary interests." The real contribution of the middle classes was entirely different: "On
   the one hand, it was a case of creating an ideological climate
   favorable to the Fascist parabola. On the other hand, it was
   a case of the injection of a petty bourgeois mentality and of
   a petty bourgeois praxis."

5. A typical case is that of Enzo Santarelli, *Storia del movimento
   e del regime fascista*, 2 vols. (Rome, Riuniti, 1967). See also
   his *Ricerche sul fascismo* (Urbino, Argalia, 1971). The group
   consists of: Alberto Aquarone, *L'organizzazione dello Stato
   totalitario* (Turin, Einaudi, 1966), in addition to several
   essays published in *Nord e Sud* (Naples), *La Cultura* (Milan), and *Il nuovo Osservatore Politico, Economico, Sociale*

(Milan), in 1964-65; Simona Colarizi, *Dopoguerra e fascismo in Puglia (1919-1926)* (Bari, Laterza, 1971); Ferdinando Cordova, *Arditi e Legionari dannunziani: Crisi ed evoluzione del combattentismo nella politica del dopoguerra (1918-1926)* (Padua, Marsilio, 1969); Renzo De Felice, *Mussolini il rivoluzionario (1883-1920)* (Turin, Einaudi, 1965), *Mussolini il fascista: La conquista del potere (1921-1925)* (Turin, Einaudi, 1966), and *Mussolini, il fascista: L'organizzazione dello Stato fascista (1925-1929)* (Turin, Einaudi, 1968); Franco Gaeta, *Nazionalismo italiano* (Naples, Edizioni scientifiche italiane, 1965); Francesco Margiotta Broglio, *Italia e Santa Sede dalla grande guerra alla conciliazione: aspetti politici e giuridici* (Bari, Laterza, 1966); Piero Melograni, ed., *Il Corriere della Sera (1919-1943)* (Bologna, Capelli, 1965), and "Confinudstria e fascismo tra il 1919 e il 1925," *Il nuovo Osservatore Politico, Economico, Sociale* (Milan; November-December 1965); Giuseppe Rossini, *Il movimento cattolico nel periodo fascista* (Rome, Cinque Lune, 1955), and *Il delitto Matteotti fra il Viminale e l'Aventino* (Bologna, Il Mulino, 1966); Salvatore Sechi, *Dopoguerra e fascismo: Il movimento autonomistico nella crisi dello Stato liberale* (Turin, Fondazione Luigi Einaudi, 1970); Paulo Ungari, *Alfredo Rocco e l'ideologia giuridica del fascismo* (Brescia, Morcelliani, 1963).

6. Delio Cantimori, "Il mestiere dello storico," *Itinerari* no. 58 (Bologna; June 1962), p. 96; reprinted in *Conversando di storia* (Bari, 1967), pp. 134 ff. Cantimori was responsible, during the 1930s, for some of the most perceptive analyses of National Socialism and its rise to power. See, for example, "Note sul nazionalsocialismo," *Archivio di studi corporativi* 5:291 ff. (Pisa; [1934]).

7. Croce, *Scritti e discorsi politici (1943-1947)*, I, 217 ff.

8. Gabriele De Rosa, *Considerazioni storiografiche sulla crisi dello Stato prefascista e sull'antifascismo*, p. 26.

9. Alan John Percivale Taylor, "Gli storici e le origini della seconda guerra mondiale," *Storia e politica* (Rome; January-March 1965), pp. 10 ff.

10. *Il Cannochiale: Rivista Bimestrale di Cultura* (Rome; January-June 1966), p. 86: introduction to a debate on Alberto Aquarone, *L'organizzazione dello Stato totalitario* (Turin, Einaudi, 1965).

11. For a bibliographical orientation on Italian Fascism, see Piero Melograni, "Bibliografia orientativa sul fascismo," *Il Nuovo Osservatore Politico, Economico, Sociale* (Milan; May, December 1966); Geneviève Bibes, "Le fascisme italien: État des travaux depuis 1945," *Revue Française de Science politique* (Paris; December 1968).

Conclusions

1. According to Bedřich Loewenstein, "Nemecky válečny zážitek a iracionální kritika civilizace. Trend od 1. svetové války k fašismu v ideologické a kulturne sociologické perspektive," *Československy časopis historicky* (Prague), 4:521 ff. (1966). This new content fell into four categories: the hope for a moral renewal brought about by the war; national self-exaltation and contempt for the rights of people in other lands; the community of the people or national solidarity expressed as imperialism or as "War Socialism"; and the elementary model of the peacetime state—for example, the transposition to it of war methods, extreme criteria, and crisis values. In this same vein, but applied to a case where these elements were largely unsuccessful, see Bedřich Loewenstein, "Il radicalismo di destra in Cecoslovacchia e la prima guerra mondiale," *Storia Contemporanea* (Bologna) 3:503 ff. (1970).

2. Federico Chabod, "Croce Storico," *Quaderni della rivista storica italiana* (Naples; October-December 1952), pp. 519 ff.

3. Cf. Palmiro Togliatti, *Lezioni sul fascismo* (Rome, Riuniti, 1970), pp. 20 ff.

4. Werner Conze, "La crise économique et le mouvement ouvrier en Allemagne entre 1929 et 1933," *Mouvements ouvriers et dépression économique de 1929 à 1939: étude et rapports préparés pour le VIIᵉ Colloque international d'histoire des mouvements sociaux et des structures sociales du Comité international des sciences historiques, tenu a Stockholm a l'occasion du XIᵉ Congres international des sciences historiques* (Assen, Van Gorcum, 1966), p. 56.

5. Gino Germani, "La socializzazione politica dei giovani nei regimi fascisti: Italia e Spagna," *Quaderni di Sociologia* (Turin; 1969), no. 1-2, pp. 11 ff.

6. The role of veterans was always very important, especially in

the early stages of Fascism. See René Rémond, "Les Anciens combattants et la Politique," *Revue Française de Science Politique* (Paris; 1955), no. 2, pp. 267 ff.

7. The differences between Fascism and National Socialism have been amply discussed. For the early years, see Klaus-Peter Hoepke, *Die Deutsche Rechte und der italienische Faschismus: Ein Beitrag zum Selbstverständnis und zur Politik von Gruppen und Verbänden der deutschen Rechten* (Düsseldorf, Droste, 1968). For the importance of these differences see Max Ascoli and Arthur Feiler, *Fascism for Whom?* (New York, Norton, 1938).

8. For an introductory analysis of Fascist culture in Italy, Germany, France, and England see Alastair Hamilton, *The Appeal of Fascism: A Study of Intellectuals and Fascism, 1919-1945* (London, Blond, 1971).

9. In a completely different vein and several years later (1931), compare Curzio Malaparte, *Tecnica del colpo di stato* (Milan, Bompiani, 1948), pp. 180 ff.

10. Daniel Guérin, *Fascisme et grand capital* (Paris, Maspero, 1965); trans. Frances and Mason Merrill, *Fascism and Big Business* (New York, Monad, 1973), p. 26.

11. Baran and Sweezy, *Monopoly Capital*, p. 156.

12. See Piero Melograni, *Confindustria e Fascismo tra il 1919 el il 1925* (Milan, Longanesi, 1972), pp. 834 ff., and Mario Abrate, *La lotta sindacale nella industrializzazione in Italia, 1906-1926* (Milan, Angeli, 1957).

13. That this took place when the "red" revolutionary trend was in decline has a relevant historical significance. The ebb was not yet clear; and, in certain situations, in the short run appearance is more important than reality; for his part, the historian must "receive historical reality as the men of the moment experienced it, believed it to be, and transmitted it to us"; Jacques Ellul, *Autopsie de la révolution* (Paris, Calmann-Lévy, 1969), p. 11.

14. Otto Bauer, "Il Fascismo," in De Felice, *Il Fascismo*, pp. 366-367.

15. Mario Abrate, "Remarques sur l'analyse de la conduite des entrepreneurs en Italie pendant la grande dépression," *Annales Cisalpines d'historie sociale* (Pavia; 1970), no. 1, pp. 3 ff. "There is no doubt that the wishes of the most powerful groups of men were extremely well reflected in legislative action, and that the stimulus to concentration, whether voluntary or coerced, enormously favored them. Nevertheless, I have the feeling that an intelligence (Alberto Beneduce?), which was not entirely disguised and operated after 1932, directed events in such a fashion that what seemed to be, or in fact were, concessions to important patronage were also revealed as the pawns in a more complex game that tended to reinforce the economic executive instruments retained by the State. The Machiavellianism of the Confederation of Industrialists, if we may speak in terms of Machiavellianism, was not revealed in 1945 and 1946 any more than it had been during the period preceding World War II. Even before the crisis, the tendency was to turn toward the reinforcement that we have just conjectured; some of the more foresighted members of the Confederation had clearly foreseen not only the end of De Stefani's "liberal" era—that is, the onset of State control of foreign exchange and foreign trade —but a tendency that was supported by the National Fascist party to gain control of the principal sectors of Italian economic life."

16. See especially Alberto Aquarone, *L'organizzazione dello Stato totalitario* (Turin, Einaudi, 1965); Hans Mommsen, *Beamtentum im Dritten Reich: Mit Ausgewählten Quellen zur Nationalsozialistischen Beamtenpolitik* (Stuttgart, Deutsche Verlags-Anstalt, 1966); S.J. Woolf, "Did a Fascist Economic System Exist?" in *The Nature of Fascism: Proceedings of a conference held by the Reading University Graduate School of Contemporary European Studies* (London, Weidenfeld, 1968), pp. 119 ff.

17. Jules Monnerot, *Sociologie de la révolution* (Paris, Fayard, 1969), pp. 7 ff.

18. Augusto Del Noce, *L'epoca della secolarizzazione* (Milan, Giuffrè, 1970).

19. For all the discussion of the revolution and its current interpretations, see Jacques Ellul, *Autopsie de la révolution*.

Selective Bibliography of Works

by Renzo De Felice
(compiled by Charles F. Delzell)

Studies of the late eighteenth century and of the Italian Jacobins:
  Note e ricerche sugli "Illuminati" e il misticismo rivoluzionario (1789-1800) (Rome, Edizioni di storia e letteratura, 1960).
  La vendita dei beni nazionali nella Repubblica romana del 1798-99 (Rome, Edizioni di storia e letteratura, 1960).
  ed., *I giornali giacobini italiani* (Milan, Feltrinelli Editore, 1962).
  ed. with Delio Cantimori, *Giacobini italiani*, 2 vols. (Bari, G. Laterza, 1956-64).
  Italia giacobina (Naples, Edizioni scientifiche italiane, 1965).
  Aspetti e momenti della vita economica di Roma e del Lazio nei socoli XVIII e XIX (Rome, Edizioni di storia e letteratura, 1965).

On D'Annunzio:
  Sindacalismo rivoluzionario e fiumanesimo nel carteggio De Ambris-D'Annunzio, 1919-1922 (Brescia, Morcelliana, 1966).
  ed. with Emilio Mariano, *Carteggio D'Annunzio-Mussolini (1919-1938)* (Milan, Mondadori, 1971).
  ed., *La Carta del Carnaro: Nei testi di Alceste De Ambris e di Gabriele D'Annunzio* (Bologna, Il Mulino, 1974).
  Gabriele D'Annunzio, *La penultima ventura: Scritti e discorsi fiumani* (Milan, A. Mondadori, 1974).

On Italian Fascism and Italo-German relations:
  Il fascismo e i partiti politici italiani: Testimonianze del 1921-1923 (Bologna, Cappelli, 1966).

ed., *Il fascismo: Le interpretazioni dei contemporanei e degli storici* (Bari, Editori Laterza, 1970). This work, a companion anthology to the present edition, contains a long introduction that supplements material in *Interpretations of Fascism*. It is divided into two sections: "The political judgment" and "The historical judgment."

I rapporti tra fascismo e nazionalsocialismo fino all'andata al potere di Hitler (1922-1933): Appunti e documenti (Naples, Edizioni scientifiche italiane, 1971).

Storia degli ebrei italiani sotto il fascismo, with preface by Delio Cantimori (Turin, Giulio Einaudi editore, 1961; 3rd rev. enlarged ed., 1972).

Il problema dell'Alto Adige nei rapporti italo-tedeschi dall'Anschluss alla fine della seconda guerra mondiale (Bologna, Il Mulino, 1973).

L'Italia fra tedeschi e alleati: La politica estera fascista e la seconda guerra mondiale (Bologna, Il Mulino, 1973).

Mussolini e Hitler: I rapporti segreti, 1922-1933: Con documenti inediti (Florence, Le Monnier, 1975).

On Mussolini (all Turin, Giulio Einaudi):

Mussolini il rivoluzionario, 1883-1920 (1965).

Mussolini il fascista, I: *La conquista del potere, 1921-1925* (1966).

Mussolini il fascista, II: *L'organizzazione dello Stato fascista, 1925-1929* (1968).

Mussolini il duce, I: *Gli anni del consenso, 1929-1936* (1974).

Mussolini il duce, II: *Lo Stato totalitario, 1936-1939* (to come).

Mussolini l'alleato, 1939-1945 (to come).

Index